EARLY CHILDHOOD EDUCATION SERIES
Leslie R. Williams, Editor
Millie Almy, Senior Advisor

ADVISORY BOARD: **Barbara T. Bowman, Harriet K. Cuffaro, Stephanie Feeney, Doris Pronin Fromberg, Celia Genishi, Dominic F. Gullo, Alice Sterling Honig, Elizabeth Jones, Gwen Morgan, David Weikart**

(Continued)

The
WHOLE LANGUAGE
Kindergarten

Shirley C. Raines
Robert J. Canady

Foreword by Bill Martin, Jr.

TEACHERS
COLLEGE
PRESS

Teachers College, Columbia University
New York ✳ London

Published by Teachers College Press, 1234 Amsterdam Avenue
New York, NY 10027

Library of Congress Cataloging-in-Publication Data

Raines, Shirley C.
    The whole language kindergarten / Shirley C. Raines, Robert J.
Canady ; foreword by Bill Martin.
        p.   cm. — (Early childhood education series ; v. 30)
    Includes bibliographical references and index.
    ISBN 0-8077-3049-1 (alk. paper) : $19.95
    1. Kindergarten—Curricula.   2. Kindergarten—Activity programs.
3. Language experience approach in education.   4. Reading
(Preschool)—Language experience approach.   I. Canady, Robert J.
II. Title   III. Series.
LB1180.R35   1990   90-41750
372.19—dc20   CIP

Printed on acid-free paper
Manufactured in the United States of America

97 96 95 94 93 92   8   7   6   5   4   3

Dedicated to

Irene and James Athel Raines

Our children, Brian, Lynnette, Scott, and Lark

The memory of Polly and Bob Canady

Contents

Foreword

One aspect of the gathering interest in Whole Language as an educative process is its relevancy to literacy. It premises that all children are expert, that they come to school already richly experienced in the use of assimilation and accommodation. Proponents of Whole Language validate their commitment to this developmental phenomenon with a variety of evaluation measures that reveal children's steady growth, emotionally, mentally, and socially. Many educators are hesitant to subscribe, however. They say that until the academic potential of the Whole Language classroom is more securely researched and established, they are content to follow a traditional curriculum that dictates what and how children learn, and sets the pace for that learning.

Indeed, there are ponderable questions: Are a child's spontaneous trial-and-error judgmental responses a secure path to cultural literacy? Is a child truly advantaged by a Whole Language classroom environment which assumes that one can learn life's essential controls by encountering and engaging in "rich conflicts" of implied meanings and self-teaching? Is Whole Language a tangible curriculum designed for the long-range needs of a child's school years, or is it, as now practiced, an experiment primarily by individual teachers in single classrooms?

The Whole Language Kindergarten collects the energies and insights of two distinguished, lifelong educators, Drs. Shirley C. Raines and Robert J. Canady, who are also husband and wife. They believe totally in the genius of children, and that kindergarten children learn the cultural necessities and adornments by involving themselves in the world of play. Their play is inspired by books, songs, poems, and art; by reading, writing, and speaking activities; by listening, thinking, and making choices; and by a continuing array of social interaction. In fact, children learn everything from the continuous undulations of their awareness of life.

"Any kindergarten literacy program," the authors believe, "which is designed to use language materials and activities that are meaningful to children, and which is designed to perpetuate the natural literacy acquisition and development process established by the child long before coming to school will, in fact, be a Whole Language program."

I concur with these recommendations and curriculum designs. They synthesize my current understandings and experiences in working with the 4-5-and-6'ers. They also release my dormant and half-realized dreams of what kindergarten education can be.

BILL MARTIN, JR.

Preface

As we ended our presentation at yet another teachers' conference, we noted with pleasure that our session had been filled. In fact, every chair was taken and there had been people sitting on the floor at the front of the room. Small groups of teachers remained at the back of the room chatting excitedly. We thanked the kindergarten teacher who brought samples of her children's writings, praised others for their active participation in the session, and anticipated the extra time we would spend with the group that had arrived early, had sat in the front row, and now guarded the door to be certain their questions would be answered. It is experiences such as these that have led us to write this book.

We are eager to bring the dialogue between kindergarten teachers, early childhood education leaders, and emergent literacy researchers from the conference-presentation level to the arena of classroom practice. In *The Whole Language Kindergarten*, we accomplish that aim in Chapter 1 by first helping the reader to understand the foundation in theory and research for the changes we recommend in classroom practice. Change is a process that requires thoughtful consideration of one's present practices and assumptions about learning, as well as a vision of the possibilities of operating a classroom differently. A view of this change process is presented in Chapter 2, where our readers, both prospective and practicing educators, can follow one teacher as she goes through her transition of becoming a Whole Language teacher. Creating Whole Language kindergartens, however, does not involve a step-by-step approach, but rather a perspective about how literacy emerges and is developed. It requires a commitment by a kindergarten teacher to make all instruction meaningful and compatible with what is now known concerning cognitive development and the acquisition and development of literacy.

The question asked most frequently by early childhood educators is, "How much of my current kindergarten program needs to be changed to make it a Whole Language program?" Although each teaching situation is unique and kindergarten teachers' concepts of a Whole Language classroom vary, in the remaining chapters of the book we answer this question and many others asked by teachers. Most are pleased to learn that, if their philosophical view of the curriculum is child centered and experience centered, and they are equipped with new knowledge about young children's emerging literacy development, they are then able to modify the majority of their present practices and become Whole Language teachers. If their view of the curriculum is not centered on the child and on experience, we provide the rationale for changes, based on theory, research, and past professional practices of successful kindergarten teachers. Teachers will be glad to know that the changes we recommend in the activities and materials, and in teacher interactions with children, are based on the criteria from three respected sources: the position paper of the National Association for the Education of Young Children (NAEYC), titled *Developmentally Appropriate Practices* (Bredekamp, 1987); and the recommendations of the Association for Childhood Education International (ACEI), in a paper titled "The Child-centered Kindergarten" (Moyer, Egertson, & Isenberg, 1987). The practices we recommend for a Whole Language kindergarten are also congruent with the International Reading Association's (IRA) position paper, *Literacy Development and Prefirst Grade* (Early Childhood and Literacy Development Committee, 1988). (See Appendixes A, B, and C for excerpts from these position papers.)

To guide teachers in implementing a Whole Language learning environment, we examine play, grouptime, the writing center, the library corner, theme teaching, art activities, music and movement activities, the science center, housekeeping and blocks areas, mathematics manipulatives, and, finally, working with parents to help them understand changes in the classroom. Readers will notice that in each chapter we give teachers a glimpse inside kindergartens and describe ways the programs were organized and how the children reacted. We share the concerns expressed by the teachers, and we provide guidelines necessary for the teachers to reshape their kindergartens to function as Whole Language classrooms. As with all successful kindergarten programs, teachers will modify the information presented to fit their particular talents as creative professionals and their particular children.

We hope we have conveyed in the few words of this preface that we have listened to the ideas of experienced teachers as well as those readers who plan to teach. We have heard your questions, concerns, frustrations, and ideals you expressed when we met you at conferences, in university classrooms, and visited your centers and schools. *The Whole Language Kindergarten* is our reply.

We are indebted to the teachers at the George Mason University Project for the Study of Young Children, the Vienna Baptist Preschool, the East Tennessee State University Child Study Center, and a group of teachers enrolled in a creative-teaching class at Northeastern State University in Tahlequah, Oklahoma, for allowing us to observe in their classrooms. Additional classroom anecdotes were provided by practicing educators enrolled in graduate classes at Marymount University and George Mason University.

In addition, we must express our appreciation to our colleagues at George Mason University and Marymount University for their support of our research and writing, as well as for their thought-provoking discussions. Throughout the book, we shared examples from many different early childhood classrooms. We appreciate those teachers who allowed us to interact with them, as well as those parents who gave permission for their children to participate in our research projects. The teachers' and children's names used throughout the book are pseudonyms, to protect their privacy.

In addition, we appreciate the excellent editorial assistance we received from Sarah Biondello, Brian Ellerbeck, and Nina George at Teachers College Press, and from copyeditor Susan Keniston.

What Is Whole Language?

Educators, like other professionals, have developed jargon to describe what they do in their profession. Recently, early childhood teachers have been introduced to terms from research which may not be familiar to them, such as *psycholinguistics, sociolinguistics,* and *emergent literacy.* Another term that teachers are hearing and reading is *Whole Language,* used to describe instruction that stems from extensive research and observation of the natural acquisition and development of literacy.

As kindergarten teachers hear terms that may be new to them, as they read about Whole Language classrooms, and as they attend inservice presentations about Whole Language, they often ask, "What is a Whole Language kindergarten, and how does it differ from my present classroom?" In the pages to follow, these and other questions they pose are answered. In this chapter, the meaning of the term *Whole Language* is clarified and related to the reading and writing processes. Also, we examine how Whole Language instruction relates to the learning process in general.

THE FOUNDATION OF WHOLE LANGUAGE IN RESEARCH AND THEORY

In this section, we will see that Whole Language recommendations are an amalgamation of findings from psycholinguists, sociolinguists, emergent literacy researchers, and educational researchers who describe children's literacy development and then recommend educational practice.

The reason many teachers are confused about the term *Whole Language* probably stems from the fact that they have been bombarded from all sides with different ways to teach reading. Auckerman (1984) documents 165 methods, approaches, and systems for teaching beginning reading. Massive research studies have been done that have produced conflicting evidence as to the best method of reading instruction (Chall, 1967; Anderson, Hiebert, Scott, & Wilkinson, 1984; Delacoto, 1959; Durkin, 1970; Flesch, 1955). It is not surprising that many teachers have questioned whether *Whole Language* refers to yet another method of teaching children to read.

Influences from Psycholinguistic Research

In order to understand why Whole Language is not just another instructional method, it is important to examine a psycholinguistic view of the reading process. In 1968, Kenneth Goodman presented the Goodman Model of Reading, published in his book, *The Psycholinguistic Nature of the Reading Process*. The purpose of Goodman's research was not to study reading instruction, but to focus on the process of reading from a psycholinguistic perspective, or to describe the relationship between thought (psyche) and language (linguistics) as it applies to the act of reading. The Goodman Model of Reading described reading not as a letter-by-letter, word-by-word decoding process, but rather as a "psycholinguistic guessing game" (Goodman, 1982a, p. 33) whereby the reader uses graphophonic, syntactic, and semantic clues simultaneously to construct meaning from print. Beginning with the prediction of what the information is about and knowledge of how language works, the reader selectively samples from the print and, using all three cuing systems simultaneously, constructs meaning.

Armed with new information about the reading process, other educators and psycholinguists conducted their own studies of the reading process, and these not only verified but expanded on Goodman's initial research (Clay, 1922; Ferreiro, 1986; Y. Goodman, 1986; Harste, Woodward, & Burke, 1984; Taylor, 1983). As teachers became aware of this new information, many of them began to reorganize their classrooms and to plan reading instruction that was compatible with the psycholinguistic view of the reading process (K. S. Goodman, 1986; Henke, 1988; Hittleman, 1988). In order to provide reading material and reading instruction that would be meaningful to the reader, they found that the materials must be "whole" and must contain "language" that is meaningful to the individual; thus the term *Whole Language*.

Whole Language, then, is not a method of instruction, but a perspective, a view of reading instruction that is compatible with the psycholinguistic view of the reading process. It is not a set of materials, a set of books, a set of experiences, or a set of practices. As Altwerger, Edelsky and Flores (1987) have pointed out, "It must become practice, but it is not practice itself" (p. 145). Teachers who have this perspective do use many practices, such as providing an abundance of children's literature in the classroom, creating a writing center, and taking a unit approach to curriculum planning. These practices, however, may exist without the teacher having a Whole Language perspective.

Influences from Sociolinguistic Research

In addition to psycholinguists, sociolinguists also have influenced the Whole Language perspective. Sociolinguists, as the term implies, examine the social aspects of language, that is, the social contexts within which language, in its spoken or written forms, is used. Crucial to the understanding of the relationship between language and thought is the premise that an intended meaning cannot be understood without examining the "communication intentions of language users" (Feldman, 1980, p. 72). The communication intentions cannot be examined without looking at the social context in which they occur.

Findings from Emergent Literacy Research

When the findings of psycholinguistic and sociolinguistic research are used as the basis for recommending changes in educational practices related to young children's reading and writing, the term *emergent literacy* is often used. This refers to the relationship of language and thought as it manifests itself in the process of a child becoming literate. The settings in which sociolinguists and educators study young children's emergent literacy are the natural or social contexts in which it occurs.

Teale and Sulzby (1986) trace the concept of emergent literacy to Marie Clay of New Zealand, a researcher whose work first appeared in the 1960s. Writings about emergent literacy surfaced in the United States in the 1970s and increased rapidly in the 1980s. It is important to note that the concept indicates an ongoing *process*, not a specific *time* when children learn to read and write. This process is compared to a growing tree by Yetta Goodman (1986). She refers to the "roots of literacy" (p. 6), which begin as children become aware of the relationship of print and meaning. Research studies of "print awareness" by Yetta Goodman (1986) (Clay, 1975; Long et al., 1982) and others have established the fact that children in a literate society grow up surrounded by print and that the roots of literacy begin much earlier than was previously realized.

Children become aware of print as a natural, functional aspect of their environment as they observe adults interacting with, discussing, and using print, both in reading and writing, to fulfill their needs or their communication intentions. They are exposed to print in their homes, in grocery stores, in shopping malls, and in fast-food restaurants; and they soon realize that written language in a variety of forms conveys meaning and "gets you things." In her study using signs and logos, Yetta Goodman (1986) found that "at least 60% of all the 3-year-old subjects and an average of 80% of the subjects ages four and five can read environmental print when it is embedded in context" (p. 7). Children become aware of the function of print in books in much the same way. Over time, they learn that reading the print high above the restaurant counter gets them a "Big Mac" and reading the print in a book gets them a "neat story." Children come to school with varying degrees of knowledge about print and how it functions in the environment, and many children already know how print works in books.

Learning, Reading, and Writing Processes

To answer questions about Whole Language and how it differs from present practice, one must examine the changing views of the learning, reading, and writing processes. Restructuring classrooms for Whole Language instruction requires that educators make a basic change in their attitude concerning these processes.

Learning. According to Piaget (1977), all learning takes place through the processes of assimilation and accommodation. Learners consider the circumstances and make predictions by sampling the general characteristics of information samples and confirming or rejecting their predictions. If the learners' predictions are confirmed, that is, if they have verified the prediction or assimilated the information, they move on to the next sample. If their predictions are rejected, they must either abandon or adjust them and move on to another sample of information. New information may cause learners to organize their information into new constructs or schemata, once again indicating a process of accommodation. The depth of the learning will be determined by the quality of the predictions and the samples of information, and the prior knowledge of the learners.

Reading. The reading process is no longer considered a word-by-word decoding process designed to unlock the meaning embedded in the print. Whole Language teachers view reading as a process of constructing meaning from interacting with the print and relating the information to what one already knows. This process follows the general process for learning just described. First the reader scans the print and predicts the meaning. Then the reader samples the print to confirm or reject the predicted meaning. If the prediction is confirmed, she moves on to the next sample. If the prediction is rejected, she either abandons or adjusts the prediction and moves on. As she moves through the text, predicting, sampling, and confirming information, she integrates the new information in with her previous knowledge. Comprehension is taking place as the reader reads and when the "whole" text is read. The depth of understanding, or comprehending, is determined by the quality of the reader's prediction, print samples, and prior knowledge. Frank Smith (1985) has said that "children do not learn to read in order to make sense of print. They strive to make sense of print and as a consequence learn to read" (p. 120). The process of reading is thus an interactive one, with the child interacting with the print actively to construct meaning.

When the Goodman Model of Reading was first published (Goodman, 1968, 1969), it was assumed that it was a description of mature reading. Recent studies (Goodman, 1982; Harste et al., 1984; Smith, 1982; Taylor, 1983; Teale & Sulzby, 1986) reveal that the process also can be applied to beginning readers and even to a young child who is determining whether a sign says "Hardees" or "Arbys." Viewing the child as an active participant in beginning reading development is a concept that may be new to many kindergarten teachers; however, understanding and accepting reading as an interactive process is essential to successful Whole Language instruction.

As we have seen, the term *emergent literacy* refers to a process that occurs over time (Sulzby, 1986). Kindergarten children are at varying stages of their development as readers and writers, so this warrants a variety of ways of interacting with them (Hoffman, 1987). For this reason, and because they already know a great deal about written language long before they enter the kindergarten classroom (Vukelich & Golden, 1984), it is developmentally inappropriate to use a preplanned skills approach to reading and writing that is designed to treat all the children the same. As teachers begin to view children as "constructors" of the process (Atkins, 1984; Ferreiro, 1986), actively engaged in reading and writing by the time they enter kindergarten, the question becomes, "What can I do in my kindergarten classroom to continue the children's development as readers and writers?" As Cambourne (1988) has said, "Learning to become literate ought to be as uncomplicated and barrier-free as possible" (p. 4). The Whole Language kindergarten teacher plans experiences, activities, interactions, and a classroom environment that support literacy development and reflect current information regarding emergent literacy (Jalongo & Zeigler, 1987; Loughlin & Martin, 1987).

Writing.   Just as readers use print to construct meaning, writers also use print to construct meaning (Clay, 1975). Young writers select a thought to be expressed and choose words and whatever print symbols they know, to convey that thought. The writer then constructs a sample of print and examines it to confirm the meaning intended. If meaning is confirmed, the writer continues. If meaning is not confirmed, the writer adjusts the print accordingly. The process is basically the same, whether the author is a mature writer or a preschooler who knows a few letters and sounds and invents a way to spell the message. A Whole Language kindergarten program allows for the various types of writing that kindergarten children are capable of doing, and provides opportunities for print exploration in a nonthreatening, environment.

Although the foregoing descriptions of the learning, reading, and writing processes are greatly oversimplified, and although research in these areas continues to reveal their extreme complexity, their similarities to one another can no longer be ignored in beginning reading and writing programs. The information given here can provide a direction for kindergarten teachers who wish to establish literacy education programs based on current research data.

Learning to read and write is complicated, but it is no more difficult a process than those used by children when they learn to talk or learn the difference between a dog and a cat (Smith, 1982). All children come to school as experts in the use of assimilation and accommodation, which are basic to Goodman's (1968) reading model and Clay's (1975) model of the writing process. Any kindergarten literacy program designed to use language materials and activities that are meaningful to the children, and to perpetuate the natural literacy acquisition and development process established by the child long before coming to school, will, in fact, be a Whole Language program.

TRANSLATING THEORY AND RESEARCH
INTO EFFECTIVE PRACTICE

Many early childhood teachers have long been concerned about the gap between what is known about how children learn (Harste et al., 1984) and current "basic skills" in beginning reading and writing programs. They disliked using "reading readiness" worksheets and preprimers from basal series, because they treated the children as passive recipients of information, rather than as active, hands-on, independent learners (Gibson, 1989). The information being gathered by psycholinguistic researchers now verifies that teachers' concerns were well founded. This demands an immediate re-evaluation of both materials and practice. Beginning reading and writing instruction, as well as "reading readiness" types of programs that are often adopted for use in kindergarten, must be very carefully scrutinized (Teale & Sulzby, 1986).

Child-centered Teachers' Concerns

Many child-centered kindergarten teachers fear that incorporating an emphasis on reading and writing in their curriculum will cause academic pressures for children and will mean giving up the hands-on active learning that has characterized their programs. Whole Language teachers, however, often find they are expanding their curriculum to include even more firsthand experiences. Kindergarten teachers who view themselves as child-centered and have designed an active learning environment find Whole Language compatible with their philosophy of child growth and development. As they learn more about emergent literacy, they combine that information with what they already know about developmentally appropriate practices for young children, continually re-evaluating their current classrooms and curricula, based on their findings.

Basic Skills Teachers' Concerns

Teachers who have a "basic-skills" orientation; who use reading readiness materials, commercially prepared workbooks, worksheets, and preprimers; and who rely heavily on the use of a lot of teacher-directed activities find themselves in conflict with the research on emergent literacy. The emphasis on skills such as learning correct letter formation, long and short vowel sounds, and colors, and matching the directionality of pictures, are just a few examples of things children are being taught that have little to do with their success as readers and writers. As proof of this lack of correlation, in 1966 Durkin reported that many children who were given reading instruction, even though they had previously failed reading readiness tests, did learn to read. Her conclusions caused educators to question many of the skills once thought of as "prerequisites" to learning to read. Many of these same teachers have searched eagerly for alternative information that will assist them in what they consider their major responsibility—helping children begin reading and writing (Gibson, 1989).

Reconciliation of Research and Concerns

The term *Whole Language* may be new to many early childhood teachers, but the concept of teaching the whole is not. Teachers know the value of using stories, poems, and songs to help children learn new concepts and specific information. When kindergarten teachers present a new song, they introduce it by singing the whole song first, and they then have the children echo the teachers' singing until the song is learned. It would never occur to most kindergarten teachers to emphasize the individual words or letters of a song until the whole song was familiar to each child. It is because of early childhood teachers' awareness of the ways young children learn that they have rejected the basic-skills curriculum, which breaks the language into such small pieces that meaning is lost for the child. In a Whole Language kindergarten, the basic skills of language are learned without destroying the song (Martin, 1988).

Whole Language teachers believe that, if the parts of language, commonly known as the "skills," are to be understood by the learner, the child must first know why he is learning the parts, and then how the part fits into the "whole." To insure that children know why they are learning the parts of language, the Whole Language teacher creates a "need" for that learning. The need might be a functional need, such as reading the instructions for playing a game, or making a sign to tell other children to stay away from a block creation; or it might be to complete a sentence in a story the teacher is reading. Learning in order to fulfill a need is basic to a Whole Language kindergarten and is in keeping with the natural development of children.

In a Whole Language classroom, the skills of reading and writing are learned through active participation in the reading/writing process (Smith, 1983). There is no set of skills the child must learn before being allowed to read or write. There is no prescribed, sequential order for teaching the skills of reading and writing, and there is no teacher's guide with step-by-step lessons.

To a Whole Language kindergarten teacher who uses a process or strategy approach to literacy instruction, the long-standing controversy among reading educators of whether to stress whole words or sound–symbol relationships (parts) becomes meaningless. Sight-word vocabulary is developed through using words repeatedly in meaningful contexts, and sound–symbol relationships are learned as a part of the natural rhythm of language and as a part of the child's construction of writing. Children construct meaning through active involvement with wordless picture books, patterned language books, big books, songs, poems, and chants, and through personal writing using their own invented means of spelling.

In a Whole Language classroom, all of the skills necessary for fluency in reading and writing are practiced over and over again, day after day. Phonics skills and sight words are learned as they relate to the total process, and when specific lessons in these skills become necessary, the children have no doubt how those skills fit into the reading/writing process.

Both types of kindergarten teachers—those who consider themselves child centered and those who consider themselves basic-skills teachers—discover that a review of the findings from emergent literacy research helps them reconceptualize the reading and writing process and view the young child's literacy development differently. Whole Language teachers design their classrooms on the belief that natural literacy begins at home, through exposure to meaningful reading and writing materials in a nonthreatening environment, without exposure to formal lessons (Y. Goodman, 1986).

Research data on natural readers and writers also support Piaget's theory of cognition as a process of constructing meaning through assimilation and accommodation (Ferreiro, 1986). Children explore the reading and writing processes in the same manner they have learned everything else—through experimentation and interaction, and by becoming involved with real reading and writing experiences. Children who become fluent readers and writers before entering kindergarten usually come from home environments where they have been encouraged to interact with print, where there are reading and writing role models, and where there is an abundance of reading and writing materials (Jewell & Zintz, 1986). In any literate society, however, even in homes and cultures where reading and writing are modeled less frequently and fewer books and writing materials are found, children develop an awareness of how print functions and do construct meaning from print before coming to school (Y. Goodman, 1986).

Natural readers and writers learn the skills of reading and writing in the same way they learn talking, listening, walking, swimming, and all of the other skills they will learn in their lives—through meaningful participation in that particular activity (Bissex, 1980; Taylor, 1983). All learners, regardless of age, tend to lose interest in any task where the purpose of learning that task is unclear. A baby is willing to learn the individual skills involved in crawling and walking because the purpose—getting to the other side of the room or becoming more mobile in order to explore more of the environment—is clear. Researchers are finding that motivation and clarity of purpose are just as essential in literacy acquisition (Ferreiro, 1986; Y. Goodman, 1986; Holdaway, 1979). Close observation of children involved in natural literacy acquisition has led to the Whole Language classroom—a new and exciting way to prepare the kindergarten environment for reading and writing.

KEY ELEMENTS FOR A WHOLE LANGUAGE KINDERGARTEN

A synthesis of psycholinguistic, sociolinguistic, and emergent literacy research reveals several key elements that teachers can use to guide their instructional practice in kindergartens.

Immersion in Language and Print

Just as the young child learned to speak by being immersed in a language environment, the Whole Language kindergarten is one where children are immersed in language and print. As young children learn, they practice what they are learning over and over, at their own initiative. They are constantly interacting with and responding to adults and each other in many ways, including speech, reading, and writing.

Opportunities and Resources

A second key element is comprised of opportunities and resources—the materials, time, space, and activities needed to support the child as a learner and thus a communicator. Young children who are immersed in a print-rich environment with interesting books and materials to read and explore, and who have many and varied types of papers, pencils, and pens, will use these materials over and over to read and write, because they are available, because they are interesting, and because young children are active and want opportunities to communicate. They want to make sense of print, and they make sense of print by using it.

Meaningful Communication

Children want to communicate, so they focus their attention on topics of discussion; on the information found in print, both in books and their own and others' writing; and on the discoveries, facts, questions, and inquiries about the activities of their lives. They are learners who are seeking and constructing meaningful communication as they make sense of their world and represent their learnings in spoken and written language. Therefore, the third key element for guiding instructional practice is meaningful communication. Just as children in the home hear adults using oral language functionally to live their lives, they also see them using written language meaningfully and purposefully (Teale, 1985).

Teacher As Communication Role Model

The fourth key element in a Whole Language kindergarten is the teacher as a role model. The teacher is the facilitator who communicates with the children and who provides the time and the materials that invite them to listen and speak with the teacher and with each other. The teacher as the reading and writing role model makes obvious to the children how print operates for communication purposes. For example, when the teacher is writing a note to one of the parents, the teacher will read the note to the child. When the teacher is writing a thank you note to the cafeteria workers who helped prepare a special holiday meal, the children may help to compose the note and watch the teacher write it, or write their own versions. The purposes and functions of written communication are made clear to each child in a Whole Language classroom.

Acceptance of Children as Readers and Writers

The teacher's meaningful and purposeful communication incorporates one of the basic premises of Whole Language, which is that the communication is seen as a whole. Whole stories, songs, poems, messages, and various examples of meaningful print become the vehicles through which reading is taught. It is the wholeness of language that makes it meaningful. Similarly, then, the fifth key element for guiding instructional practice is acceptance of the children's communication as a whole. When a child scribbles a note in a play situation, it is accepted as a whole communication. When children experiment with print in order to write a message to other children or the teacher, that print is considered a whole, meaningful message from the writer.

The teacher accepts the children as readers and writers (1) because they are already readers and writers when they enter school and (2) because they will refine their reading and writing as they become more aware of how print works and as they continue constructing their own print. As already noted, children come to kindergarten at various stages of literacy development. Some are scribblers, yet others are composing sentences in print. Some are pretend readers, while others are already reading favorite books aloud. All children come as emerging readers and writers.

While reading stories to children has long been standard practice in the kindergarten classroom, the research on emergent literacy has lead teachers to observe more closely the individual ways children read stories. Some may be pretending to read by retelling the story of a familiar book. Whether or not this retelling closely approximates the actual print, it is a sign of literacy development. Just as parents who hear their child attempting a new word will accept and applaud any approximation, the teacher in a Whole Language classroom accepts children's natural attempts at reading without correcting them. Much of the success children achieve in learning to speak is due to adult encouragement of their efforts, however imperfect they may be. Similarly, when children are learning to write, teachers do not expect perfection. They accept scribbles and or mock letters, as well as the ways children use the letters they know to invent ways to spell what they want to communicate.

Attitude of Expectancy

A sixth key element from the emergent literacy research is an attitude of expectancy. Teachers encourage and support children in their process of becoming literate. Parents expect all children to learn to listen and talk, and Whole Language teachers expect all children to read and write, regardless of their socioeconomic, linguistic, cultural, or other background experiences. When the emphasis in the kindergarten program is shifted from knowledge of basic skills to actual reading and writing processes, most teachers are relieved to discover how much children in a literate culture already know about print before they enter kindergarten.

Literacy emerges in a Whole Language kindergarten in a supportive, encouraging environment of acceptance and expectancy, where children are allowed to explore and arrive at their own conclusions concerning the reading/writing process, and are free to take risks as they struggle to communicate through written language. When children use the few words or phrases they know in a particular book, and then pretend to read the rest of the story, their efforts are applauded. When they use a few letters to write their names, those letters are accepted as representations of their whole names. The Whole Language kindergarten teacher expects each child to expand her reading and writing and to be successful, and this is reflected in a classroom that has been carefully organized to insure that each child is allowed to continue the process of becoming literate, which was begun long before coming to school.

Summary

The Whole Language kindergarten, then, is a whole environment where children are immersed in language in both its spoken and written forms, where there is an emphasis on listening, speaking, reading, and writing. The emphasis is always on Whole Language and meaningful communication. The teacher as a communication role model is a good listener, speaker, reader, and writer and views the teaching role as a whole process of communicating. Children are actively involved in meaningful communication as they construct knowledge by using the whole of an experience, the whole of a piece of literature, or the whole of some meaningful message to others. The children's reading and writing are accepted, and their efforts to communicate are accepted as whole and meaningful, rather than as incomplete because they do not have all the adult features of communication. The Whole Language kindergarten program builds on the recognition that young children are already readers and writers. They are capable of whole communication, even while they are constructing concepts of how print functions in the environment and in books, and even as they learn to construct meaningful print on their own. It then becomes the responsibility of the teacher to provide the time, materials, opportunities, and encouragement needed for meaningful communication, so that the children can continue the literacy process. The whole environment, the teacher's attitude, the time, the materials, and the opportunities for communication are arranged because the teacher is confident in young children and fully expects them to continue to develop and refine their listening, speaking, reading, and writing.

RECOMMENDATIONS FROM EDUCATIONAL LEADERS

Kindergarten teachers who restructure their classrooms to implement Whole Language learning environments will find that the changes they make are compatible with the views of large numbers of educational leaders. They will find support and guidance for a Whole Language kindergarten in the recommendations contained in the International Reading Association's position paper, *Literacy Development and Prefirst Grade* (Early Childhood and Literacy Development Committee, 1988). The same position paper also has been adopted by the Association for Childhood Education International, the Association for Supervision and Curriculum Development, the National Association for the Education of Young Children, the National Association of Elementary School Principals, and the National Council of Teachers of English. The recommendations are as follows:[1]

1. Build instruction on what the child already knows about oral language, reading, and writing. Focus on meaningful experiences and meaningful language rather than merely isolated skill development.
2. Respect the language the child brings to school, and use it as a base for language and literacy activities.
3. Ensure feelings of success for all children, helping them see themselves as people who can enjoy exploring oral and written language.
4. Provide reading experiences as an integrated part of the broader communication process, which includes speaking, listening, and writing, as well as other communication systems such as art, math and music.
5. Encourage children's first attempts at writing, without concern for the proper formation of letters or correct conventional spelling.

---

[1]Reprinted with permission of the International Reading Association. See Appendix C for the entire position paper.

6. Encourage risk-taking in first attempts at reading and writing, and accept what appear to be errors as part of children's natural patterns of growth and development.
7. Use materials for instruction that are familiar, such as well-known stories, because they provide the child with a sense of control and confidence in their ability to learn.
8. Present a model for students to emulate. In the classroom, teachers should use language appropriately, listen and respond to children's talk, and engage in their own reading and writing.
9. Take time regularly to read to children from a wide variety of poetry, fiction, and nonfiction.
10. Provide time regularly for children's independent reading and writing.
11. Foster children's affective and cognitive development by providing opportunities to communicate what they know, think, and feel.
12. Use developmentally and culturally appropriate procedures for evaluation, ones that are based on the objectives of the program and that consider each child's total development.
13. Make parents aware of the reasons for a broader language program at school and provide them with ideas for activities to carry out at home.
14. Alert parents to the limitations of formal assessments and standardized tests of prefirst graders' reading and writing skills.
15. Encourage children to be active participants in the learning process rather than passive recipients, by using activities that allow for experimentation with talking, listening, writing, and reading. [pp. 6, 7]

These 15 statements are consistent with the findings of psycholinguistic studies about how young children construct language and symbols to represent thought. The statements also fit well with recommendations made by sociolinguists and emergent literacy researchers regarding the importance of the context within which language occurs. Kindergarten teachers who plan and implement practices based on these 15 statements can be confident that they are creating a Whole Language environment where children are recognized as active learners and respected as individuals.

The Whole Language kindergarten program is also in agreement with a position paper entitled *Developmentally Appropriate Practice* (Bredekamp, 1987), developed by leading early childhood educators from the NAEYC. Our recommendations are also compatible with those in "The Child-centered Kindergarten" (Moyer et al., 1987), a position paper from the Association for Childhood Education International (ACEI).[2] The descriptions of appropriate practices in these position papers fit well with the concept of emergent literacy, which in turn is based on findings from psycho- and sociolinguistic research. The Whole Language kindergarten program, then, is a child-centered approach in which teachers design and implement activities in a learning environment that is developmentally appropriate for the young child, and in which literacy evolves as a natural part of the communication process.

Proponents of the Whole Language concept are quick to point out that the information gathered by psycho- and sociolinguistic research concerning the nature of the reading/writing process should in no way be used to develop future step-by-step literacy instruction programs (Watson, 1987). This book, then, is not a "how to" teacher's guide, but rather a description of Whole Language kindergartens, which include learning centers, activities, and units organized by teachers. Skills such as left-to-right progression, sound–symbol relationships, capitalization, and punctuation, commonly referred to as "sub" or "basic skills," are never taught in isolation. Instead, throughout this book, examples will be given of Whole Language classroom environments, activities, and teacher interactions that allow children to develop as listeners, speakers, readers, and writers through the active involvement in the communication process. Through these examples, teachers will be able to evaluate their existing kindergarten programs and make their own decisions regarding changes they may need to make, to create a Whole Language kindergarten.

SUMMARY

When kindergarten teachers are exposed to new terms and new findings from research, their natural inclination is to seek to understand what is meant and discern what effects this new information will have or could have on their present practice. Such has been the case with the introduction of the term *Whole Language* into the jargon of the profession. Information from psycholinguistics, sociolinguistics, and emergent literacy has provided the foundation for a new understanding of the reading, writing, and learning processes. This in turn has led reading researchers, early childhood specialists, and practitioners to

---

[2]Excerpts from *Developmentally Appropriate Practice* are given in Appendix A, and excerpts from "The Child-centered Kindergarten" are reprinted in Appendix B.

recommend changes in the kindergarten classroom, because some present practices are in conflict with the findings.

Key elements from psycholinguistic, sociolinguistic, and emergent literacy research can be translated into guidelines for teachers who wish to implement a Whole Language kindergarten. The key elements are:

1. *Immersion.* Immerse children in a rich language and literacy environment.
2. *Opportunities and resources.* Provide time, materials, space, and activities to be listeners, speakers, readers, and writers.
3. *Meaningful communication.* Focus on the whole, because the mind makes sense of or constructs meaning from experiences, whether the experiences are spoken or listened to or read or written about, when they are communicated as wholes.
4. *Modeling.* Act as a communication role model in listening, speaking, reading, and writing, so that instruction, function, and purpose are meaningful.
5. *Acceptance.* Accept young children as readers and writers capable of whole—and thus meaningful—communication.
6. *Expectancy.* Create an atmosphere of expectancy, an affective, attitudinal climate that is encouraging and supportive, where children are expected to continue in their literacy development.

Teachers can find good support for changing to a Whole Language learning environment, particularly from the position papers from educational leaders in national and international associations. Three we recommend are

1. The IRA's *Literacy Development and Prefirst Grade* (Early Childhood and Literacy Development Committee, 1988);
2. The NAEYC's *Developmentally Appropriate Practice* (Bredekamp, 1987);
3. The ACEI's "The Child-centered Kindergarten" (Moyer et al., 1987).

Clarifying what Whole Language means helps kindergarten teachers determine which practices are consistent or inconsistent with this view of beginning reading and writing. As teachers assess their current kindergarten practices as they relate to emergent literacy, their next steps are to decide what needs to be added, modified, or eliminated.

❋ 2 ❋

The Language Experience Approach and a Whole Language Kindergarten

When kindergarten teachers first learn about Whole Language, the question that often follows is: "How does the Language Experience Approach fit into a Whole Language classroom?" The Language Experience Approach (LEA) to reading instruction is based on the premise that the first reading material used for instruction should be meaningful, and that the most meaningful words are the ones the children speak when they tell about some experience they share. For example, after children share an "experience," such as taking a walk together, then they talk about it. The teacher writes down their words, taking dictation from them. The teacher may take dictation from individual children or choose to print a group of children's sentences on a large chart called an experience chart. The children watch the teacher convert their spoken words into written ones. After the dictation process, the teacher reads what the child has said or invites the child to read. As the children become more adept at reading the language they have dictated about their experiences, then the teacher uses those language samples to extend the reading lessons. The children read other students' dictations, write and read group stories, and even bind their writings into books that can be kept in the class library.

There are numerous variations on the Language Experience Approach and even recognized leaders of LEA, such as Roach Van Allen (Allen & Canady, 1979), Russell Stauffer (1980), Mary Ann Hall (1981), Veatch et al. (1973), and Sylvia Ashton-Warner (1963) do not agree on all aspects of the approach. For that reason, when we refer to LEA, we will be using Allen's interpretations, including his organization of LEA into three major strands having a total of 20 substrands (Allen & Canady, 1979). These are shown in Figure 2.1.

Figure 2.1   The Language Experience Approach Strands

Strand One: Experiencing Communication
   1. Oral sharing of ideas
   2. Visual portrayal of experiences
   3. Dramatization of experiences
   4. Responding rhythmically
   5. Discussing and conversing
   6. Exploring writing
   7. Authoring individual books

Strand Two: Studying Communication
   8. Recognizing high-frequency words
   9. Exploring spelling
   10. Studying style and form
   11. Studying language structure
   12. Extending vocabularies
   13. Reading nonalphabetic symbols

Strand Three: Relating Communication of Others to Self
   14. Listening to and reading language of others
   15. Comprehending what is heard and read
   16. Organizing ideas
   17. Assimilating and integrating ideas
   18. Searching and researching multiple sources
   19. Evaluating communication of others
   20. Responding in personal ways

Source: Adapted from R. V. Allen, *Language Experiences in Reading: Teachers Resource Guide* (Level 1), pp. 9–11. Chicago: Encyclopedia Brittanica Educational Corporation, 1974. Used with permission of the publisher.

It is important to note that, even though the use of dictated stories, experience charts, and classroom publishing has long been identified with LEA, Allen's strands include other aspects of the communication process. Kindergartens that are planned and implemented according to these 3 strands and 20 substrands more closely resemble Whole Language kindergartens than those where LEA activities are used to supplement a reading readiness type of kindergarten program (Allen & Canady, 1979).

Whole Language educators recognize the contributions LEA has made to the evolution of Whole Language literacy instruction. LEA has been referred to by some Whole Language educators as "a necessary precursor to Whole Language" (Altwerger, Edelsky, & Flores, 1987, p. 148). In order to clarify some of the differences and similarities of an LEA classroom and a Whole Language learning environment, we will examine one teacher's transition as she restructured her classroom to Whole Language.

Kathy, a kindergarten teacher in a small southwestern town, was first introduced to the concepts of Whole Language while taking early childhood education graduate courses at a local university. Previously she had organized her classroom around the three strands of LEA and over the years had incorporated suggestions from her school's curriculum guide. Kathy was recognized in her school as an eclectic teacher who had integrated other forms of instruction and LEA into the school's established sequential-skills approach to reading and writing. But, as Kathy gathered more information concerning recent studies on literacy acquisition and the reading and writing processes, she began to question some of her kindergarten instructional practices.

LEA DICTATED STORIES, EXPERIENCE CHARTS, AND CHILD-AUTHORED BOOKS

Perhaps the three instructional activities most associated with the Language Experience Approach are dictated stories, experience charts, and child-authored books. Kathy, like many other kindergarten teachers, used dictated stories and experience charts extensively in her classroom as meaningful materials for beginning reading instruction. For example, after drawing pictures, children would tell her about their drawings. Whatever the children said, Kathy wrote below their drawings and then read back to them. The children were then encouraged to read the words they had dictated. Sometimes children dictated whole stories about their drawings. These were shared at grouptime, posted on bulletin boards, and eventually sent home. Some teachers bound individuals' stories or groups of children's stories into books and kept them in the class library, or gave them to the school library, or sent the books home to appreciative parents. The captioned pictures, dictated stories, and child-authored books are examples of some of the activities Kathy used as part of strand one, "experiencing communication" (refer to Figure 2.1).

Group experience charts were also a tool Kathy and other LEA kindergarten teachers used regularly. When a special event happened in the classroom, Kathy had the children gather around her and discuss the event. For example, after a visit from some puppeteers from the city library, Kathy's students discussed the puppet show, then dictated several sentences about their favorite parts of the entertainment (see Figure 2.2). As the children dictated, Kathy wrote. When the experience chart was completed, she read it back to the class. Then individual children read back their own sentences. If any of them wanted to change the way they phrased their sentences, Kathy added the words.

Teachers often use experience charts functionally, throughout the classroom and throughout the curriculum, for meaningful communication. When new materials are added to the science center, for example, a teacher may have the children dictate some safety re-

Figure 2.2 Experience Chart About a Puppet Show

Some people came to our room. They had puppets. I thought Miss Piggy and Kermit would be here.

The man said, "They stayed home." We like the girl puppet. She was pretty. The mean old witch was ugly.

They made the puppets move with strings. The man and woman stayed behind the red curtain. When they got out, they showed us how to jiggle the strings and the puppet move.

At the library, we can see more puppet stories.

minders, which she then writes on a chart. Experience charts may also be used in the block corner, for the builders to tell about their skyscrapers and how they were constructed. When a mother brings a new baby to class, the children may follow the experience by dictating sentences for the experience chart about changes in families when a new baby is in the house. These group experience charts help students relate their personal language to the language of their peers; in the process, the children see their spoken words being converted into printed form. Each experience chart can be displayed in the room, and the children will return to it often to discover they can read what they have said and what others have said, even when the teacher is not around.

A favorite pastime for some children in Kathy's classroom was finding all the words on the experience charts that start with the letters of their first names. In addition to offering a means of "experiencing communication" (strand one), experience charts are good examples of strand two, "studying communication." As children reread the sentences from the experience charts and from their personally dictated captions and stories, they discover sound–symbol relationship, describing words and words of movement, and they also internalize the relationship of the structure of oral language and the structure of written language.

CHILDREN'S LITERATURE WITH THEME TEACHING

Kindergarten teachers often depend on the librarian's assistance to help them select books to accompany the themes or units of study of the kindergarten curriculum. Whether it was a unit on community helpers, families, seasons, transportation, or simple machines, the librarian at Kathy's school helped her find good books to be read to the children and to be displayed in the library corner of the classroom.

Regardless of the theme or unit, Kathy read aloud to her class at least twice a day, once during morning grouptime and again after the children came in from playing outside. Exposing children to good literature is an important part of the third strand of the language experience approach, "relating the communication of others to the self" (Allen & Canady, 1979). Children relate their personal language to the books that are read to them in the same way that they discover the similarities of each other's language when they share dictated stories and experience charts.

Kathy observed that even the children who came from limited home reading environments chose to go to the library corner more often when there were familiar books there that had been read aloud in class (Raines & Isbell, 1989). She also kept a variety of other good children's books, poems, jokes, riddles, and magazines in the library corner.

HOW IS A WHOLE LANGUAGE LEARNING ENVIRONMENT DIFFERENT FROM AN LEA CLASSROOM?

At the university, Kathy was introduced to the six elements of a Whole Language learning environment that are discussed in Chapter 1. They derived from the research and writing of Marie Clay (1975), Kenneth Goodman (1968), Yetta Goodman (1983), Donald Graves (1983), Don Holdaway (1979) and Dorothy Watson (1987), among others. Kathy decided to use the six elements to evaluate her current classroom operation. In this section we will take a look at her thinking in these areas.

Immersion

Kathy felt that her LEA classroom certainly met the first key element—immersion in language and print. The children in her room had ample opportunity to talk, listen, and role-play through the many choices of activities they found at the various learning centers. They also were surrounded by print. As she looked around her room, she saw the signs she had printed concerning the rules of the classroom, the children's names over their cubbyholes, and the printed labels she had attached to the furniture and storage areas throughout the room. She had even labeled the face of the clock high up on the wall. There were captions under bulletin boards, labels on puzzle boxes, and signs giving directions.

As she thought about the key element of immersion in language and print, Kathy realized that, even though the spoken language that was generated in her classroom was the children's own personal communication, the written language room was not theirs—it was hers. She decided to keep some of the signs, labels, and charts, but only those that were meaningful communications from her to the children. She planned to engage the children themselves in writing more of the print for signs and directions.

Opportunities and Resources

The second key element, which involved providing time, materials, space, activities, and opportunities for children to be listeners, speakers, readers, and writers, certainly fit with Kathy's existing schedule, materials, and space. She provided many activities and opportunities for the children to be listeners, speakers, readers, and writers. However, her view of the reading and writing processes and, for that matter, learning itself, had been altered considerably since her coursework at the university. She realized that she needed to re-examine some of the activities—and thus the opportunities—she had been providing as means for children to learn to read and write.

She had learned that the reading process is a "psycholinguistic guessing game," a process of using graphophonic, syntactic, and semantic cues simultaneously to construct meaning from print (Goodman, 1982a). In her notes, she had written, "Children predict what the print means by scanning and sampling the print, then reject or confirm their predictions, and either integrate new information into existing concepts or restructure the concepts when faced with conflicting information. Readers use the three systems of semantic, syntactic, and graphophonic cues to engage in the reading process of predicting, sampling, confirming, and integrating information."

When Kathy recalled the read-aloud activities she had seen when she visited Whole Language classrooms, she remembered that many of the teachers brainstormed with the children and discussed several ideas related to the book, before beginning to read the story. One teacher spent almost five minutes having the children tell what they already knew about the two characters, Frog and Toad, before she read to them. Then the children looked at (sampled) the picture and the print on the outside cover of the book, to make predictions about the story. As the teacher read to the children, she paused periodically to let the children confirm that their predictions were accurate or to change their predictions, as they heard new information in the story. As the story unfolded and after the reading was completed, the children integrated what they knew from previous Frog and Toad adventures about the usual way the two characters interacted, with the surprises in this particular story.

As Kathy reviewed her notes on the classroom visits, she decided that in the future when she read aloud to the children, she would concentrate more on helping them make connections with the characters, events, actions, and problems of the story, thus helping the children to develop the strategies they must use when they read on their own. She planned to incorporate many more strategies for focusing on reading as a process. The following sources provide a variety of reading process strategies: Goodman, 1983; Lynch, 1986; Martin, 1988; Raines and Canady, 1989; Raines and Isbell, 1988; Rhodes, 1981; and Watson, 1987.

After examining the research data describing young children's writing (Clay, 1975) and research on the writing process (Graves, 1983), Kathy also decided to make some changes in the way she helped the children become writers. She recognized that, in the dictation process, when she wrote captions and stories for the children's drawings, she did not allow the children to use their own knowledge of how print works. This practice was causing the children to view composition as something that is done before, instead of during, the writing process. She planned instead to encourage children to form their own letters and to use their own invented spellings to write captions for pictures they drew, as well as to write longer messages and stories. She decided to continue to use experience charts to record whole-class and small-group activities, but she would eliminate individual dictation, unless the child asked for it.

Kathy's decisions concerning children's writing were derived not only from the research she had read but also from examining young children's writing samples she had collected for her university class. She noted how the children progressed from using a single letter to represent a whole word and gradually acquired more letters and combinations of letters, until their writing approximated correct or "standard" spelling (Temple, Nathan, Burris, & Temple, 1988). Kathy suddenly realized that the dictation process, where the teacher prints exactly what the child says, does not allow the children to use the knowledge they already possess about print, but makes them dependent upon the teacher.

Meaningful Communication

The third element of a Whole Language learning environment is meaningful communication. Using the language experience approach, Kathy had always included many firsthand and hands-on experiences, such as field trips into the community, cooking the children's favorite recipes, nature walks, growing plants, and caring for real animals in the classroom. She provided as many firsthand or whole experiences as possible because she felt the children learned more from them. She had found that each experience had stimulated meaningful communication. Kathy often took notes on what the children said about their experiences. She then used their descriptive words to make charts of vocabulary words associated with their experiences. Taking the words from the charts, she alphabetized them and placed them on a wall, to make a "wordwall." She was amazed at how well the children remembered words that they could associate with meaningful events.

Kathy realized she had always placed a strong emphasis on individual words and in recent years had been emphasizing decoding skills, breaking the words down into individual sounds. She wondered if the time she used teaching such skills might not be better spent on having the children read signs, logos, directions, books, and other meaningful print, as well as asking them to write about their experiences on their own. Kathy began to think of "communicating" an experience as being part of what makes the experience whole and meaningful.

Modeling

The fourth key element in a Whole Language learning environment is modeling, where the teacher acts as a communication role model in listening, speaking, reading, and writing, so instruction, function, and purpose are meaningful. Kathy was already aware of her significance as a role model; however, after reviewing the emergent literacy research and observing Whole Language teachers, she recognized she could do more to model the reading and writing processes. She thought of many new ways throughout the day and throughout the curriculum where she could let the children see her engaged in these processes. For example, she always did the snack count early in the morning and wrote the number on a form for the cafeteria. She could include the children by having them count with her, and then write the numeral on a large sheet of paper with a message to the cafeteria workers. She also often wrote notes home to the parents, which she pinned on the children's coats to make sure the notes got home, but she had not read the notes to the children. She decided to include them by reading the message to them or having them help her compose what the message might say.

Similarly, as a role model, she planned to emphasize her own reading by showing the children the written materials she had read in preparation for the grouptime lesson, how she determined what ingredients were needed for a recipe, and where she read about the seashells she had displayed on the science table. There were many ways she could help the children to figure out that print provides adults with information.

Acceptance

Although Kathy thought of herself as an accepting person who knew about young children's needs, she found that she unwittingly had conveyed a different feeling to the children when it came to their reading and writing attempts. Accepting young children as readers and writers capable of whole and thus meaningful communication would be a change for Kathy. After tape recording some of her verbal interactions with the children, she found that she often pointed out to them what was wrong or incorrect with what they read or wrote. While she always accepted children's art work and appreciated each artist's individuality, when it came to reading and writing, she had thought it was her responsibility to correct the children so that they "got it right."

After learning more about early natural readers and writers, Kathy decided to try to make her kindergarten classroom as much like a home reading and writing environment as possible, to be accepting of children. Studies of natural readers and writers—those children who already are reading and writing when they enter kindergarten—show that children learn to read and write in much the same way they learn to listen and talk (Baghban, 1984; Bissex, 1980; Clark, 1976; Clay, 1972; Durkin, 1966). They learn through interactions with other language users in their homes, in a supportive, accepting environment where they are encouraged for what they attempt, rather than being overcorrected for what they do not know.

Kathy realized that, since she already provided large blocks of time for the children to choose their activities, she could use these to interact with the children in a natural, conversant manner. This is in contrast to the "teacher's voice," which is often overly probing and questioning and causes the child to think, "Something must be wrong with what I'm doing, because the teacher keeps on needing me to clarify what I'm saying." Likewise, Kathy recognized that young children begin to explore written language as an integral part of their environments. These natural readers and writers are rewarded for their efforts, and their mistakes or "miscues" are accepted as a natural part of the learning process. When teachers think of reading as a process, they encourage children to read for meaning, even if it results in minor changes or "miscues" in their reading (Goodman,

1983). Kathy decided she would treat the children's reading and writing similarly to how she responded to their artwork. She would accept whatever they read or wrote and ask them in a more natural, conversant tone to tell her more about it.

Expectancy

As Kathy thought of a positive attitudinal climate in her classroom as being an accepting environment where children were seen as readers and writers, she also thought of it as one of expectancy. From writing samples she had collected from one child, she had recognized how a child's writing changes over time. From tape recordings she had made of a child's pretend reading over several weeks, she realized that young children's reading changes very rapidly. She already expected the children to develop in their reading and writing abilities. But, with her new emphasis on all the things the children already knew how to do, rather than on how much more they needed to learn, Kathy felt she would create an even more positive atmosphere in the classroom—one of expecting the children to succeed.

INTERPRETATIONS OF WHOLE LANGUAGE

During her university coursework, when Kathy reflected on what she taught and how she taught, she realized that her views of appropriate kindergarten practice were changing. She came to view reading readiness differently. She recognized that the information about emergent literacy had influenced her view of how young children develop as readers and writers. She also felt that she could make changes in her kindergarten by keeping the three strands of LEA, but interpreting them differently than she had in the past.

Changed View of Reading Readiness

When Kathy examined various approaches to teaching reading, she recognized that, regardless of her emphasis on LEA, her school primarily had a skills-based program. At the end of the kindergarten year, the reading readiness tests that were given were designed to determine if the children knew the sounds the letters represented. Her reports on the children's progress, which she sent forward to the first-grade teachers, also emphasized the phonics skills of the reading readiness tests. There were no observations of the children's understanding of stories they heard read to them and no checklists of the students' interactions with books, such as reading on their own, pretending reading, and questions about stories.

This skills-based approach, commonly called a part-to-whole approach, is often associated with kindergarten reading readiness programs (Jewell & Zintz, 1986). On the other hand, the approaches that assess young children's interactions with the content of stories are called comprehension approaches. Certainly in the Whole Language program, the major emphasis is on comprehension. The child is expected to construct the meaning from the print by bringing prior knowledge to the story (such as remembering the two characters of Frog and Toad) and by predicting what the story might be about by using cues from the cover, the title, and finally from the print. This view of reading is sometimes called a whole-to-part program (Jewell & Zintz, 1986).

When Kathy had first begun using the Language Experience Approach, she thought she had solved the "skills" problem by introducing the children to the "basic skills" of reading through the words they used to describe their experiences. She recorded their words through dictated stories and experience charts. From poetry, songs, children's literature, and many other resources, she took key words and displayed them on charts and wordwalls. From those words, she helped the children to learn skills such as directionality, letters, and sounds, as they related to what had started out as whole and meaningful language.

Even before Kathy's introduction to Whole Language, however, she had been disturbed by the fact that so many of the children who had enjoyed dictated stories and experience-chart reading in her kindergarten classroom suddenly lost their enthusiasm when she drilled them on the letter sounds. They also were even less enthusiastic about reading from the controlled vocabulary readers in first grade. Several of the first-grade teachers had voiced concern about the effect of the nonsensical primers and preprimers, but they did not want to get the children out of sequence for the basal reader series, which included specific skills at each grade level.

Psycholinguistic and Sociolinguistic Influences

Kathy recognized that there were at least three major differences between the Whole Language kindergarten teachers' view of reading and writing instruction and her own practices. First, the teachers in the kindergartens she visited had allowed the children to write in whatever form they were capable of, whether it was scribbling, using a few letters, or writing long sentences and stories where the children "invented" ways to spell the words using whatever letters they knew. One Whole Language teacher said the children were "constructing writing." Second, these teachers seemed to have a different concept of "skills." Third, the teachers were able to explain the reasons for the ways they taught and why they had made certain changes in their classrooms. They were operating from a different theoretical base. If this base made sense to Kathy and she expected to use it for planning her curriculum, she would have to be able to explain it to the other teachers, the principal, and the parents.

Constructing writing. While visiting Whole Language kindergartens, Kathy had noticed the abundance of stories on display that the children had written themselves using invented spellings. The teacher had shown her samples of the children's writing from throughout the year. Kathy was fascinated with how the children went from scribbling and writing a few letters to writing sentences and stories that she could read and understand. She recalled that, when she had asked her kindergartners to write, they had said, "But we don't know how to spell." The children in this classroom were writing without concern for exact spelling. Kathy knew these children were actually writing, while her students were telling her what to write.

A different concept of skills. When Kathy made her first visits to Whole Language kindergartens, she noticed the lack of skills lessons. She agreed that reading and writing skills should not be taught in isolation, as separate drills on each of the letter sounds. But she failed to see how the Whole Language teachers could possibly know whether or not the children were learning the skills necessary to decode unknown words, if there were no direct lessons in the use of these skills. Kathy soon observed that Whole Language kindergarten children did know the basic skills of reading, and they were applying those skills when they encountered new words. The difference was that the skills were learned during real or "whole" reading situations, and mastery of those skills was evaluated during the process of reading, not through the use of paper-and-pencil tasks.

Kathy also noticed that, with reading as with writing, the children were at many different levels; however, the Whole Language kindergarten teacher called all of the children "readers." Some were listening to tapes the teacher had recorded of some of the students' favorite books, and they would join in with the reading on the tape by saying some of the recurring phrases throughout the book. She remembered one child listening to the tape, then suddenly saying aloud (reading aloud) several times, "Run, run, as fast as you can. You can't catch me, I'm the Gingerbread Man." Kathy also recalled a little boy who invited a friend to hear him read *The Very Hungry Caterpillar* (Carle, 1981). At the time, Kathy thought he had memorized the book, but the teacher called him a reader. She also remembered the little girl who was poring over a copy of *Chickens Aren't the Only Ones* (Heller, 1981), and appeared to be searching for a certain word. She was reading under her breath, then stopped, pointed to the word, and called her teacher over and said, "I found it. *Oviparous.* That's the hard word." Kathy remembered then that was the book the teacher had read for the morning grouptime. While she certainly would have thought of this child as a reader, before she changed her concept of reading skills, Kathy would not have thought of as readers the children who remembered a recurring phrase or had memorized a book. The Whole Language kindergarten teacher said they were all readers because they expected to comprehend the story.

Explaining teaching differently. Perhaps the main difference between Kathy's approach to LEA and the Whole Language teachers' view of literacy acquisition lies in the theoretical base that forms the foundation of their teaching. Kathy recognized how her own thinking had changed as she had been exposed to more information. Thus, before any meaningful change could take place in any educational program, it would be important to evaluate that program in terms of what the teacher believes is best. As she thought about her skills-based school and her own modified version of LEA, she knew many of the teachers believed that reading is best taught by reducing the English language into its most basic elements—letters, sounds, and words. They thought it advisable to teach those elements first, and then slowly and methodically put the language back together until the child could read whole stories. Variously labeled "phonics" or "whole-word instruction," the theoretical base for this method is a part-to-whole approach to learning (Jewell & Zintz, 1986).

As Kathy learned more about the theoretical base of the Whole Language perspective, she began to understand the frustration she had felt in recent years as she had attempted to conduct a holistic kindergarten program and still meet the demands of a skills-based approach. The foundation of the Whole Language view of instruction is a constructivist perspective of how children build and refine their concepts of reading and writing by being involved in real reading and writing, rather than in instruction about reading and writing. As Kathy began to restructure her program as a Whole Language kindergarten, she realized that her theory of how children become readers and writers had changed.

ADAPTING THE THREE STRANDS OF LANGUAGE EXPERIENCE APPROACH TO THE WHOLE LANGUAGE KINDERGARTEN

Many kindergarten teachers who, like Kathy, learn more about Whole Language recognize that in many ways they are already Whole Language teachers. Their classrooms are rich with language and print; they appreciate the young child as a developing reader and writer; they recognize the significance of their role as a communication model for listening, speaking, reading, and writing. Armed with new information about emergent literacy, however, they often decide to make some changes in the curriculum, in the resources, and in their interactions.

Kathy's decision to evaluate her classroom by reviewing each of the three strands of the language experience approach was a helpful device for her. When she looked at strand one, experiencing communication, she became eager to incorporate more of the children's own writing, rather than dictation. She recalled that the children she had observed writing their own captions for a drawing appeared to do so quite naturally, but she had been using dictation for so long that it felt a bit unnatural to her not to be writing for the children. She would not draw a picture for a child, yet she felt compelled to write the caption for it. She recognized that the children were constructing the written language in much the same way they constructed the picture, by bringing to the task what they then knew and were able to do. She recalled the child in her case study, a little girl who wrote *A* for her name, Amy. She wrote what she knew at the time. A few months later, she wrote "AMY HOS" under the drawing of her house, and it reflected her expanded knowledge of spelling gained from freely exploring reading and writing.

Kathy thus planned to limit her use of dictation for individual children, while still continuing to use group and experience-chart dictation to help show the relationship between written and spoken language. She recalled how the experience charts helped children expand their reading and writing vocabularies. While she saw some need for change in the second LEA strand (studying communication), she realized the charts were still valuable tools. She remembered the children going over to the charts and pointing out their names and a few familiar words, so she planned to take advantage of their interests and encourage them to read and reread the charts that drew their attention. She would help them recall the incidence that prompted that particular group dictation and then let children who were interested read their sentences and those of their friends. Kathy planned to encourage them to read on their own, without correcting the "miscues," so readers would approach the print without fearing they would make mistakes. She had come to regard miscues as natural in beginning reading, not as mistakes.

Basic-skills and reading readiness teachers often like the second LEA strand, "studying communication," because it sounds like the emphasis is on skills. For example, a common basic skill and a reading readiness skill is the recognition of rhyming words. The basic-skills teacher may ask the child to complete a worksheet by matching printed words that rhyme, and the reading readiness teacher may direct the child to circle pictures of sets of objects that rhyme. Whole Language teachers prefer to use the rich resources of children's poems, songs, and patterned language stories. They read and reread the selections, so that children learn to actively reconstruct the poet's or author's language by recognizing the rhyming patterns. The verbal cloze process works well with rhyming words. For example, when the teacher says, "Twinkle, twinkle, little *star*, how I wonder what you ____ ," the children immediately can predict the rhyming words. The Whole Language teacher's primary purpose is for the children to experience the language and to predict what the author might say in the next rhyming couplet, based on what they already know about their own language, or to enjoy the rhyme of the poem as it moves along and stops at the end of the verse. All three types of teachers are involved in language study, but the Whole Language teacher is capitalizing on the children's natural rhyming ability. She is helping them to use what they already know, to predict what the writer might say. The children can hear how a writer works with the words to create a whole.

The third LEA strand, relating the communication of others to oneself, also needs some attention if it is to take advantage of the new knowledge about emergent literacy, and if the kindergarten classroom is to be turned into a Whole Language environment. While many kindergarten teachers, and Kathy as an LEA teacher, recognize the importance of reading to their children every day and providing books in the library corner, many need help in showing children the relationship between their personal written and spoken language and that of others. Some teachers place too much emphasis on exactness or correct, word-by-word reading. When they have children join them in repeating the recurring phrases in a story in which a new character is added to each scene, they insist on exactness. They do not allow for the natural "miscues" that are caused by personal language and personal experiences. When children construct meaning through the processes of speaking, writing, listening, and reading, many times they make changes in the original language without changing the meaning intended. For example, when a child reads, "The caterpillar made an egg," and the text says, "The caterpillar laid an egg," the "miscue" makes sense.

When teachers listen to children's early reading attempts and observe their early writing attempts, it is the effort and what the children bring to the task that are significant. With time and with new experiences of seeing and hearing the language read and written by the teacher and their friends, children will become more knowledgeable. They will add to their constructions through the study of the language that the teacher provides, and by exploring language in its written and spoken forms on their own.

PUTTING IT ALL TOGETHER

Many kindergarten programs, like Kathy's, are designed around a curriculum guide which is often written by a group of teachers and administrators working together. Teachers in a particular school or child-care center agree to design their instructional programs around the goals listed in the curriculum guide, and they agree that any basic changes made in the program should be consistent with the goals that have been established.

After teachers learn more about emergent literacy, one of the first tasks they often want to undertake is a reassessment of their school's curriculum guide. It is not unusual to find that the overall goals and aims of the curriculum are compatible with emergent literacy. The guides often make such statements as, "Children should be treated as individuals." "Consider the whole child and each aspect of development—cognitive, language, physical, social and emotional." However, when the proposed goals become translated into activities stated in behavioral objectives, the resulting "skills and drills" seem at cross purposes to recognizing individual differences. Fortunately, many principals and program directors understand that young children need hands-on experiences in order to learn and are willing to have informed teachers make changes in their classrooms, if the teachers can explain them.

To encourage curricular changes, Whole Language teachers often share their plans with their peers in their schools, join with other kindergarten teachers who are making similar efforts, and invite principals and supervisors for regular observations. When administrators observe the children reading and writing on their own and see progress over time, and when parents display those child-authored stories with pride, then there is less concern over whether or not the "basic skills" are being taught.

Those parents, fellow teachers, and administrators who are anxious about whether the children are acquiring skills can be shown the many ways Whole Language teachers evaluate their children's progress. Teachers can share examples of the children's writing and tapes of the children's reading, and they can invite direct observations of the children's progress (Fields, 1988). In so doing, they help parents and administrators to become better informed.

Incidentally, principals and child-care-center directors recognize that they can save money on copying paper, dittoes, and workbooks when the kindergarten becomes a Whole Language classroom. Teachers should request that the money saved from those supplies be used to purchase more children's literature, such as patterned language books and wordless picture books, as well as writing supplies and materials for binding and publishing the children's own writing.

As teachers like Kathy review books and articles on Whole Language teaching and become aware of the reciprocal relationship between beginning reading and beginning writing in natural literacy acquisition, they feel comfortable making changes in their classrooms. Throughout this book we will provide glimpses into Whole Language classrooms, explaining teaching practices and interaction patterns between the children and the teacher that are indicative of a Whole Language classroom. The following are some of the basic changes that many Language Experience Approach teachers who want to become Whole Language teachers find they must make:

1. Include more writing activities;
2. Continue the practice of reading to the children at least twice a day, with more emphasis on strategies that focus on the reading process;

3. Surround the children with print in the environment;
4. Use print as often as possible to convey messages to the children and to help them see how writing is used to communicate (Loughlin & Martin, 1987);
5. Provide more "environmental" print for children to interact with, such as signs, logos, advertisements, and other print children find in their homes and communities;
6. Use children's literature and the classroom library more actively.

Teachers also often find themselves ordering more books and expanding their own knowledge of children's literature. With the changes in materials come changes in room arrangement. Often teachers create a special center for writing and publishing, sometimes near the art area because of the close relationship between writing and artistic expression. Similarly, writing materials often find their way into the library corner because young children are inspired to write based on what has been read to them or what they have read on their own. Additional information about changes in materials and room arrangements are provided throughout this book.

As the library corner is expanded and furniture is rearranged to make space for the writing center, materials and equipment throughout the room soon begin to reflect changes in the teacher's attitude of acceptance and expectancy toward the children as constructors of their own reading and writing. Some changes include placing pens and pencils in the housekeeping corner and leaving markers and poster board near the science and blocks areas. As the classroom takes shape, the teacher brings the kindergarten program more in line with the key elements of a Whole Language learning environment. Teachers who learn more about emergent literacy rapidly develop what Goodman (personal interview, 1988) says is a prerequisite for Whole Language reading and writing instruction: a Whole Language "attitude" toward literacy acquisition and development.

SUMMARY

Important contributions to literacy instruction have been made by LEA leaders, such as Allen and Canady (1979), Hall (1981), Stauffer (1980), and others (e.g., Ashton-Warner, 1963). Now, as teachers are influenced by recent research on emergent literacy, many decide to make basic changes in their LEA kindergartens.

In this chapter, we shared the experience of one LEA kindergarten teacher who became a Whole Language teacher. Kathy kept the three strands of the LEA as a way of organizing the reading and writing program in her classroom, but she made changes in her interactions and her acceptance and expectations of the children as readers and writers, thus necessitating changes in the activities under those strands. Most important, Kathy changed her attitude about her teaching responsibility as she saw herself as a reading and writing teacher. As she learned more about how young children develop naturally as readers and writers, she modified her reading and writing instruction.

Many LEA teachers, like Kathy, have restructured each of the three strands in specific ways, to make their kindergartens into Whole Language learning environments.

In order to promote "experiencing communication," they have

1. Made more materials available for independent writing, encouraging children to use their own invented spellings;
2. Continued to use experience charts to record group experiences.

To promote "communication study," they have

1. Continued to use experience charts as one way to introduce their children to the conventions of writing,
2. Eliminated all reading readiness worksheets and allowed children to show their "mastery of skills" through the use of real reading and writing activities,
3. Helped the children understand the construction of written and oral language through the use of more children's literature.

In the third LEA strand, designed to help children "relate the communication of others to the self," these teachers have

1. Used more prediction strategies, such as verbal cloze, while reading with the children, and encouraged them to use their knowledge of their own language to predict the language of the author;
2. Realized miscues made by children when they read and write are important to learning and that reading and writing samples should therefore be analyzed for what children demonstrate they do know, instead of what has still to be learned.

Finally, these LEA kindergarten teachers have changed their attitudes to make them compatible with the Whole Language view, by recognizing children as constructors of their own knowledge and by accepting children as communicators of whole and meaningful language, whether in spoken or written form.

As LEA teachers transform their classrooms into the Whole Language learning environment, they recognize that it is imperative that the children's parents, the principal or child-care-center director, and the teachers' colleagues become observers and interacters with the children in the kindergarten. By evaluating their past practices and their curriculum, and by carefully planning changes, Whole Language teachers can take the first steps toward creating an environment where children continue developing their literacy.

3

The Role of Play in the Whole Language Kindergarten

Whatever the child's age, the desire to play and the act of playing itself fill a child's attention and energy. All young children have the need, and from quite a young age they know the word *play*. A two-year-old will toddle over to her father, grasp his finger with her tiny hand, and tug him toward a stack of toys on the patio, repeating over and over, "Play, play." A five-year-old will sit at the dinner table and attempt to bribe her aunt by saying, "If I eat my green beans, then will you play 'Candyland' with me?" A mother we know sleepily answered the doorbell at seven o'clock on a Saturday morning to find the familiar sight of little Jonathan, his bright eyes looking up at her, asking, "Can Scott come out and play?" After being told Scott was away at his grandparents' for the weekend, Jonathan turned slowly to leave, then asked, "Can *you* come out and play?"

Adults can identify with these scenes because play is what children do. Adults recognize children's various invitations to play, their creative attempts to manipulate others to play, and the intrinsic need for play that all experience. As adults watch children at play, they recall the joys of their own childhoods.

While adults may enjoy romanticizing their own play as children, kindergarten teachers realize that play is more than that. Early childhood educators have learned that play meets some very basic needs of young children. These needs must be identified and explained when parents ask, "But when do you teach them? Every time I come to the classroom, I see them playing." Much of the success of a Whole Language kindergarten program depends on the teacher's ability to protect the child's right to play and to assure parents that their child, indeed, is being taught and is learning through a carefully planned play environment.

WHY PLAY IS CENTRAL TO THE CURRICULUM

While it is easy for parents to think of play as a means for young children to occupy their time and energy while at home, they often expect that, because kindergarten is a part of school, it should be more like school than play. Teachers must help parents understand play as a vehicle for meaningful learning in all areas of child growth and development. In the NAEYC's *Developmentally Appropriate Practice* (Bredekamp, 1987), teachers are reminded that "the child's active participation in self-directed play with concrete, real-life experiences continues to be a key to motivated, meaningful learning in kindergarten and the early grades" (p. 4). In the ACEI position paper, "The Child-centered Kindergarten" (Moyer et al., 1987), it is said that one of the characteristics of quality programs is that they

> view play as fundamental to children's learning, growth and development, enabling them to develop and clarify concepts, roles and ideas by testing them through use of open-ended materials and role-enactment. Play further enables children to develop fine and gross motor skills, to learn to share with others, to see others' points of view and to be in control of their thoughts and feelings. [p. 239]

Growth Across Areas of Development

The ACEI statement offers guidelines encompassing all of the major areas of child development. Through clarifying concepts, roles, and ideas, children develop *cognitively*. As they use materials that challenge their fine and gross motor skills, they develop *physically*. Through sharing with others and seeing others' points of view, children develop *socially*. As they retain control of their own thoughts and feelings, they develop *emotionally*.

The Whole Language kindergarten teacher who recognizes the value of play for the development of the whole child—physically, cognitively, socially, and emotionally—is also aware of the importance of play in the language development of young children. Vygotsky (1962) and Piaget (1974) have written extensively about the reciprocal relationships that exist between language acquisition and cognitive development through play. One aspect of language development that becomes most evident during the observation of play is a child's representational competence. As Yawkey (1983) states, "Pretend play and language growth are related through representational thought" (p. 1).

Representational Thought

The levels of representation children demonstrate through their use of language and props is evident in the following play scene from a study of representational thought (Raines, 1990a). Four children were playing in the housekeeping corner, which they had converted into a pizzeria, using props a girl's father had provided from his franchise pizza business. The children decorated the center with a red and white checkered tablecloth; set the table with napkins, glasses, and plates that had the restaurant's logo on them; and began to play. As the children negotiated for their roles, a chef and a server volunteered, and the two remaining children were told that they were the customers.

The observer noticed that, as soon as the play began, the vocabulary of the various players changed. The chef used the terms *oven, pizza cutter,* and *'rella cheese.* The server used *order, menu, thick and chewy,* and *thin and crispy.* The customers specified *pepperoni, super deluxe,* and the names of their favorite soft drinks. Not only was the vocabulary rich, but the intonation and inflection verified the roles the children played. The players expressed complete confidence as they represented their roles in words and actions.

An unexpected representation was observed, however, as the play continued. The server, who was dressed in an apron, came to the table to take the customers' orders and asked, "What do you want to eat?" and then abruptly left to search for a pad and pencil. Another child, who had wanted to be the server, jumped up from her seat at the table, held up the palm of her hand, and, using her finger like a pencil, asked, "May I take your order, please?" Then, hearing the customer's reply, proceeded to press on her palm and say aloud, "Pepperoni, thick and chewy."

For the first server to play this role, a red apron, a real pad, and a real pencil were needed. For the second server, a hand and finger were sufficient for an imaginary pad and pencil; moreover, her phrasing was more indicative of the comments of a "real-life" server. Both children knew their roles well, but they varied in their need for props to represent their knowledge. The language and actions in their play were evidence of the children's representational competence. According to Copple, Sigel, and Saunders (1979), "Representational competence develops fully only in response to interactions with the appropriate physical and social environments" (p. 24).

Play is central to the Whole Language kindergarten, because play is a representation of the real world, and because it is through play that children often employ layers of symbols in their representations.

For example, the children in the pizza parlor play scene were representing a real-world experience they had enjoyed, but they also used symbols to represent real objects. When one player wrote with her finger, she represented symbolically the server using symbols to write, or what Sinatra (1986) terms the "double knowledge of representational thought" (p. 11). As the children played in their pizza parlor, they understood that what they were creating was a representation of the real. As Garvey (1977) has said, "All play requires the players to understand that what is done is not what it appears to be" (p. 7). While some children need more authentic symbols to represent their worlds, for others play is layered with symbols.

From the pizza parlor play scene, each player's responses can be examined and their vocabulary and ability to represent their roles competently can be assessed. However, if we examine the evolving play throughout the interaction, even more evidence of the children's learning can be seen. After ordering, cooking, waiting for the pizza, eating, and paying, the role players exchanged roles. The first server began to imitate the second, writing with her finger on the palm of her hand. A quiet customer who had let someone else place the orders later used new vocabulary to place an order. Despite the fact that some of the phrases got mixed up, such as "thin and chewy" instead of "thick and chewy," through play this child's social confidence and competence in the role of customer grew.

Play As Story Making

Another area of language development that occurs in play is that of story making. As children play, they are constructing stories (Harste et al., 1984; Roskos, 1988). Within a few sentences, the children organize themselves into characters, set the scene, and decide on a plot or storyline that will engage them in connected dialogue and action. Someone will suggest, "You be the Daddy. I'll be the Mommy, and let's pretend we're going to a party." The resulting play contains a clear sequence of events, including getting ready for the party, going to the party, and being at the party. Through play, teachers can observe all the elements of a good story, such as development of character, location, scenes, a central theme, problems solved, and satisfactory endings.

Educators and researchers have much to learn about the dynamics and complexity of children's representations with props, their uses of vocabulary, and the ways they construct stories through play. Nonetheless, the ease with which children move in and out of play reinforces the value of play in the curriculum as an avenue of natural learning. The dynamics of the play are observable when one sees the roles and the problems change throughout the play episode. At first, the play takes on a comfortable rhythm; then conflict arises and the play changes as a problem has to be solved. Again, the play regains its equilibrium and continues through creative sequences of interactions, until another problem has to be solved in order for the story or the episode to continue. Teachers can help parents to see that play contributes to growth across all areas of development, including language development, growth in representational competence, and in story making.

INVITATIONS TO PLAY

Outside the classroom, children may have to resort to hand tugging, promises to eat their green beans, or even doorbell ringing to solicit a playmate, but in a Whole Language kindergarten, teachers issue invitations to play. Teachers invite play by the creative ways in which they arrange the schedule, encourage the players, and prepare the classroom environment for play.

Arranging the Schedule for Play

Play is the heart of the kindergarten day. At intervals throughout the day, children are free to play. There are three major time periods designated as play times in the schedule listed in Table 3.1—the tabletop activities (arrival time), freeplay, and outside play. While schedules may vary slightly, this basic structure is recommended by early childhood curriculum specialists (Fromberg, 1988; Seefeldt & Barbour, 1986; Spodek, Saracho, & Davis, 1987).

Tabletop activities or center time. As the children arrive one by one, they are greeted by the teacher and then encouraged either to select from materials placed on tabletops or to go to one of the play or learning centers. For example, when tabletop activities were observed in one classroom, we saw the teacher had placed puzzles and Tinker Toys at one table. On another, the teacher's aide was supervising a cut-and-paste art activity related to a fall theme. On the third table, Play Doh was available. While at first glance it appeared that the tabletop materials were simply for manipulating, closer observation revealed how children use these materials for constructive play.

Table 3.1   Half-Day Kindergarten Schedule

8:30–9:00	*Arrival time—individual greetings, tabletop activities, or center time
9:00–9:30	Circletime or grouptime
9:30–10:30	*Freeplay inside, often at labeled centers
10:30–10:40	Snacktime[a]
10:40–10:45	Preparations for outside play
10:45–11:15	*Outside play
11:15–11:25	Toileting, washing hands, browsing through books while waiting for others
11:25–11:50	Storytime
11:50–12:00	Departure[b]

*Designated for play activities.

[a]Snack may be served during freeplay time, with children coming to the snack table as they choose. With an open snack plan, the freeplay period could be extended.

[b]For a full-day program, lunch is served; children nap, rest, or engage in quiet activities while resting for 30 minutes to an hour. This is followed by a repeat of the time frames of grouptimes, freeplay either outside or inside, and culminating in a group activity to complete the day.

Two children on one side of a table were working with puzzles, while two other children were helping each other construct an elaborate design by connecting plastic Tinker Toys. Damien, working with a new farm scene puzzle, systematically tried each piece until it fit. Roberto, playing with a familiar puzzle, held each piece like a toy airplane, waved it over his head, and talked to other imaginary pilots before flying the piece into its spot in the puzzle. When the two other children at the table, Michael and Latrice, extended their Tinker Toy construction into Damien's workspace, they received a reprimand. "Get out of here!" Damien yelled. "I'm the policeman."

With the expansion of each added section, the Tinker Toy builders transformed their structure. At the beginning, Michael said it was going to be a robot, but, by the time the structure had invaded Damien's workspace, it had become a spaceship. What appeared to be simply the manipulation of materials soon escalated into constructive and even dramatic play.

Freeplay inside and outside.   The second time period designated for play is the freeplay period (refer to Table 3.1). At this time, children are free to choose their own playmates and play activities and to decide, within the schedule limits, how long the play is to continue. Some teachers feel that the term *freeplay* may be misunderstood and choose to call this period of the day "choice time," "center time," or "interest time." Regardless of the label, a time for individual choice of partners and play activities is essential to the kindergarten program.

In addition, the freeplay period must be long enough to allow the children time to: (1) explore the possibilities of new materials and activities; (2) practice the developmental skills appropriate to individual needs; and (3) establish elaborate roles and interactions in dramatic play. The need for adequate time during freeplay can best be observed by following Eric as he plays in various areas inside the classroom.

In the woodworking area, where there was already an array of the usual carpentry materials, the teacher had assembled hammers, nails, and an old tree stump. Eric and several other children spent a few minutes on their own examining the tree stump. Then they consulted the teacher to gain information about the kind of tree it was, how it got into the classroom, and what happened to cause it to die. While most of the other children then moved on to other areas of the classroom, Eric and Shannon remained while the teacher demonstrated how to hold the hammer and nails and how to nail the different types of nails into the tree stump. After a few successful attempts at nailing roofing nails into the tree stump, Eric pretended he was building a house. Next he started using the hammer to strike the side of the stump, as if he were chopping down the tree. Finally he invited Shannon to help him push on the stump while saying, "Timber!"

After sustaining this activity for about 15 minutes, Eric wandered around the room, touched various objects, and talked to the teacher and other friends, before settling into the art center, where three other children were already busy. One was quietly engaged in cutting tiny pieces of many colors of construction paper, then pasting the pieces on his drawing of a tree trunk. The teacher had asked all the children to complete this activity at some time during the next few days, so Eric sat down to begin his cut-and-paste picture. When another child left an easel, Eric changed his mind about the cut-and-paste picture and selected a painting shirt from a nearby hook.

Leslie, who was on the other side of the easel, painting, periodically peered around at Eric's painting. After some conversation back and forth about what each was painting, Leslie offered a suggestion, "Make it orangey like this," while swirling red over the yellow paint on Eric's paper. Just over the artists' heads, a branch of brilliantly colored fall leaves hung from the ceiling, almost touching the top of the easel. When Leslie dripped paint on the floor, Eric paused and said, "I'll get it," went over to a nearby sink, wet a sponge, and mopped up Leslie's paint.

At the art center, Eric selected what he wanted to create and the medium he wanted to use. He not only practiced the skills necessary to paint, which were appropriate skills for him, but he had the opportunity to interact socially with Leslie. When he finished painting, Eric returned the painting shirt to the hook and then asked the teacher's aide to help him hang his picture up to dry. "I made mine orangey just like that," Eric told the aide as he pointed to the leaves above the easel. After a few minutes of conversation about the artwork and other possibilities for activities, Eric began glancing around the room. Sensing Eric's eagerness to join another activity, the aide concluded their conversation, and Eric rushed over to the block area.

The block area had been recently vacated by some children who went to play in a tent that had been set up in the classroom. In a few minutes, Eric was joined by three other players. He enthusiastically divided up the construction trucks and vans for the shopping center he told them they were going to build. The players seemed content to let Eric direct the activity, deciding where each delivery and each block was to go.

This arrangement worked well until Eric decided he also wanted to drive Derrick's cement truck. Allison, who had been driving her van along the edge of the carpet, looked up and observed the boys arguing. Carlos, who had been driving the flatbed truck with a load of long blocks, waited a few minutes and then said, "I'll be the boss," and dumped his blocks at the edge of the structure. With his next load, Carlos began directing Allison and engaged her in the play. The shopping mall suddenly changed to houses, while Eric went on negotiating with Derrick over the cement truck. The children continued to establish and change their elaborate roles and interactions in this dramatic play activity until the teacher began singing the "cleanup" song. At this point, Eric took charge again and directed the children where to store the blocks and trucks.

After cleanup time, the children enjoyed their snacks, then went to the playground to claim their favorite outside activities. Eric, who for days had been practicing throwing a small basketball into a lowered hoop, raced to a large plastic basket where the balls were kept. Finally, two basketballs were located. He and Derrick threw the basketballs at the goal and chased after their missed goals for about 10 minutes. Then the activity dissolved into chasing each other instead of the balls. They ran back and forth the length of the entire playground fence until finally, in total exhaustion, they collapsed onto the grass, giggling.

Children learn best when they are actively involved in the learning situation, when they are given the opportunity to initiate the activity, interact with other learners, and reflect verbally and nonverbally on what has been experienced. What may appear to the casual observer to be "just playing" is to the Whole Language kindergarten teacher an essential part of the kindergarten program.

Encouraging the Players

The second way a teacher invites play is by encouraging the players. No matter how carefully the teacher has planned the schedule and arranged the environment, the success or failure of freeplay depends on the attitude of the teacher. During Eric's inside and outside freeplay experiences, there were two significant encounters with adults where his play was encouraged and the value of play was recognized in ways that may appear incidental. During the nailing experience in the woodworking area, the teacher encouraged Eric's play by answering his questions about where and how she got the tree stump and what had happened to the tree, and by demonstrating the proper use of new materials.

In the second instance, the teacher's aide, who assisted Eric by hanging his wet painting on the clothesline, engaged Eric in conversation about his painting and suggested further activities to extend his work. As he secured Eric's painting to the clothesline, the aide commented, "When everyone finishes painting with fall colors, we're going to write about our nature walk and where we found those leaves." Eric then burst into an animated version of the part of the walk he liked best, when they raked the leaves into piles and played in them. The excited exchange between Eric and the aide as they recalled their playing together were ways that the aide encouraged play and recognized its value.

Teachers also encourage play by knowing when to leave children alone. Children like Eric require very little encouragement during freeplay. Eric's teacher and the aide have learned, though many hours of interacting, just when to direct, when to encourage, and when to back off and allow children to survey their options and make their own decisions. With children who are reluctant to engage in an activity during freeplay, teachers or aides may initiate an activity, get the child involved, and then carefully remove themselves from the situation. For example, in order to get Allison involved in the construction play with the blocks, the aide interjected himself into the play by saying, "I'll be Allison's partner. We'll drive this truck delivering bricks." After making a few deliveries, the aide said, "Okay, Allison, it's your turn to deliver the bricks. Carlos wants you to build with him."

During freeplay in Whole Language kindergartens, children learn as they play constructively, through participating in the process of play. Teachers and aides also learn the art of successful encouragement of players by active involvement when needed in the indoor and outdoor activities.

Preparing the Classroom Environment for Play

The third way a teacher invites children to play is by preparing the classroom physical environment for play. Looking back through Eric's morning play activities, it is important to realize that, even though Eric was an assertive, self-motivated learner, much of his success in the classroom was dependent on the preparation of the environment.

Eric's classroom was organized into centers. Eric went to the woodworking center, the art center, and the block corner, but there were numerous other centers he could have chosen. He also could have gone to the housekeeping corner, with its child-sized table and chairs, dress-up clothes, dolls and stuffed animals, chest of drawers, and bedroom furniture. He could have chosen the library corner, with the open-shelved display of books, puppets and a puppet stage, a listening station, a flannel board, and soft cushions. Eric might have gone to the writing center, which was supplied with a variety of papers, writing utensils, a primary typewriter, and materials for binding books. He could have visited the science area, which contained the aquarium, some hand-held magnifying glasses, a small balance, and a display table that was covered with brightly colored fall leaves. Or, there was the manipulatives area, with its open shelves of puzzles, unifix cubes, and cuisenaire rods, as well as small plastic and wooden building blocks and toys. There was also the snack and cooking area, where fresh fruits and vegetables were prepared by the children and where, on some occasions, the teacher led baking and other food preparation demonstrations. Because of the careful preparation of the freeplay environment, Eric was free to choose from many valuable centers and activities.

In addition to the materials normally found in the kindergarten classroom, the teacher had planned some areas of special interest. The tree stump, for instance, was added when the teacher had it removed from her yard. She sawed off some of the roots so the stump would sit up straight and brought it to school for the children to explore. Eric's kindergarten teacher enjoyed bringing interesting materials into the classroom, including ones the children did not expect to find there. She enjoyed listening to the conversation among the children and answering questions about her "surprises."

Eric also could have chosen to go to the tent, which the aide had brought in, complete with sleeping bags and outdoor cooking equipment. In the area where Eric lives, fall camping is an activity many families enjoy when the leaves are in full color.

Eric's teacher arranged the environment in centers and displayed the learning materials so that they would be interesting and inviting, as well as easily accessible. Consideration was given to the traffic patterns in the room, the need to have materials and equipment used in more than one area, and the need for grouping quieter centers near each other. The art center, library corner, and writing center, for instance, were located together because the children often move from one to the other, using materials across the centers. The art center, cooking area, and science center were near each other because water from the sink is needed in all these areas. The small-manipulatives/mathematics area was placed near the science center because many of the materials are used in both areas. When children played in the housekeeping, blocks, and woodworking areas, their play was often loud, so those areas were adjacent to each other. The circletime area, where the teacher has musical instruments, a record player and tape recorder, and display easels and charts, can also be used by the children for musical activities they select. Each piece of equipment and the materials have been carefully selected to help 20 kindergartners learn as they learn best—through active, hands-on experiences—and to encourage the children to interact with teachers and their peers in ways that have been determined as appropriate for five-year-olds.

The teacher arranged the environment as an invitation to play by scheduling for play, encouraging the players, and arranging a classroom that supports play. Since play is central to the curriculum of the Whole Language kindergarten, its environment is planned to accommodate the young child's social, emotional, physical, and cognitive development. To appreciate more fully the Whole Language kindergarten as an active, dynamic environment conducive to play, it is important to examine the types of play individuals and groups of children are engaged in around the classroom.

TYPES OF PLAY IN CENTERS AND ACTIVITIES

Kindergarten teachers have various creative ways to signal the time to begin and end classroom activities and to move the children within the classroom. On one particular day at the close of grouptime, while the children were still sitting around the edge of the carpet, the teacher used the kinds of shoes they were wearing to determine the order in which the children would leave the carpet and go to centers. The children with velcro fasteners were allowed to go first, followed by those with slip-on shoes, and then those with shoes that tied. This is just one of many ways teachers can begin the transition from teacher-directed grouptime to child-directed freeplay time.

In a few short minutes, after leaving the carpet, all the children were actively engaged in a variety of types of play. Along one wall of the classroom there were children in the mathematics/manipulatives center, in the science area, and in the cooking area. At the mathematics/manipulatives center, a girl and three boys were at a table where they were putting puzzles together and building small towers with the wooden blocks and logs. Some were engaged in manipulative or functional play, while others were engaged in constructive play as they created with the materials. One boy was standing at the end of the water table, holding on and rocking back and forth while he tried to persuade his friend to leave the science area and come over to the big Tinker Toys. In the cooking area, a boy and a girl in chef's hats were helping the teacher grate carrots for snacktime. Another child was telling the teacher's aide a long story about his trip to Cleveland.

Along a second wall, where the housekeeping corner, block area, and tent were located, there was evidence of parallel play, associative play, and cooperative play (Parten, 1932). In parallel play, children use similar materials and play beside, but not with, each other. In associative play, children interact with each other while following their own line of play. While engaged in cooperative play, children assign themselves different roles and then interact with each other and adjust their language and behaviors to fulfill a mutually agreed-upon play theme.

In the housekeeping corner, children were involved in cooperative sociodramatic play, which Garvey (1977) calls social play, which occurs when "successive, nonliteral behaviors of one partner are contingent on the nonliteral behaviors of the other partner(s)" (p. 163). The sociodramatic play began as one girl placed a doll in a stroller with several stuffed animals and then told the father, "You cook supper while we go shopping."

In the block corner, four children engaged in all three levels of play—parallel, associative, and cooperative (Parten, 1932). Two laid out an intricate highway of long hollow blocks and were driving a variety of trucks through their maze. Their play was cooperative, as they interacted socially and physically while driving the trucks and unloading the blocks to construct their highway. A third child engaged in parallel play, driving the trucks next to the others but not interacting with them. Another child hid in the tent on the edge of the block area. As he heard the builders drive their trucks near him, he drove his truck out of the flap of the tent, got their attention, talked with them about his truck, then waved goodbye and darted back under the door flap. Parten would call this associative play, because the child was playing in the same area, using the same toys, and interacting with the other players, but was not playing the role of highway builder.

In a quieter zone of the classroom, where the library corner, writing center, and art area were located, children were engaged in a variety of activities. In the library corner two children listened to a tape of *The Teddy Bears' Picnic* (Kennedy, 1983). One child was holding the book like the teacher, while the other looked at the pages. In the art area, one child was painting at the easel while two others were sitting at the table squeezing paint from plastic mustard bottles, making multicolored squiggly designs on construction paper. No one was in the writing center.

The level of interaction among the children, between the children and the teacher, and between the children and the materials was very high. The classroom was typical of a Whole Language kindergarten that has been carefully planned to allow children to do what children do best. The children were involved in functional and constructive play. Some were fulfilling their needs through physical activities, such as the chefs grating the carrots, or the constructors building the small block towers.

For other children, the primary focus of their play was the interaction with their peers in intricate roles, as with the highway builders and with the mother and father with the baby carriage. Even the child peeking out from under the tent flap was playing, as he attempted to capture the attention of other children passing by his campsite.

When children are free to choose their play activity and allowed to explore that activity uninterrupted, their play takes on many forms. Some are more subtle than others. There was one little girl at the listening station who imitated the teacher by turning the pages of the books and saying, "When you hear the ding, turn the page, then you will see the right picture and the right words." Another child attempted to persuade his friend to join him by saying, "We can build a spaceship and you can be the flyer, if you come get the Tinker Toys." Even the child who recounted his trip to Cleveland related his journey in terms of the games they played, the songs they sang, and the playgrounds where they stopped during the long ride.

Within a few minutes, the classroom changed. The children moved in and out of centers and in and out of the various roles they played; and their play changed from functional to constructive to dramatic play and back again, depending on the materials and inter- actions they encountered. They engaged in parallel, associative, co- operative, and sociodramatic play. The children were invited to en- gage in the many forms of play because the teacher arranged the schedule for play, encouraged the players, and organized the space and materials to support the play (Isenberg & Quisenberry, 1988; Smilansky, 1968).

CHANGES NEEDED FOR A WHOLE LANGUAGE ENVIRONMENT

The kindergarten classroom described in this chapter had a well- prepared physical arrangement of materials and centers, a schedule with ample time devoted to play, and two adults who encouraged the players. A kindergarten teacher may ask, "What could possibly be changed to make this excellent classroom a better Whole Language environment?" The answer is simple, and it reflects the primary message of this book. The emphasis in the kindergarten just de- scribed was on children constructing representations through their own role playing and use of manipulative materials, and through the teacher's acceptance of children's personal language as they became involved in meaningful listening and thinking activities.

Play in this kindergarten could be improved, however, by provid- ing more activities and materials for reading and writing. It is clear that listening and speaking have been emphasized, but more activities and materials need to be added to support reading and writing during freeplay. It is important that teachers view their children as readers and writers at the time they enter the kindergarten. That attitude must be reflected in the materials and activities that are available for the children to use throughout the day.

Adding Literacy Materials to Greeting and Tabletop Activities

As the children arrive at the beginning of the day, they are greeted by the teacher and usually engage in a bit of dialogue. Then they move on to tabletop activities such as puzzles, Tinker Toys, Play Doh, or a cut-and-paste art activity. An attendance board could easily be added to this routine. Children could place a clothespin beside their names upon arrival. Or the teacher could cover a posterboard with library-book pockets, each of which has a child's name printed on it. The children place their namecards in the proper pocket. In these ways, they can practice reading their names (Loughlin & Martin, 1987). During this greeting time, the teacher might also solicit a news item from each child, asking, "Is there anything special you want me to write about you for our news bulletin board?" Or the teacher might enjoy casual conversation at the tabletop activities and engage the child in a longer dialogue later in the morning during center freeplay.

At the tabletop activities, reading and writing could be added to the art project. For example, recall that the teacher requested that over the course of a few days all the children would complete the cut-and-paste art project using fall colors, to go along with the fall unit. When the children finished their project, the teacher could ask them to dictate a caption or to write their own caption about the picture. With the addition of literacy materials to the greeting time and the tabletop activities, children could associate reading and writing as being both a natural beginning for the day and a natural adjunct to what they draw and construct.

Adding Literacy Materials to Freeplay

While the freeplay time in the classroom we described was rich in terms of materials, equipment, and room arrangement, with the addition of a few literacy materials throughout the play centers, children could continue their development as readers and writers.

In a research project conducted by Raines (1990b) where reading and writing materials were added throughout the classroom, certain literacy behaviors were noted. For example, when cookbooks and cake decorating books were added to the housekeeping corner, children were observed looking at pictures, reading common nouns such as *cake* and *bread,* and then pretending to read and follow the recipes. With the addition of "cents-off" coupons clipped from newspapers and magazines and pads of preprinted grocery lists, the children began reading and writing in their pretend grocery shopping. With the addition of paper, index cards, crayons, and markers to the block center, the road builders designed traffic signs and drew pictures and scribbles on index cards, which they then taped to the sides of their trucks. In the mathematics/manipulatives area, with the addition of notepads and markers, the children counted, then wrote numerals to remember how tall was the tower they had built. Adding materials for reading and writing to freeplay activities also had a positive effect on the centers of the classroom where literacy materials are usually already found, namely, the library corner, writing center, and the art center. When the teacher added posterboard and markers to the library corner, two puppeteers drew a picture and wrote, "Pupit so" (puppet show). When one of the children walked around the room and pointed to the sign while wearing the puppet on her hand, the sign and her insistent invitation brought several friends over to be an audience.

When the researchers returned a few days later, the library corner was papered with signs and writing (Raines, 1990b). The teacher explained that the girls' puppet show had begun a rash of writing and pretend and real reading activities. The children made a schedule to show who would give future puppet shows. Then the children's writing appeared in written directions on how the listening station should be operated. They formalized their library corner play by assuming the role of librarians, checking out books, writing cards, making signs, and writing an announcement for the storytelling hour. Later they pretended to be the teacher and read books to small groups of children. When other children were not available for an audience, the readers brought dolls and stuffed animals into the library to listen. According to Yetta Goodman (1986) and Holdaway (1986), such pretend reading is a necessary foundation for successful beginning reading.

A similar explosion of reading and writing took place when the teacher arranged the classroom so that writing materials were available in the art center. Before this change, the teacher and the aide stationed themselves in the art center and added labels or captions to the children's pictures by taking dictation, writing down exactly what the children told them to write. However, after seeing the children's writing during play in other areas of the classroom, the teacher decided to let the children write their own captions for their pictures. Eric wrote, "Lsle, lpd mak rnj" (Leslie helped make orange). After several weeks, some children extended the caption writing to writing stories. With others, the teachers continued to take dictation for long stories, but encouraged the children to write their own captions on their pictures. The children discovered for themselves the integral relationship between the art and writing centers.

Adding Literacy Materials to Outside Play

The children's need for functional writing, especially for making lists and writing instructions, extended to the outside play activities. Jim and Nathan decided that a list of playground equipment was needed, and Eric, who had found a new vehicle for expressing his authority, wrote the rules for playing basketball and taped them under the backboard of the basketball goal. The teacher became involved in the outside writing by taking a notebook outside and jotting down things children said while they were playing. These statements later were used in the writing center for a dictated group story.

Nature walks also were occasions for adding writing materials to outside play. For example, while the children played in the leaves and then later collected leaves and made comments about the signs of fall, parent volunteers listened to the casual exchanges, recorded a few on index cards, and read them at the following grouptime (Raines & Canady, 1989).

When children see adults writing their words down or making notes to be kept and read aloud at another time, then they learn a valuable communication lesson. They learn that writing is a way to record and to recall what was said and what happened. Functional writing for the purposes of labeling, directing, and recording can be a natural extension of the children's play.

SUMMARY

The young child's world revolves around play. On any given day in a Whole Language kindergarten, children represent their real and imagined worlds through listening, speaking, reading, writing, painting, and building—all forms of play. They are growing in their competence to represent what they have learned, to use materials functionally and constructively, to imagine themselves in roles they know, and to adopt those roles for awhile.

In a Whole Language environment, an informed teacher and aide support children as players by planning time in the schedule for play; by creating a relaxed, unhurried, positive atmosphere of encouragement; and by arranging a physical environment to support play. By adding literacy materials throughout the centers, the play environment can be made conducive to young children continuing the process of becoming literate. Teachers can observe young children incorporating reading and writing into their play, using writing functionally, and engaging in pretend or real reading and writing, which enables the children to continue in their development as readers and writers.

❉ 4 ❉

Changing Grouptime
to Emphasize Whole Language

The times during the day when kindergarten children come together as an entire class are called by a variety of names: grouptime, circle-time, circle, opening exercise, sharing time, or storytime. A teacher may refer to the first grouptime in the morning as the opening exercise or sharing time, while the grouptime after the children re-turn from outside play is called storytime, and the last one of the day may be designated as music time. Whatever the label, grouptime provides five-year-olds with a time to sit together comfortably, usually for 20 to 30 minutes, and interact with a carefully planned but flexible lesson.

Kindergarten teachers value grouptime because it provides infi-nite possibilities for the children's language growth and development. In a Whole Language environment, the frequency of grouptime, the types of interactions involved, and ways it is organized are the same as in most effective kindergartens. Many kindergarten teachers, how-ever, are discovering new ways to strengthen grouptime as a means for children to develop their language as they improve as listeners, speakers, readers, and writers.

Grouptime for children is talking time, sharing time, giggle time, "thinking-about-something-new" time. For teachers, it is a time to explore new topics, entertain, inform, and pique the curiosity of kindergartners. Teachers use grouptime to create a sense of commu-nity among the learners, set the stage for the special activities of the day, and share new knowledge and information related to the unit or theme being studied. Most important, children learn to communicate with their peers and their teacher through the active involvement in the grouptime setting. They learn to listen and respond to the teacher's directions and to interact with other children through teacher-led discussion.

In *Developmentally Appropriate Practice* (Bredekamp, 1987) and "The Child-centered Kindergarten" (Moyer et al., 1987), teachers are urged to focus on the needs of the child and the experiences that naturally interest children, as well as those experiences that will captivate the students' interests if the teachers present them in an inviting manner. Grouptime, then, becomes a major component of the thematic unit of study, a means of organizing the kindergarten curriculum around the children's needs and interests, as well as a means of introducing new information and experiences to the children. The unit not only provides the organizational theme for the activities that comprise grouptime, but it also is the unifying topic around which the teacher integrates other experiences into the plan for the day. Further discussion of units of study and themes are presented in chapters on thematic units and science.

SCHEDULING GROUPTIME

Whole Language kindergarten teachers usually plan two or three grouptimes per day, scheduled at approximately the same times each day. If the kindergarten is a half-day program, the first one may come at the beginning of the morning, after some tabletop activities or center activities, while the second may come after outside play. If the program lasts a full day, there may be an additional grouptime at the end of the day.

The length of grouptime will vary according to the time of the school year and the interests and abilities of the children. It is important that the children think of grouptime as a positive experience. The Whole Language kindergarten teacher, knowing that constructive listening and interacting during grouptime is a process that must be learned by the children, might start with brief grouptimes at the beginning of the year, which may be increased to over 30 minutes by the end of the year. However, as the amount of time increases, teachers must plan several movement activities for each session. The length of time and the format for grouptime may vary, but the goal for all teachers is meaningful listening and interaction.

ORGANIZATION OF MATERIALS AND SPACE

The seating arrangement plays an important role in the success of grouptime. Provisions should be made for all the children to sit comfortably and have a clear view of the teacher and the materials. The most common seating arrangements for grouptime include children sitting around a large oval carpet, on squares of carpet placed in a semicircle, or around a wide strip of tape placed on top of the carpet. Whether the teacher sits on the floor, on a small pillow, or in a low chair, the teacher and the materials must be close to the children's eye level, so they can see without holding their heads back. In planning for grouptime, it is important that the most frequently used teaching tools (e.g., tape recorder or record player, flannel board, an easel to hold display material or chart tablets) be easily accessible to the teacher.

A SAMPLE GROUP TIME

Many Whole Language kindergarten teachers begin grouptime with a particular signal or song. One creative kindergarten teacher we know begins every grouptime by singing. Promptly at nine o'clock, after the children have played at tabletop activities or worked in the interest centers, she calls the children together to sit around the edge of the large oval carpet for the first grouptime of the day. She has a collection of "special songs" she has composed, some about the day of the week or the weather, others based on the children's names. While not every teacher has the talent to compose songs, Whole Language kindergarten teachers find various ways to begin grouptime through music or through the "music" of language (Martin, 1988). They may begin with familiar fingerplays or by playing one of the children's favorite records. They have found that beginning grouptime with music, singing, and rhythmic movement helps bring children together in unison and creates a harmonious atmosphere, which sets the mood for successful group interaction.

Children learn to communicate with the teacher and with each other through active participation in the communication process. Therefore, grouptime must include a balance of teacher-led talk and children's talk, with the teacher acting as a model. After the children are settled around the rug and the beginning song has ended, many Whole Language kindergarten teachers invite children's talk by asking for various news reports. Children may give a weather report, a news item about themselves or their family, or make an announcement of a special event scheduled to occur in the classroom that day. Using the teacher as a model, the children learn to organize their thoughts and report information to others in an interesting and meaningful manner. Children who are personally involved in group-time reporting become better listeners not only to each other but during the time the teacher is talking. Whole Language kindergarten teachers believe that good listening cannot be mandated by the teacher, but it can be developed by careful grouptime planning.

Whole Language kindergarten teachers also use the first group-time of the day to brainstorm about the particular unit or theme currently being stressed and to insure that any new knowledge is related to the children's existing knowledge. For example, in a unit discussion where the theme was nutrition, one teacher asked the children to tell some of their favorite fruit snacks, then proceeded to add new information by placing a basket of fruit in the middle of the circle. The basket contained some of the fruit snacks the children had mentioned, as well as some tropical fruits the children had not mentioned. After identifying the new fruits, comparing them to familiar fruits, and discussing their nutritional value, she gave the basket to the parent volunteer to place in a special learning center where the children could go later in the morning and wash, prepare, and sample the fruits.

In leading the discussion, the teacher connected the known information from the children to new information. They associated the new vocabulary words with the experience of seeing, touching, smelling, and naming the real fruits. Later the new information was reinforced when they had their tasting party during center time. After the nutrition discussion, the teacher read Bruce Degen's *Jamberry* (1983), followed by a "Jamberry" parade to some marching music. The teacher ended grouptime by once again asking the children their favorite fruit snack. After each child answered, that child was allowed to leave and select a learning center or activity center in which to play.

Although carefully planned and directed by the teacher, group-time is a time for group interaction, and children need to feel that they are active participants even when listening to the teacher. Sitting quietly during grouptime does not always mean that learning is taking place. Group lessons need to include verbal and physical interactions to better insure kindergartners will learn. The pattern during the grouptime is to have the teacher in charge, but to include the children throughout the interaction. Time needs to be reserved for the children to listen to the teacher, but always followed by some time for the children to respond verbally and listen to each other.

ANALYZING THE EFFECTS OF GROUPTIME

To plan better grouptimes—ones that are sensitive to the needs of the whole child—teachers use the strategy of viewing an activity from the child's perspective. In fact, the best teachers often predict the effects of the activities they plan and then, after the grouptime is over, review the effects on specific individuals as well as on the class as a whole.

Balancing Individual Children's Needs

One excellent teacher we know has shared her practices in case-study interviews conducted by Raines (1990b). When planning grouptime, once she gets her initial ideas of what she will present during grouptime, she almost immediately starts thinking of the effects of her planned activities on individual children who are having problems.[1] For example, she had two children, Melitta and Riley, who had special social-emotional needs. This teacher predicted that Melitta, an ESL (English as a second language) student who was adjusting to the classroom environment, would wander around the room rather than joining the group, unless the aide invited the child to sit in her lap. This invitation often precipitated several other children wanting to sit on the aide's lap as well and distracted even more students. The teacher, empathizing with Melitta's adjustments, described how it must feel to be in a strange environment with a new language, and how significant it must be to have someone who spoke Spanish to provide the comfortable lap. The dilemma of Melitta's individual needs versus the need to have a grouptime that was not disrupted was not settled before grouptime began; the teacher decided simply to watch and see what happened, to see if her predictions were accurate.

After the grouptime was over, the teacher found that her predictions had been accurate, so she evaluated the situation and planned steps to solve the problem. Indeed, as grouptime began, Melitta wandered around the room, the aide went over and said something to her in Spanish, and they returned to the grouptime circle where Melitta perched in the aide's lap. Then a scramble for lap space ensued with

---

[1] It is interesting to note that she does not refer to such students as "problem children," but rather "children who are having problems."

three other children also wanting to be held. The proposed solution for the next day was an easy one. The teacher asked the aide to invite Melitta to the circle area before grouptime began and explain to her that she would sit beside her during the entire time, but to discourage lap sitting. Their plan worked, but it had to be repeated for several weeks to become a part of the routine for grouptime.

Riley's needs were quite different, though also grounded in his social-emotional development. During earlier observations, the teacher interpreted Riley's eagerness as a sign of intense interest and intellectual curiosity. After a few grouptimes, however, she decided he needed to be the center of attention. If the teacher did not stop her presentation and listen to him, he would come over and get right in front of her face or tug on her sleeve until finally she gave in and listened. Each question directed at the group and each discussion point about the variety of nutritious snacks brought comments from Riley, sometimes on the subject and other times completely unassociated. The teacher predicted another difficult day with Riley, but planned to continue her usual responses of using both verbal and nonverbal cues, such as gently moving him back into the circle with her arm, ignoring some comments, and including him as often as she could.

After the grouptime, when the teacher discussed Riley's behavior, she determined that she must think of some new strategies, both because she was beginning to be irritated with the boy and because she was noticing that the other children were starting to show their irritations as well. Rather than deciding on a solution immediately after the grouptime, she said, "I think I need to give this problem some thought." She offered no solution until the next morning. Normally, she noted, she would simply ask the aide to assist with Riley, but, with Melitta's arrival and her needs, she had to look elsewhere. So, she tried having a talk with Riley before grouptime, asking him to listen more, indicating that the other children wanted to have turns to talk as well. Riley's difficulties persisted, however; he was not able to change them simply at the teacher's request.

After grouptime, the teacher again analyzed Riley's behavior, predicting that, if she did not make some changes, his attention-getting actions would continue to be disruptive. She decided to try a different tack. Since his need was for her attention, she decided to spend a few minutes with him before grouptime, really listening to whatever he wanted to say. She planned to engage him first in helping her during cleanup time, finishing quickly and then getting together while the other children continued straightening up the room. While the plan sounded like a good one, when she and Riley sat down to talk, Riley didn't seem to have anything he wanted to say; he seemed simply to enjoy her company.

Recognizing it was apparently not a matter of listening to Riley but simply of being with him, the teacher involved the child in helping her assemble the materials she planned to use during grouptime. As he assisted, he talked constantly about what they were doing. The teacher commented, "Riley, we will talk some more after grouptime is over. I need to have the other children talk to me now. As soon as grouptime is over, please help me put these things away" (indicating the cassette tape, flannel board, and the book). It worked. As soon as the teacher finished the song with the children, she handed Riley the tape, which he held. When she finished with the flannel board, he moved over and sat beside it. After she read the book, she handed it to him, and he put it under her rocking chair, where she usually placed it when she finished reading. Riley interrupted less, although he still spoke out impulsively at times; however, he allowed others to receive more of the teacher's attention.

The teacher decided to continue this strategy of more talking and attention time before and after grouptime. Riley responded well; while he was still an eager participant, he was better able to control his movements and verbal responses. The teacher was not sure how long she would be able to let Riley be her special grouptime helper, but she was certain that for the next few weeks talking with Riley before and after grouptime would become part of her daily routine, just as the aide's daily routine would include getting Melitta comfortable and ready for grouptime.

Grouptime Planned with Whole-class Responses in Mind

Experienced teachers often orchestrate grouptime like the movements of a great symphony. When the listeners are lulled into a slow pace, as when the woodwind section is playing a musical movement, then the conductor will pique the listeners' interest, make them sit up and take notice with an unexpected change, like the sudden interruption of the trumpets. So, too, may the teacher change the pace, with the singing of a fingerplay or the chanting of a rhyme. Attention—sitting up and taking notice—is the goal of grouptime, but the teacher does not mandate attention by harsh reprimands or strictly enforced rules. Instead, the teacher plans a session that, by the nature of its activities and the information shared, will captivate children's interest.

When the teacher plans for the ebb and flow of children's attention, this goal will be accomplished. Children will attend to the teacher, to the activities, and to each other. Some inexperienced teachers, concerned that the children may "get out of hand," plan too little excitement; they lull the children into boredom, to the point that the listeners create their own excitement by talking to each other or even leaving the circle altogether. Other inexperienced teachers, concerned that, if they do not have several exciting activities, the children will talk too much and become disruptive, plan too many trumpets. Often, too little excitement and too much excitement have the same effect—the children "get out of hand."

Balancing teacher talk and children's talk helps, but experienced teachers also have learned to pace the grouptime so that children have a more relaxed listening activity followed by one that stimulates them to talk or to move, then return to a calmer activity. For example, the teacher may begin grouptime with a familiar song or fingerplay followed by several children sharing news. The teacher may then regain the students' attention, set the stage for a book that has been selected for reading aloud, read it, and allow for comments. This may be followed by a surprise or unexpected event that will excite children.

Surprises, new or novel objects, and familiar items found in unusual places will excite young children during grouptime. Teachers often use the surprise ploy of placing a covered box or basket in the circle, sometimes mentioning it at the beginning of grouptime and other times allowing the suspense to build as the children wonder what is hidden there. Recall that the teacher who used grouptime to discuss nutritious fruit snacks placed a covered basket of fruit in the circle. Novelty excites young children. It can take the form of a new pet, the unexpected smell of food cooking, new toys or equipment, or new fruits that the children do not recognize. Placing a familiar object in an unusual place also will capture young children's attention. For instance, placing the balance from the science table in the middle of the circletime rug, or a truck from the block area on the snack table, or a costume from the dress-up corner in the library will pique curiosity.

Planning for a balance between teacher talk and children's talk, between relaxing and stimulating activities, and between the familiar and the novel will make it easier to get and sustain children's attention. This carefully orchestrated plan, however, must be flexible enough to allow for the unexpected. There are times when teachers should abandon their plan and follow some spontaneous interest that arises. For example, if an interesting subject comes up, or if the children are enjoying singing together so much they want to continue, or if a book sparks some puzzling questions, then departing from the original plan seems appropriate.

In addition, when an activity is not working, the teacher needs to decide when to move on to something else. One teacher, for example, planned a discussion of pets, which deteriorated into giggles about monsters as pets. The teacher joined in the fun briefly, but her comments fueled the gigglers and soon most of the class was thoroughly distracted. Feeling that there was no point in continuing the pet discussion, the teacher began clapping and chanting a favorite rhyme, and eventually all the children were involved. Then she dismissed the children to the learning centers for freeplay by calling on individuals to tell the names of their pets, or, if they did not have a pet, what kind they would like to have. The teacher thus recovered the children's attention by improvising something that was not in her plan.

EVALUATING GROUPTIME ACCORDING TO STANDARDS OF APPROPRIATE PRACTICE

Grouptime is a major communication time for children and their teacher. Children learn to participate as individuals and also as a group. Experienced teachers learn to read their children's verbal and nonverbal responses as they follow a carefully thought out plan designed around their expectations of individual children's needs, as well as how the group will probably respond. In addition, experienced teachers have learned to

1. Evaluate the grouptime after it is over;
2. Analyze special problem situations;
3. Judge their own orchestration of grouptime in terms of
   a. The balance of teacher talk and children's talk,
   b. The balance of the familiar and the surprising,
   c. The teacher's agility in deciding when to follow and when to change the plan.

These criteria for a good grouptime do not change when the kindergarten teacher decides to become a Whole Language teacher.

This book is written on the premise that Whole Language kindergartens meet the standards established by the NAEYC's position paper,

Developmentally Appropriate Practice (Bredekamp, 1987), the ACEI's "The Child-centered Kindergarten" (Moyer et al., 1987) and the IRA's *Literacy Development and Prefirst Grade* (Early Childhood, 1988). In the teaching strategies section of the NAEYC position paper, the standard is clear: "Children are expected to be physically and mentally active," and it is considered inappropriate practice if "a major portion of time is spent passively sitting, listening, and waiting" (p. 50). In the program implementation section of the ACEI position paper, there is support for the aims of the Whole Language kindergarten teacher, who "responds to the needs of children as developing, thinking individuals by focusing on the processes of learning rather than disparate skills, content and products" (p. 238). In the IRA position paper it is recommended that teachers "build instruction on what the child already knows about oral language, reading and writing. Focus on meaningful language rather than on isolated skill development" (p. 6).

According to these standards, grouptime should be a flexible time where the teacher initiates interactions, leads activities, and expects and responds to a variety of answers that reflect children's own lives and preferences.

The grouptimes discussed in this chapter are consistent with the statements in these position papers and reflect the current knowledge that exists concerning the physical, social, emotional, and cognitive development of five-year-olds. However, for a Whole Language kindergarten teacher, grouptime also should reflect recent research findings regarding emergent literacy and the oral language development of children at this age.

Grouptimes planned with five-year-olds in mind consider the physical needs of young children. The length and interaction patterns of grouptime are planned for active learners who are supposed to be talkers and movers. Likewise, the social and emotional needs of young learners are recognized. Guided by the teacher, who facilitates the verbal interaction, children learn to respect others' talking turns, to hear each other, and to enjoy the companionship of shared ideas and singing and of realizing that in many ways they are like others. Yet the teacher also recognizes the individual's needs to contribute. Individuals are respected for their knowledge and opinions, as when sharing a news item and answering the teacher's questions.

The grouptime discussion of fruits for nutritious snacks, mentioned earlier, met many of the standards established by NAEYC, ACEI, and IRA. While the teacher planned a grouptime in which children's physical, social, and emotional needs were respected, their cognitive growth also was considered. The teacher built the new information about healthy snacks on meaningful feedback from the children about the fruits they enjoy. Their knowledge was expanded by first-hand experiences of seeing, touching, and later tasting some new fruits, as well as learning their names and using new descriptive terms.

One of the appropriate-practices statements in the NAEYC position paper is, "Children are provided concrete learning activities with materials and people relevant to their own life experiences" (Brede-kamp, 1987, p. 50). The teacher's use of real fruits for the lesson and allowing the children to tell about their own preferences were com-patible with this guideline. The grouptime also met this standard from the ACEI position paper: "Provides multiple opportunities for learning with concrete, manipulative materials that . . . keep them actively engaged in learning and discovering through use of all the senses, leading to more input upon which thought is constructed" (Moyer et al., 1987, p. 238–239). The tasting party and use of real fruits in the grouptime indicated that the teacher planned multiple opportunities for experiences with concrete materials. The teacher remembered that young children need sensory experiences coupled with new descriptive words, to build new information into their previous knowledge.

RECOMMENDED CHANGES FOR A WHOLE LANGUAGE EMPHASIS

The teacher who led the nutritious-snacks grouptime was an excel-lent communicator, planner, and motivator and was able to reflect upon her own practice. The children were allowed to listen, speak, sing, and move around. The teacher integrated the theme by selecting a book to read aloud that not only related to berries, but captured the imagination of the children. How could this well-planned and well-executed grouptime be improved to make it more of a Whole Lan-guage approach?

Whole Language Connections
to Children's Special Needs

This excellent teacher was concerned before and after grouptime about two of her children with social and emotional needs. The teacher correctly analyzed the needs of the new ESL student, Melitta, but overlooked one possible bridge to the child's participation. The teacher correctly identified that the child's most important need was to feel secure in the new environment, and the identification with an aide who spoke Spanish was critical. However, if the teacher, even with her limited Spanish-speaking abilities, had learned the names of the fruits in Spanish and used the English and the Spanish names, Melitta would have recognized that the teacher was trying to communicate with her. The children also could have practiced saying the names of the fruits in both languages. Even if the kindergarten teacher had only spoken a few words in Spanish, she would be following one of the recommendations from the IRA about literacy development and prefirst grade, which Whole Language teachers try to remember: "Respect the language the child brings to school, and use it as a base for language and literacy activities" (Early Childhood, 1988, p. 6).

The teacher struggled with and correctly analyzed Riley's need to communicate with her. While trying several strategies to keep Riley's comments from intruding on the participation of the whole class in grouptime, the teacher was following another of the recommendations from IRA: "Foster children's affective and cognitive development by providing them with opportunities to communicate what they know, think, and feel" (Early Childhood, 1988, p. 6). Riley needed the teacher's attention; she, by responding to his affective needs, made it possible for them both to communicate better during grouptime and in their informal times together.

Talking "with" Children

Whole Language kindergarten teachers plan specific times when their major objective is to engage individual children in casual conversation. During arrival and departure times, during freeplay both inside and outside, and during snacks and meals, Whole Language kindergarten teachers talk "with"—rather than "at"—their students. Adults conversing with children use a different language register than when they are teaching them during group instruction. Skilled conversationalists are able to follow the lead and response of their partners. Teachers who work on their conversing-with-children skills have learned to control their tendency to talk "at" children. They also have noted that both they and their children are so much more relaxed at the end of the day than when they were constantly "quizzing and questioning" their students. The sort of questioning needed to extend someone's understanding and lead them to seeing another's point of view can be accomplished by good conversation.

One teacher noticed that her new aide, a woman in her fifties, seemed immediately to draw the children to her. Sensing that the woman's abilities were worth observing, the teacher asked permission to place a tape recorder at the snack table while the aide and the children prepared the snacks. At first the aide was hesitant and not comfortable with the machine eavesdropping, but afer a few days she became acclimatized and her conversation returned to normal. After the teacher and aide listened to the tapes, the teacher determined to work on sounding more like the aide, a wonderful conversationalist who skillfully listened, responded to what the children said, and kept the conversation alive. Kindergarten teachers who recognize that spoken language as meaningful communication is the very foundation of a Whole Language classroom must learn to be good listeners, good speakers, and thus, good conversationalists.

Adding Reading and Writing Steps

Whole Language kindergarten teachers also realize that they must build in many opportunities for children to use language in its printed form, in reading and in writing. The teacher who led the grouptime on nutritious fruit snacks could improve this lesson for the whole class by adding two brief writing and reading steps. Using a large tablet or sheet of posterboard, she could write the list of fruits the children like as snacks. The children would be able to see their spoken words become written words, and this would help them discover "the purpose of written language—that it preserves oral language" (Teale, Hiebert, & Chittenden, 1987, p. 774). In addition, after showing the children the fruits they do not know, those names could be listed. The list could be taken to the tasting party, and children could decide whether or not they want to change their favorite snacking fruits. Or, as the children come to the snacking area in small groups, the teacher or parent volunteer could jot down comments the children make while snacking. At the next grouptime of the day when discussing their "tasting" party, the teacher then could read what the children said about the "furry fruit, the kiwi," or about the fact that Tina's mother likes cantaloupe with ice cream, or that José mainly eats pears that come in cans.

A reciprocal reading possibility would be to have the children read with the teacher the list of favorite snacks and new fruit names. The fruit names could be written in colors that correspond to the fruits. Again, the emphasis would not be one of calling on individual children to read the list, but the teacher would go over the list and the children would read it with her as part of a restatement or summary of their discussion.

The teacher read *Jamberry* (Degen, 1983) during this grouptime, and the children delighted in the recurring phrases, "One berry, two berry, pick me a blueberry." The rhythmical and rhyming selection would have been an excellent one to use a verbal cloze process. As the teacher reread the book, she could pause and have the children join her in repeating the rhyme each time. Whole Language kindergarten teachers find ways to connect the grouptime presentation of a read-aloud book to the children's reading it in the library. (There are numerous suggestions for making these connections in Chapter 6, on the use of the library.) After the reading, the teacher could ask a child with limited interest in books to place the selection in the library corner (Raines & Isbell, 1989). When children are familiar with a book through repeated readings and active participation, they are more likely to interact with it on their own (Martinez & Teale, 1988).

The addition of some writing activity and an emphasis on participation in reading, as well as noting that children can explore the book on their own in the library corner, would strengthen the grouptime as a Whole Language experience. Good kindergarten teachers will find such additions easy to assimilate into their planning. The suggestions made here are only a few of the many that could have been added to the grouptime. It is important for kindergarten teachers who want to become Whole Language teachers to think of grouptime as an opportunity for children to experience the reading and writing processes in as lively a fashion as they communicate through listening and speaking.

Connections to Other Curricular Areas

In addition to encouraging more effective listening and speaking and making more connections to reading and writing in grouptime, a Whole Language kindergarten teacher will find ways to build bridges between the grouptime presentation and the other curricular areas. For example, to link reading and music, the teacher could print the recurring phrase from the book on a posterboard and have the children read it and repeat it rhythmically as they enjoy marching to music, as Jamberry Bear did in the book. In the snack area, an important science lesson also could take place. The teacher could write down the names of the berries and fruits in her basket and leave them for display. Another science comparison could be made by letting the children taste the berries in a variety of states—fresh, frozen, and made into jams and jellies. Making a graph of the children's likes and dislikes for fruits in the various states would be an excellent connection to mathematics.

After the tasting party, the children might use the writing center to compose a grocery list of their favorite snacks, using invented spelling. Or, at the end of the day, the children might be encouraged to write in their journals about some of the things they did that day and what they learned about nutritious fruit snacks. The Whole Language kindergarten teacher will find ways to integrate grouptime activities with reading and writing in other related areas.

SUMMARY

Grouptime works well when teachers plan brief, interactive sessions, alternating teacher talk and children's talk; when they incorporate a variety of activities connecting the children's prior knowledge to new knowledge; and when they respect the children's opinions and individual contributions. Experienced teachers who reflect on their practice can often predict how individual children will respond during grouptime, as well as what the responses of the whole class will be. They also take time to evaluate after grouptime is over, to plan more effectively for individual children's needs and for the whole of the grouptime presentation.

Most kindergarten teachers are already using many Whole Language activities in their grouptime sessions. However, in light of current information regarding literacy development, Whole Language kindergarten teachers are including opportunities for more children's talk and child participation. These successful kindergarten teachers are demonstrating developmentally appropriate practices (Bredekamp, 1987) and implementing program standards from "The Child-centered Kindergarten" (Moyer et al., 1987). By listening and speaking more effectively, by adding some brief writing and reading activities, and by building connections from the theme of the unit of study to other areas of the curriculum, the children will be able to communicate meaningfully, which is the basic premise of the IRA's *Literacy Development and Prefirst Grade* (Early Childhood, 1988).

｜5｜

Writing in the
Whole Language Kindergarten

Perhaps the most misunderstood and neglected aspect of the kindergarten curriculum is the area of developmental writing. The gap that traditionally exists between educational research and classroom practice becomes obvious in kindergarten programs, where beginning writing instruction still consists primarily of forming the letters and numerals correctly or copying handwriting lessons on worksheets. Whole Language kindergarten teachers view writing as an integral part of the emergent literacy process and provide writing centers where children are encouraged to continue their exploration of writing as a means of self-expression and communication. In a Whole Language kindergarten, the skills of writing are not taught by preplanned drills in letter and word formation. Rather, they are learned by providing children with the tools and the encouragement they need to continue their natural desire to construct meaningful communication through the medium of print—a process they began long before coming to school.

Children emerge in their literacy over time (Sulzby, 1986). When teachers view children as "constructors" of print (Ferreiro, 1986), they also recognize that children are at varying stages of development as writers. When concern for the individual's development is taken into account, teachers interact with children in a variety of ways, rather than through preselected whole-group lessons (Hoffman, 1987). As teachers begin to view children as actively engaged in reading and writing at the time they enter kindergarten (Vukelich & Golden, 1984), the question becomes, "What can I do in my kindergarten classroom to continue the children's development as writers?" Just as the teacher's interactions patterns change, in a similar fashion the experiences, activities, and classroom environment are changed to support literacy development (Jalongo & Zeigler, 1987; Loughlin & Martin, 1987; Raines, 1986). A carefully planned writing center is essential in a Whole Language kindergarten program, to allow for the various types of writing kindergarten children are capable of doing and to provide opportunities for print exploration.

PLANNING FOR CHILDREN'S DEVELOPMENT AS WRITERS

Kindergarten teachers who organize and evaluate writing activities on the basis of the three position statements we discussed earlier—from the NAEYC, the ACEI and the IRA—will support their children's development as writers. In the NAEYC's position statement, developmentally appropriate practice includes children "experimenting with writing by drawing, copying, and inventing their own spelling" (Bredekamp, 1987, p. 51). The ACEI position paper on the child-centered kindergarten states that "the activity/experience-centered environment, essential if young children are to reach their maximum potential, provides for a far richer and more stimulating environment than one dominated by pencil-and-paper teacher-directed tasks" (Moyer et al., 1987, p. 237). And in the IRA's position statement on prefirst-grade literacy development, teachers are advised to "encourage children's first attempts at writing without concern for the proper formation of letters or correct conventional spelling," as well as to "encourage risk-taking in first attempts at reading and writing, and accept what appear to be errors as part of children's natural patterns of growth and development" (Early Childhood, 1988, p. 6). The guidelines for appropriate practice reflect the current information being gathered by educators and researchers in the area of writing. Before kindergarten teachers attempt to organize Whole Language writing centers, they need to be aware of the results of that research and the implications the information has for writing instruction.

KINDERGARTNERS' WRITING DEVELOPMENT

The research and theory upon which the position statements from the NAEYC, the ACEI, and the IRA are based have established two important concepts concerning early writing: (1) young children progress through various stages as they develop as writers (Bissex, 1980; Ferreiro & Teberosky, 1982; Lamme, 1984); and (2) children already know a great deal about print before entering school (Clay, 1975; Durkin, 1966). Researchers have helped teachers to interpret the features of young children's writing at various stages in order to

1. Observe and infer meaning from the children's writing forms,
2. Recognize their construction of print in various stages and contexts,
3. Value their compositions and refinements of print forms.

Observations of Meaning in Children's Writing Forms

While observing Kirsten in the dramatic play center, which had been organized to look like a veterinarian's office, the teacher noticed the child scribbling a note. She overheard Kirsten say, "Take this to the drugstore and give your dog this medicine. He won't be sick no more." Later, when the teacher retrieved the small scrap of paper during cleanup time, she noticed the writing was just scribbles. The teacher was a bit surprised that Kirsten was scribbling. Even though it was near the beginning of the school year, she recalled how Kirsten had printed the letter *K* very carefully and had said, "That's my name." Clay (1975), however, has observed children moving back and forth between scribbling and writing, as the situation demands. The quick and easy scribbling was representative of the veterinarian's prescription and allowed the child to write without getting bogged down in the formation of letters. Even more important, her action was indicative of a powerful learning. Kirsten understood that the writing was meant to convey a specific message, not that she was incapable of writing in letter form.

Many kindergarten teachers will recall children coming to school at the first of the year, pointing to a letter, and saying, "That's my name." The explanation is not surprising when we recall young children learning to talk. We remember how one word, *mama*, had a variety of meanings, depending on the intonation and gestures that accompanied the word. An angry cry of "mama" meant something entirely different than a delighted shout of "mama." Similarly, as children use whatever simple words they can speak to convey a variety of greater meanings, they also use whatever printed forms they know and can make to represent a variety of meanings. For example, Kirsten's printed letter *K* with hearts added means one thing on a card to grandmother, while a *K* printed on a scrap of paper and placed beside the last piece of cake in the refrigerator means, "Do not eat this. It belongs to Kirsten." It was Temple and colleagues (1988) who explained that young children first perceive their world and display their perceptions from "gross distinctions to progressively finer ones" (p. 21).

Therefore, when teachers encounter a child who is using very simple printed symbols, it does not necessarily mean that the printed message is simple; on the contrary, this gross differentiation may convey a complex concept. In fact, even simple scribbles can do this. To illustrate, Michelle, who watched her older brother write his name in his books at home, climbed the stairs to her room, took all the books from the bookshelf, sorted the ones that were hers from those of her older sister, and scribbled lines across the inside covers. When her mother reprimanded her for writing in her books, Michelle went downstairs, searched her brother's room for his books, and brought them to her mother. She lacked the verbal skills to say she was just doing what her brother did, but she did not lack the understanding that writing one's name in a book means ownership.

Likewise, teachers of young children need to recognize that the purposeful writing of young children, even scribbling, contains meaning. While at times children may scribble at random, much as adults doodle at random for the sheer enjoyment of the activity, young writers are usually emulating what they have seen as purposeful activity from the writers in their environment. Therefore, given the understanding that young writers will write using simple symbols for quite complex meanings, Whole Language kindergarten teachers will interact with children differently.

Recognition of Children's Construction of Print in Various Stages and Contexts

As teachers observe children constructing print, they see some kindergartners scribbling, while others are using a combination of mock and real letters, and still others are inventing ways of spelling words and beginning to refine their compositions. As noted already, depending on the context, five-year-olds at play may generate print in scribbles and may also use letter forms. Young children are constructing their knowledge of print by observing adult writings, by using it in their play, and by writing for a variety of functional purposes. As teachers observe children constructing print, it is important to note the context in which the writing occurs (Dyson, 1985).

The features of children's writing change over time, from scribbles to mock- and real-letter combinations, to sound–symbol relationships in invented spellings, to children manipulating the print to refine their compositions (Raines & Canady, 1982; Temple et al., 1988). How teachers respond depends on their abilities to interpret the implied

Figure 5.1   Richard's Dragon Story

The Jragon
The Jragn sad This iszT
a PlasTo liv SadThejrdgn
I WOTa nas plos To
liy I wil Taka hik
and Fid mea home
The Jragn sad nok hok
and Sunb ddeoisrd
ae   Sad The wmunM
ad The Jnagn No and seh
Sld The dn No Wadme I ms wal
gin up BuT I wil Tnia gnin
hok nok   one The dun
he lo   Wil you Kipme
yes   Sdd The wunmem
The ind

meanings of the writing samples within the context in which they originate. As children progress from Michelle's scribbling stage to Kirsten's stage, which includes scribbling in play situations but also includes letters and graphics, they are demonstrating the knowledge they have constructed about how print works as a symbol system for meaning. However, there will be interesting variations in the forms children's writings take. For example, Hugo, a five-year-old, wrote the word *fish* as follows:

$$\Gamma \; | \; C \; \wedge$$

The incomplete *F* and the upside-down *Y* or pitchfork shape are forms that have a letter appearance, but are not letters (Raines, 1986). They are mock letter forms (Temple et al., 1988).

As children learn more letters, they continue to use real letters and mock letters, sometimes even resorting to scribbling long after they know all the letter forms and have established sound–symbol relationships. Often when fatigue sets in, as after composing a long piece, the kindergartner will resort to scribbling or using fewer letters to convey the same meaning (Raines & Canady, 1982). An example of this phenomenon is shown in Figure 5.1, where Richard's story about a dragon is reprinted.

The translation of Richard's story, line by line and edited for spelling and punctuation, is as follows:

THE DRAGON

The dragon said, "This isn't
a place to live," said the dragon.
"I want a nice place to
live. I will take a hike
and find me a home."
The dragon said, "Knock, Knock,"
and somebody answered.
"Ee," said the woman,
and the dragon no and she
slammed the door. "No one wants me I might as well
give up. But I will try again."
Knock, knock on the door.
"Hello, will you keep me?"
"Yes," said the woman.
The end.

Sometimes, even within one piece of writing, a child will experiment with several different spellings of the same word. For example, in Richard's story, he wrote "woman" two different ways, "wmunm" and "wunmem." Also, near the middle of his long piece, he graphically represented *answered* with a combination of real and mock letters in his sentence about the woman who was scared when she answered the door and saw a dragon. In the beginning of his story, Richard indicated the dialogue by using the phrases, "The dragon said," but as he continued, he dropped the dialogue markers. Children will often vary the forms of the print, depending on the function of the writing, the intended audience, and, in a long piece of writing, their shortened sentences and phrases may result from fatigue.

Valuing Children's Compositions and Refinements of Print Forms

As children make transitions from letter forms to invented spelling using letters, their writing samples will include a variety of print forms. Yet, as children continue to explore written language, their use of print becomes more consistent. They discover that, when a group of letters is arranged to form a word, if that same combination is repeated, both words have the same meaning.

For example, in a research project with Head Start children (Raines, 1983), Sheila was asked to write a "pretend" grocery list (see Figure 5.2). For the first item on the list she wrote "EABIL." For the second item, she again wrote "EABIL," and then continued the list using various combinations of letters she knew how to write, many of them in her own name. When she finished the list, the researcher said, "Tell me what you have written on your grocery list." Sheila pointed to the first group of letters and replied, "Bread." When the researcher asked what the second item was, Sheila examined the letters briefly, and then with a gesture one uses when explaining the obvious said, "Bread. It says, 'Two loaves of bread.'"

Sheila thus demonstrated an important stage in the transition from letter forms to invented spelling. Even though she has not yet discovered the relationships between sounds and symbols, she has discovered the importance of letter arrangement in written language. Sheila realizes that, in order to say the same thing, the print must be written in the same way. The remainder of Sheila's list contained only one repeated configuration of letters, indicating she also is aware that, in order to say something different, the print must look different. She probably did not realize she had repeated the "AIE" arrangement

Figure 5.2   Sheila's Grocery List

EABiL } Two loaves of bread
EABiL

AEA   Bacon

AiE   Grits

EiA   Meal

EAi   Potatoes

AEi   Cookies

AiE   Pineapple

of letters at the bottom of her list, since it was separated by five other items. Sheila's writing is an example of what Clay (1975) calls the "generative principle." Children use a few letters and reconfigure them in a variety of ways to generate new combinations.

As early as 1936, Hildreth found that the letters in children's first names play an important role in their beginning writing. While it has been common practice in kindergarten classrooms to use children's first names in beginning reading, letter recognition, and letter formation exercises, observations of young children's writing indicate they begin to manipulate the letters they know—such as the letters in their first names—long before they establish sound–symbol relationships. In a research study comparing written-language samples collected over a period of a year, it was found that children consistently use the letters in their first names before they discover sound–symbol relationships (Raines & Canady, 1982). When they establish sound–symbol relationships, they generate long lists of words that start with the first letters of their names. Later they are able to create new words by using the other letters of their first names, the letters of other children's names, and then the letters of other familiar words in their environment.

Studies of children's early writing attempts reveal a natural progression in the use of symbols to represent the sounds, or more accurately, the "meaning," of oral language. This progression, or process, is commonly referred to as "invented spelling." Donald Graves (1983) describes five steps of invented spelling. The word *grass*, for instance, is first represented by the beginning consonant "G," next by the first and last consonant, "GS," then by adding an interior consonant, "GRS," followed by the inclusion of an interior vowel, "GRES," and finally by the use of standard spelling, "GRASS." Other researchers have made similar observations (Gentry & Henderson, 1978; Henderson, 1980; Read, 1975).

These research reports have caused teachers of young children to take a second look at children's early attempts to relate sounds and symbols. For example, one mother shared her daughter Caroline's writing with a researcher who spoke at a parent's meeting. Under a photograph, Caroline had written, "AME S QT" for "Amy is cute." Caroline used her knowledge of the letter names for *A* and *E* to write "Amy," but she also used her knowledge of the consonant sound of *M* as an interior letter. For *is*, she used the consonant sound of "S." When writing "QT" for *cute*, she used a letter name, *Q* followed by the consonant sound of the letter *T.*

Children often approximate the sounds of words and spellings by combining the strategies of letter names and consonant sounds to invent a spelling. Throughout an extensive story Kevin composed about a bear hunt, he wrote, "I wnt n" for "I went in." The *I* represents a letter-name strategy for spelling, while "wnt" corresponds to his understanding of consonant sounds, followed by the *n*, a letter-name strategy. From writing samples collected over the period of a year, it was observed that Head Start and kindergarten children's invented spellings progressed from the use of a few letters from their own names to using letters of the other children's names, and then to including new letters as they became more familiar with the alphabet (Raines & Canady, 1982). As children are exposed to writing, see others constructing print, and structure their own writing based on their understanding of how print works, teachers will observe children using more elaborate combinations of letters to represent blends, digraphs, and vowel sounds.

Extensive studies of early spelling conducted by Read (1975) provide strong evidence that children refine their invented spellings using specific strategies that have profound implications for literacy instruction in the kindergarten program. Teachers must respect that children enter kindergarten at various stages of spelling and writing development, and that they should be given the opportunity to continue their exploration of the writing process in a supportive, nonthreatening environment. It is important for the teacher to recognize that each child will use writing idiosyncratically, but each child's writing also will contain some features that make it like the writing of other children. Therefore, teachers must observe and interact with children during meaningful writing activities in which the child is the constructor of the writing, rather than simply rewriting what the teacher has constructed.

INTERACTING WITH YOUNG WRITERS

Many teachers find that creating and maintaining a system of writing folders is essential to ensure that they systematically review all the children's writing and interact with each child. The writing samples collected over a period of time also help document the children's progress as constructors of written language, and they let the children know that their writing is valued by the teacher. The writing samples provide valuable resource material for the teacher to observe each child's development, to share with parents, and to call individual children's attention to their progress.

Although proper interaction with children about their writing can be the key to a successful writing program, many teachers feel insecure when faced with a long string of print, laboriously written by a motivated young writer. The best advice to a kindergarten teacher who is attempting to establish a writing program in a Whole Language kindergarten is to remember that the concept of "Whole Language" is an attitude about literacy development and not a step-by-step prescription. Value the children's attempts, consider the natural stages of writing, and then respond honestly to the child's writing.

Remember that writing is meant to be read. Ask the child to read the message, regardless of whether the writing is scribbles, mock letters, or printed letters the child has used to invent a way to spell words (Hoffman, 1987; Martinez & Teale, 1987). Occasionally a writer will insist on the teacher reading the message, without giving a clue to its meaning. The teacher should respond honestly, "I know you have written a message, but I don't know how to read it. Please read it for me." The positive request to read what was written acknowledges the child is a writer and that the work does convey meaning. This basic understanding, or attitude, forms the foundation for interacting with the child as a writer.

The writing center is designed to reflect the total environment of a Whole Language kindergarten. It conveys the message that this is a place where personal language is valued and where children are not only provided the opportunity to continue their development as writers, but are "expected" to experience success in writing. Many kindergarten teachers who rely heavily on direct instruction to teach writing are uncomfortable in the role of observer and reactor, but a step-by-step program of direct instruction designed to teach "correct" writing is incompatible with what is now known about emergent literacy. Kindergarten teachers who wish to realize the success that Whole Language teachers are experiencing must accept children as "constructors" of language. They must be given the opportunity to construct written language through active participation and experimentation (Hansen, 1987; Willert & Kamii, 1985). Teachers must trust their children to discover the conventions of spelling and writing through developmentally appropriate reading and writing practices.

It is imperative that kindergarten teachers who want to become Whole Language teachers recognize that their responsibility is to support the child's own constructions and inventions, not to instruct the child in what to write and how to write it. If one recalls that a kindergartner is in the stage of "emergent" literacy, then the "constructivist" perspective is acceptable. There are no right and wrong answers to the children's writing. They are displaying in written form what they know about writing and how print functions. As they learn more from being exposed to more reading and writing in their classroom and from constructing more print on their own, then their writing will move more toward the conventions of spelling and writing.

Kindergarten teachers have long been aware of the importance of their own reading as a model of reading for their children. Whole Language kindergarten teachers also provide their children with a writing model. During a typical day, teachers may model writing in a variety of ways. They may create a cognitive map on the chalkboard as the children brainstorm or share new information learned in grouptime about nutrition; they may take dictation for the entire class, to read one child's news item; make a large duplicate copy of an open house invitation. They may write the names of the children who made the special castle creation for a sign in the block center; they may print the words to a favorite fingerplay on posterboard; or they may write a group story and edit it, to be bound into a class book. (See Appendix D, "Steps in Binding a Book.") The teacher models the function of writing for a variety of purposes, while teaching the basic skills of writing.

In a Whole Language kindergarten, the reciprocal relationship between reading and writing and their functional roles are never in doubt. The children observe the teacher reading what they have written and what other authors have written in books, as well as various school announcements; classroom instruction; notes from parents; communication to and from librarians, custodians, and guest speakers; and a wide range of other printed materials. In the writing center, children are encouraged to read their own writing, whether it is scribbles, mock letters, real letters, or entire stories with many invented spellings. The expectation is that what is written is meant to be read (Calkins, 1986; Graves, 1983).

To insure continued development of the reading and writing processes and to build on what the children already know when they enter school, a writing center designed to meet the appropriate practice recommendations from the NAEYC, ACEI, and IRA is essential in the Whole Language kindergarten.

DESIGNING THE WRITING CENTER

Writing centers in Whole Language kindergartens are designed to help children learn the skills of writing through active participation in the process, and to allow teachers to observe and interact with the children in meaningful writing situations. Although the physical appearance of writing centers may vary, a typical center accommodates four or five children, is located near the art center and the library, and contains an abundance of writing supplies. Loose sheets of a variety of textures and sizes of mostly unlined paper are available. Some paper is stapled together into bunches of three or four sheets, and some writing projects are bound together to form a book that later may have a permanent cover added.

There are a variety of writing instruments in a multitude of sizes. Pens, pencils, markers, and crayons are displayed in baskets on the shelves. On top of the shelves, there are two large bins. One is filled with the children's writing folders, with covers they have decorated, which contain pieces of writing the children have completed at the writing center. Another bin contains a journal for each child, constructed of large sheets of paper stapled together with a decorated cover. The journals may be learning journals where teachers ask children to record observations from some special class activity, or they may be used more personally for the children to write and communicate their feelings (Harste, Short, & Burke, 1988; Parry & Hornsby, 1985). In addition to the writing instruments, folders, and journals, there is a magnetic board with letters and numerals, small chalk slates, letter stencils, alphabet stamps and an inked printing pad, and even a salt tray. The salt tray is a large rectangular covered cake pan filled with salt which the children write in with their fingers, then shake to erase their writing. There are other materials that stimulate the tactile sense as well, including sandpaper letters and numerals, a tray of wet sand for writing in, and cutouts of letters from fabric.

Displays of children's writing are mainly found in three different areas of the classroom. Across the corner of the art area, the teacher strings a clothesline for drying paintings. A number of different children's writings and drawings are displayed on a low bulletin board on the wall across from the writing center. An open shelf in the library corner contains a display of some of the child-authored stories that the teacher has bound into books.

The library corner, the art center, and the writing center are positioned near each other to allow easy access for children, who often move from exploring a story in a book, to drawing a picture, to writing a story. At the beginning of the year, it is common for children to draw first and then write, but by the end of the year some children choose to write first, then illustrate. With the close arrangement of these areas, children move freely back and forth as they talk, write, and draw. Since talking is considered an essential part of the composing process (Genishi, 1985), the writing center has been located in an area that encourages verbal interaction among the children.

Scheduling of children into the writing center may vary with each teacher. Some feel that children should visit the writing center every day, while others recommend the freeplay approach and believe children should be free to choose the writing center, just as they are free to select other centers. A question often asked by kindergarten teachers is, "What do I do about the children who seldom choose the writing center?" In a Whole Language kindergarten, it is unusual for children not to want to go to the writing center, but, when that occurs, the teacher may decide to give them a gentle nudge, as in the following example.

Four young friends who seldom chose the writing center but who were regulars in the block area took great pride in the heights they were achieving with their hollow block structures. The tall towers were tempting, however, to some of the other children, who liked to dart in and knock over the building, delighting in the commotion it created. The block builders complained to the teacher, who led a problem-solving discussion with both the builders and the demolishers. It was decided that only the kids who built the stucture got to knock it over. When asked how they would remember this rule, one child who had observed other children posting rules and instructions around the room said, "Make a sign and tape it in the block corner." The teacher suggested the builders get a piece of posterboard from the writing center and make a poster for the other girls and boys to read. All four children ran to the writing center and quickly returned with a piece of blue posterboard and a handful of markers. One of the writers drew a picture of children building with blocks, and another wrote, "DNT NK OVR," for "Don't knock over!" After a few minutes' debate about the message, they decided something else was needed. Underneath the first line of writing was added, "NLS YOU BLT IT," for "Unless you built it."

The teacher extended the poster-writing experience by asking the children to tell about their poster at grouptime and by having the listeners think of other classroom rules that were needed. Several were suggested: "Be friends, don't hit." "Wash your hands before snack." "Ask before feeding the fish." "Clean up when the teacher says to." The block builders were asked to come to the writing center the next day and design and write posters for these classroom rules, which they did. In the weeks that followed, the four children continued to spend a lot of time in the block center during freeplay, but they have also become writers. There are numerous other examples throughout this book of teachers connecting children's playful activities and writing.

FOUR YOUNG WRITERS USING THE WRITING CENTER

To children in a Whole Language kindergarten, the writing center is a place where they have access to materials and the space and time to write, but another essential element of a successful writing center is *reason* to write. The writing center provides a place not only to support the young children as writers, but also for teachers to interact daily with children as they engage in purposeful writing. The following is a typical example of four kindergartners interacting with each other and with their teacher as they explore the writing process. In this case, the processes of personal expression and individual exploration were given high priority, as they are in most kindergarten programs. The teacher allowed these four children to explore writing and to express themselves in their own unique ways.

Jason, who was drawing a picture with markers, paused occasionally to fly his marker through the air like an airplane. When the teacher moved near Jason, he looked up and said excitedly, "When I'm done, I'm gonna glue it [the picture] right here," pointing to the back of several pages stapled together.

Nicki and her best friend, Christy, sat across the table from Jason. Nicki had been working on a long story that she had started the day before, but at the moment seemed to be taking charge of her friend's writing. Nicki suggested to Christy that she should "write it this way," and proceeded to write an *N* on her friend's paper. The *N* was leaning over at a strange angle, and the two girls put their hands over their mouths and giggled. It was not evident from the few letters on the paper what they had written, but when the teacher said, "Tell me about your writing," Christy replied, "It's gonna be about me and Nicki."

Stephan, the fourth writer, mumbled to himself as he stood at the end of the table with one knee on his chair and looked down at several pictures he had drawn. He was writing captions for each of the pictures, which seemed to be placed in a definite order. He wrote a string of letters as he slowly muttered each word to himself. He left spaces between the groups of letters to tell where the words began and ended.

Each of these writers was demonstrating a unique, personal approach to a writing project and a particular level of development in the writing process. The teacher recognized the various levels and interacted with each child as an individual writer. Jason was eager to share his writing with his teacher. He was illustrating his completed work and was obviously pleased with his accomplishment. The teacher moved over to look at what Nicki had written. She knew that Nicki was a self-motivated writer and that she would soon return to her own story, after she demonstrated her expert knowledge of how to make an *N* and enjoyed a few giggles with Christy. The teacher asked Christy, who had just begun her story, what the story was going to be about. When Christy replied, "It's about me and Nicki," the teacher recalled that when Christy had started her story she had said it was going to be about her dog. The teacher recognized this procedure as a normal stage in early writing and commented, while smiling to the observer, "I wonder what the story will be about by the time it is finished." The teacher did not interrupt Stephan, the writer who was deeply engaged in writing captions for his pictures, using his own invented spelling.

As the children progress as writers, the teacher makes notes of each child's strengths and may choose to give direct instruction on a particular skill or convention of writing. However, Whole Language teachers have found that when a particular feature of print, such as leaving space between words, is brought to the children's attention during grouptime, many students who are ready for that knowledge tend to apply it to their future writing. These teachers believe that even the formation of the letters is best learned by creating within the child a need for learning to form the letters. Children learn to speak correctly in order to communicate more effectively, and that same need for effective communication applies to written expression.

THE INSTRUCTIONAL DILEMMA

For some teachers, the most difficult aspect of creating a Whole Language writing program is knowing when to correct children's writing. Whole Language kindergarten teachers are aware of their children's need to communicate effectively, and they know that, through daily exposure to "correct" or effective oral and written communication, their students will not only be receptive to suggestions for improvement, but will reach a stage where they themselves insist on correct writing. It is important to remember that the children "own their writing" and progress through stages of development as writers at their own speed.

The teacher, however, is still very much in control of the program, and the conventions of writing are taught daily through various reading and writing activities. They are taught as the children observe the teacher writing a story for them; during a dictated group story, as the teacher reconstructs the words of the children on an experience chart; or when the teacher calls attention to the distinguishing features of print in children's tradebooks, a classroom-published big book, the print on a child's T-shirt, or a sample of the children's own writing. One of the major instructional aspects of a Whole Language kindergarten writing program is to make children aware of print as it exists in books, in environmental print on signs and logos, and in the writing the teacher models.

In a Whole Language kindergarten, children also learn that the importance of correct spelling is sometimes determined by the purpose of the writing activity. For instance, Nicki, who was writing her older brother's name on an index card as the teacher spelled it for her, explained, "I want to spell it right because I'm making him a birthday card." Nicki has learned that, just as there are times for careful or "correct" reading, there are times when she wants the spelling to be, as she says, "Just right." Many kindergarten teachers are concerned that, if conventional writing is not taught directly, the children will remain in the stage of invented spelling and enter first grade unaware of or unconcerned with correct spelling. In order for children to own their own writing and continue to grow as writers, they must be allowed to discover, through personal and purposeful writing, the need for conventional writing.

It is important for the teacher to know whether the writer just wants to spell the word correctly or is indicating a concern for the reader. The following is a personal example of a kindergartner named Amy who visited our home. A prolific writer, she was accustomed to having her writing read by her teacher and her parents. When writing a thank-you note to us after her visit, she complained to her mother, "They won't know how to read my writing." She knew her grandmother sometimes had difficulty reading her writing, and she generalized that difficulty to us. Although we had written notes to her in the past, and we had read the many examples of her invented spelling that her parents had enclosed in letters to us, Amy had never seen us read her writing. After a bit of coaxing from her mother, Amy wrote the note, using invented spelling, but was careful to point out to her mother the words that we probably could not read. Amy had advanced to the point in her writing where she realized that some of her writing did not comply with the conventions of "standard" writing and might not communicate as intended with her audience. Later letters to us included erasures and carefully printed words that reflected Amy's growing concern for correct spelling.

Kindergarten teachers who ask when children should be told how to spell a word have a limited understanding of the Whole Language concept. When children have ownership of their writing, they will decide when a word must be spelled for them. Teachers new to a Whole Language writing program may have difficulty reading invented spelling in the beginning, but very quickly they will discover the same excitement in reading the children's writing as the child experiences while producing it. Teachers who have attended a meeting where Whole Language kindergarten teachers are sharing samples of invented spelling on the overhead projector are amazed at how teachers who have never seen the writing before are able to read most of the words and interpret the message with little difficulty.

The guide for when to correct spelling in a Whole Language kindergarten is very simple: Correction is needed when individuals determine that their inventions are not adequate and when they are concerned about the reader. If children are reluctant to use invented spelling in their early writing because they have entered kindergarten already "indoctrinated" to correct spelling, they should be encouraged with statements such as, "Write it the way you think it should look" or, "Use the letters that you know" or, "Spell it like it sounds to you." Continued encouragement and the teachers' learning to read invented spelling will insure the children's active participation in the process.

Martinez and Teale (1987) recommend that, from the beginning of the kindergarten year, the teacher establish the expectation that children will write. Teachers can show some examples from previous years of kindergarten children's writing, including scribbles and mock letters. Also, writing samples using all letters but without sound–symbol relationships help, as well as writing that uses invented spelling. Teachers can read what the previous kindergarten children said they had written and then display the writing and transcriptions in a prominent place for the children and their parents to see.

CHILDREN'S WRITING TOPICS

While teachers of older children often hear children complaining that they don't know what to write about, kindergarten children are prolific in their choices of topics. When they draw or paint pictures, they include their families, their pets, their friends, the games they like to play, and their favorite characters from children's literature and television. They also write about their personal experiences, which provide the motivation for children's self-expression through print.

Similarly, as children become involved in the many hands-on learning experiences the teacher has planned for the classroom, they discover a new purpose for writing. Just as children express a need for sharing what they are learning through conversation, they also begin to reflect on what they are learning through writing, thereby learning new ways to record information. Graphs, lists, and labels begin to appear in the children's own writing after they observe the teacher creating these devices to recall information. The teacher may formulate a bar graph in the mathematics area when students tell their favorite fruit snacks, or make a list of fruits for the nutrition unit, or label the seeds from fruits for a display on the science table.

One way for children to follow their own learning is by writing what they have learned into journals, sometimes referred to as learning journals or learning logs. Children are asked to write about one thing they learned each day. The most important aspect of journal writing at the kindergarten stage is the process that is involved, not the clarity of the writing. One child may draw a picture of an apple as his favorite snack. Another may write a list of fruits, using the beginning letters of the words, while another may write in complete sentences. The important function is for the child to recall the information, to decide how to depict the learning, and to create a permanent record that can be reflected upon at a later date.

How the learning logs or journals are used depends on the particular kindergarten teacher. Some Whole Language kindergarten teachers have the children share their journals with other children, while others use the journals for an exclusive communication between the child and the teacher. Others allow each child to determine when the journal information is to be shared. In many kindergartens, the journal is read by the teacher, who then writes a response.

Soon the journal becomes a vehicle for written correspondence between the child and the teacher.

SUMMARY

Kindergarten teachers demonstrate their knowledge and understanding of young children's growth and development as they plan learning centers to reflect what they believe to be developmentally appropriate practices. Whole Language writing centers are also planned according to what is now considered to be developmentally appropriate for young developing kindergarten writers. Given a supportive, nonthreatening environment for writing, five-year-olds continue to demonstrate their expanding knowledge of how print functions. Just as they began speaking by using simple utterances and refined those sounds to communicate a deeper meaning, young children use simple symbols to convey complex concepts. They move from scribbling to mock letters and correctly formed letters. They write first by using the letters of their first names, after which they begin developing an awareness of sound–symbol relationships, starting with the names of the letters of the alphabet and with beginning consonant sounds. They use all of these strategies to invent ways to spell words. They learn to communicate in whole sentences and stories through the use of invented spellings. Although the sequence of children's writing has been described in numerous studies, it is apparent that children employ a variety of strategies as they experiment with print.

It is not possible to establish a step-by-step writing program that will apply to all children; therefore, it becomes the role of the teacher to provide the time, the materials, and the prepared environment for interacting with the children as individual writers and for supporting each child's development. In this chapter, some ways of observing and interacting with the children in various stages of the writing process and for various writing functions were suggested. Suggestions were also made as to how a writing center might be organized to allow children to function independently and interactively as writers.

Teachers face an instructional dilemma as they attempt to allow children to emerge naturally through the various stages of writing, while providing the instruction they feel is necessary to support children's learning. It is the children themselves who provide the cues for action in this regard. This is consistent with the underlying message of this chapter: No book and no package materials can create a Whole

Language kindergarten writing program. Five-year-olds create the writing program. Kindergarten teachers must accept their young students as writers in various stages of development and then create an environment that will best encourage the children to grow. The learning-center approach has proven essential for other aspects of the kindergarten curriculum, and a writing center is essential to a Whole Language kindergarten writing program.

Getting Children Interested
in Books

The complaint that children lack interest in books and seldom choose to go to the library corner is common among many kindergarten teachers. Yet in Whole Language kindergartens the library corner is one of the most popular spots in the room. The kindergarten teacher's philosophy about reading and the kind of reading instruction the children receive at grouptime creates an attitude about books and reading that is reflected in the children's feelings about the library corner. If, during grouptime reading instruction, a teacher stresses letter and word recognition and word-by-word reading, children will see reading as something too difficult for them. The library corner becomes for most the domain of a few "special" children who can read—an attitude no kindergarten teacher wants to create.

Whole Language teachers do not view reading as the end result of mastering reading readiness worksheets and word recognition skills. They believe that children construct knowledge about reading through the processes of assimilation and accommodation. Smith (1976) states that "children probably begin to read from the moment they become aware of print in any meaningful way" (p. 299). The primary purpose of grouptime reading instruction in a Whole Language kindergarten is to encourage the children's natural curiosity about reading, to help their discovery of sound–symbol relationships through meaningful print, and, most important, to continue their love of a good story (Bettelheim & Zelan, 1981; Cullinan, 1987).

Recommendations for appropriate practices established by the NAEYC, ACEI, and IRA can guide kindergarten teachers as they plan ways to interest young children in books. In the language development and literacy component of the NAEYC's position paper (Bredekamp, 1987), appropriate practice is described as follows:

Children are provided many opportunities to see how reading and writing are useful before they are instructed in letter names, sounds, and word identification. Basic skills develop when they are meaningful to children. An abundance of these type of activities is provided to develop language and literacy through meaningful experience: listening to and reading stories and poems; taking field trips; dictating stories; seeing classroom charts and other print in use; participating in dramatic play and other experience requiring communication; talking informally with other children and adults; and experimenting with writing by drawing, copying, and inventing their own spelling. [p. 51]

In the IRA position paper (Early Childhood, 1988, p. 6), literally all 15 of the recommendations have implications for effective use of reading in the kindergarten classroom. The following four recommendations, however, are imperative if teachers are to build their kindergartens into effective literacy environments.

Build instruction on what the child already knows about oral language, reading and writing. Focus on meaningful experiences and meaningful language rather than on isolated skill development.
Encourage risk taking in first attempts at reading and writing, and accept what appear to be errors as part of children's natural growth and development.
Use reading materials that are familiar or predictable, such as well known stories, as they provide children with a sense of control and confidence in their ability to learn.
Present a model for children to emulate. In the classroom, teachers should use language appropriately, listen and respond to children's talk, and engage in their own reading and writing.

Young children build their concepts of books and reading through many experiences with print throughout their early years (Willert & Kamii, 1985). Attitudes formed by children in the kindergarten classroom concerning reading and reading instruction may last a lifetime; therefore, the importance of an appropriate classroom reading environment cannot be overemphasized. Teachers can improve the kindergarten reading program by focusing on the following areas:

1. Reading to the children more effectively,
2. Building upon what children already know about print,
3. Recognizing the benefits of literacy play,

4. Supporting children's explorations of reading materials in the library corner.

READING TO CHILDREN MORE EFFECTIVELY

Reading to children during grouptime is part of the daily routine in most kindergartens (Nurss & Hough, 1986), and the positive effects are well documented. Reading to children increases knowledge of story structure (Jensen, 1985; Mandler & Johnson, 1977), aids language and vocabulary development (Chomsky, 1972; Cohen, 1968), and develops awareness of how print sounds when read from books (Holdaway, 1979). The teacher also acts as a role model, demonstrating the various functions of reading during grouptime and throughout the day.

Although story reading at grouptime provides the teacher with an excellent opportunity for reading instruction, it is important to remember, as already noted, that the primary purpose for reading to children is to share and enjoy a good story with them (Trelease, 1989). Through exposure to good children's literature, students in a Whole Language kindergarten develop a lasting love of reading and develop a concept of authorship.

Thinking with Authors

According to Allen (1986), "Learners must be involved in the process of thinking with authors" (p. 147). When teachers read aloud to children, they must select a piece of literature that will capture the imagination of the students. As the students become involved in making and confirming predictions and integrating the story as they hear it unfold, they will engage in "thinking with the author."

The following suggestions for involving children during storytime are designed to increase their awareness of authors and authorship. The teacher needs to remind the children that the book was written by a real person and point out the names of the author and illustrator. The title of the selection should then be noted, and the children should be asked to predict what the story might be about. After listening to a few predictions, the teacher can begin reading the story. The teacher should use a voice that sets the mood of the piece of literature, conveying, for example, that the story is dramatic, suspenseful, humorous, playful, sad, or joyful. The teacher should pause occasionally and ask the children to confirm or reject the predictions made at the beginning of the story and give them the opportunity to make new predictions based on what has been read.

Meaning is constructed by each child based on that child's prior knowledge, and although prediction is essential to comprehension (Goodman, 1982a), children must learn to alter or reject their predictions at any point in the reading and listening process. It is particularly important to allow children to alter their predictions during the open discussion at the end of the story. When the story is completed, children should be allowed time to react to the story and accept all responses, being careful not to judge responses as right and wrong.

For example, having noticed that Latrice, who sometimes has trouble following a story, was obviously piecing the day's story together from the comments of the other children, the teacher might encourage Latrice to join the discussion by asking her to retell a particularly interesting part of the story. When children retell a story in their own words, they are "re-authoring" the story.

Predictable Books

Kindergarten children take great pride in their abilities to remember stories, songs, and chants. Five-year-olds particularly enjoy books that have predictable language and story patterns, because they are easy to remember. While the popularity of predictable books is well known, recent research studies on emergent literacy have now established important links between early listening experiences and early reading experiences (Rhodes, 1981; Routman, 1988). As children use prediction to make the transition from listening to a story to reading a story, they establish effective reading and thinking strategies.

Children will enjoy the repetition and cumulative patterns in such stories as *The House that Jack Built, The Little Red Hen*, or *The Gingerbread Boy* (Galdone, 1961, 1973, 1975). The language patterns and predictable story-sequence patterns make them easy to remember for retelling as flannel-board stories and for rereading with the teacher. When teachers read *The Three Little Pigs* (Galdone, 1984), *Goldilocks and the Three Bears* (Cauley, 1981), and *The Three Little Kittens* (Galdone, 1986) on successive days, children discover the similarities and differences in the patterns of characters, interactions, and problems. It is not too early to introduce kindergartners to story maps or semantic webs as a way to make predictions before reading, check predictions during reading, and retell the story after reading. A variety of types of story maps—such as character webs, plot webs, story patterns, circle stories, and flowcharts—can be used to help children become more aware of the scaffolding or underlying structure of a story and to develop concepts of how the different elements of a story work together (Bromley, 1988).

Figure 6.1 gives an example of a story map for *The Three Little Pigs*. It can be used as follows. At storytime, the teacher stands at the chalkboard or a chart tablet and asks the children to guess which story he will read to them today. After a few guesses, the teacher gives the children some hints. As he draws three circles and places them in a triangular formation, he says that the story is one of their favorites and that it has three main characters. Before the children can guess again, the teacher draws another circle in the middle of the three circles and tells them there is also a "special" character in the story.

At this point, the children are sure it is either *Goldilocks and the Three Bears* or *The Three Little Pigs*. The teacher then draws the ears and faces on the four circles, and the children all agree that the story is *The Three Little Pigs*. As the teacher reads the story, he draws the houses around the three pigs and then a line from the wolf to each of the pigs, as he comes to their houses. After the wolf "blows their houses in," the teacher draws a dotted line as the pigs run to another house. After the wolf goes to the last little pig's house and is unsuccessful, he wanders aimlessly back into the woods.

Naturally, the teacher may choose any number of variations when using the story map. He may want to map the story as the children tell it from memory or encourage them to use the story maps to tell or write their own versions of the story.

Perhaps the most popular of all patterned language books is *Brown Bear, Brown Bear, What Do You See?* (Martin, 1983). *Brown Bear* contains a rhythm that invariably produces a pleasing listening response among young children: "Brown bear, brown bear, what do you see? I see a red bird looking at me. Red bird, red bird, what do you see? I see a yellow duck looking at me." The chained question and answer pattern allows children to "think with the author" as they predict the phrase patterns. Whether children are listening to the exciting adventure of Curious George (Rey, 1941) or enjoying the rhythm of *Brown Bear*, predictable stories encourage active participation. To further involve the children in the listening/reading experience, the teacher might have the children predict what will happen next to Curious George or what the next question-and-answer pattern will be in *Brown Bear*.

Patterned language books with repeated phrases or cumulative characters can also be used in a verbal cloze procedure, with the chil-

Figure 6.1   Sample Story Map

dren completing sentences or phrases. For example, after having read *Brown Bear* through in its entirety, the teacher could reread the book and pause for the children to fill in what comes next. The teacher would read, "Brown bear, brown bear," and then pause for the children to complete the phrase, "what do you see?" With another rereading, the children will probably read most of the book with the teacher.

In addition to the many old folktales that are excellent patterned language books, there are several predictable books that, once shared with the children, tend to be among their favorites. For a unit on families the teacher might read *Me Too!* (Mayer, 1983). The children will join in repeating the phrase, "Me, too!" which the baby sister says throughout the book. For a touch of family humor, the teacher can read *No Jumping on the Bed* (Arnold, 1987), and the children can repeat Walter's father's warning about jumping on the bed, then listen for the hilarious scenes that follow. The family theme is also found in *Jesse Bear, What Will You Wear?* (Carlstrom, 1986). The children enjoy the rhyme, as well as Jesse's predicaments throughout the day, which cause him to change clothes so often.

In addition to these patterned language books, which use rhyming words, recurring phrases, or repeated characters, there are numerous others that are based on songs, poems, and counting rhymes. Several popular ones for kindergartners are *Roll Over: A Counting Book* and *Mary Wore Her Red Dress and Henry Wore His Green Sneakers* (Peek, 1981, 1985), *The Green Grass Grows All Around* (Hoffman, 1968), and *Over in the Meadow: A Counting-Out Rhyme* (Wadsworth, 1986). The children enjoy reading or hearing the books because they can predict what the author will say next.

Shared Book Experiences

As kindergartens change the emphasis of their reading programs from skills-based to literature-based instruction, teachers are planning learning experiences that are appropriate for the developmental level of the children in their particular classrooms. Kindergarten teachers operating within skills-based reading programs were being told that children who come from homes where reading is not a high priority are at-risk children and will need a lot of work on their "basic reading skills." Against the better judgment of most kindergarten teachers, those at-risk children were placed in reading readiness programs that consisted primarily of filling out meaningless worksheets. Whole Language kindergarten teachers know that children who have had few experiences sharing a good children's book while sitting on the lap of a parent have missed an extremely important stage of natural literacy development. These teachers have devised reading activities that involve children in some of the same early reading experiences they may have missed at home. Volunteers and foster grandparents are used to read stories to individual children as a part of the daily routine, to compensate for the lack of early lap-reading experiences.

One shared book experience teachers have found valuable is the use of "big books," which are enlarged versions of regular books. They may be either homemade or commercially produced. Holdaway (1979), who has written extensively on emergent literacy, recommends using big books as a means for children to share a book experience. While listening and hearing the predictable language patterns, the children can also see the patterns in the enlarged print. There is no replacement for holding a child on one's lap and reading, but the shared book experience does allow for many of the same elements of the lap-reading experience. Through the use of big books, the children can see the illustrations and print while the text is being read aloud.

Big books have become so popular among kindergarten teachers that many are starting to make their own big books of children's favorite songs, poems, experience charts, and child- and teacher-authored books. They also are using them to retell some of the children's favorite stories. Teachers should read big books in much the same way they read other picture books, using the "thinking-with-the-author" steps described earlier. Some teachers also add steps to build on the value of the patterned language book. The verbal "cloze" procedure of pausing for the students to complete the recurring phrases or repeat the cumulative patterns becomes even more meaningful when using big books. Children can actually see the words they are saying.

The large print found in big books is a good instructional aid when teachers want to direct the children's attention to reading strategies such as prediction. When children use semantic cues to figure out a word, they look at the words surrounding the unknown word, as well as recall what they already know about the story; then they predict what the word might be. When readers use syntactic cues to determine what word might come next, they are making predictions based on the natural pattern of our language. When children use graphophonic cues by looking at the beginning letter of the word for a sound and graphic cue, they are predicting. Readers learn to use these three cue systems—semantic, syntactic, and graphophonic—as they sample the print for the purpose of gaining meaning from the story (Goodman & Watson, 1977). As with all reading instruction in the Whole Language kindergarten, the emphasis during storytime is always on whole-to-part instruction. Reading stategies are introduced and developed from print that is meaningful (the whole) before any attention is placed on the word or letter recognition (the parts).

Although big books offer an excellent format for presenting instruction in reading strategies, their use should not be confused with the big-book versions of preprimers in a basal reading series. The primary purpose of the big-book primers is to teach groups of children to read "controlled-vocabulary" stories word by word. The primary purpose of big books in a Whole Language kindergarten is to allow the children to follow along as an interesting story is being read to them. One of the best means for selecting a good big book is to see if the book was originally printed as a book for individual reading. If it was successful as a little book, then it probably has good story content for a big book. Seeing the enlarged print allows the children to discover the connections between the words their teacher is saying and the words as they appear in print. It is not until that connection is made that the teacher will emphasize individual sentences, phrases, words, and letters.

Shared reading through big books is a favorite grouptime activity of many kindergarten children. As children become familiar with the story pattern and the rhythm of the language in some of their favorite books, they are able to "think with the author." In addition, some kindergartners want to become authors themselves and construct their own versions of the story.

In one classroom, the children's first big book activity was an extension of *Brown Bear, Brown Bear, What Do You See?* (Martin, 1983). The children added more animals to the story and attached their new pages at the end of *Brown Bear*. Later they began writing more big-book stories based on other literature selections. They made a whole series of "seed books" based on the classic story, *The Carrot Seed* (Krauss, 1945), only their seeds were popcorn, radish, tomato, corn, watermelon, and cantaloupe. Using the basic structure of *The Carrot Seed*, the teacher helped the children write their own stories on the chart tablet that she used for experience charts. They made posterboard covers for each of the seed books. Soon the children found they no longer needed the scaffold of the controlled pattern of other books and began to produce big books of their own compositions. The children who had "thought with the author" when listening to stories at grouptime and when writing their own patterned language books were now sharing their own stories during grouptime. They used the same reading strategies to read their own books to other children as the teacher had modeled for them earlier.

Children learn fluent reading strategies by listening to fluent reading, and it is through practicing fluent reading strategies that they begin to read independently. The shared big-book experience just described helps children to understand the reading process and to become fluent readers.

USING CHILDREN'S KNOWLEDGE OF ENVIRONMENTAL PRINT

It has been established that the term *Whole Language* refers more to an attitude about literacy and literacy development than to a particular method of instruction. The success of a Whole Language kindergarten reading program depends not only on the attitude of the teacher toward literacy, but also the attitude of the children. Many children think they are not readers until they come to school and are taught to read. The concept of being taught to read and of reading readiness must be re-evaluated. Kindergarten teachers cannot be expected to "begin" something that was already begun long before the children entered school (Canady, 1983).

The IRA's position statement (Early Childhood, 1988) recommends that teachers "build instruction on what the child already knows about oral language, reading and writing. [Teachers should] focus on meaningful experiences and meaningful language rather than on isolated skill development" (p. 6). One of the areas of oral language, reading, and writing that young children have a great deal of knowledge about is referred to as "environmental print." Few types of print have more meaning to them.

While parents and teachers have observed their children reading logos from fast-food restaurants and softdrink signs and labels from cans and cereal boxes, they usually do not think of these early experiences with print as "real" reading. Reading has been taught from a part-to-whole perspective for so long that many people confuse the reading process with reading instruction. They think erroneously that, unless their children are "sounding out" the letters and piecing them together to make words, then they are not reading. When reading is viewed as part of a literacy process that emerges from the time children first become aware of print, then children's early experiences with the print they find in their environment become an integral part of that process. For children who have not been read to at home, environmental print often provides them with their first meaningful encounters with print.

Studies of young children from a variety of socioeconomic and ethnic backgrounds have shown that they already know a great deal about print in the environment (Canady, 1982b; K. S. Goodman, 1968; Y. M. Goodman, 1986; Torrey, 1969; Ylisto, 1967). Teachers eager to build on what children already know must realize that, regardless of their students' socioeconomic status or ethnic background, young children have already begun the reading process when they construct meaning from signs, logos, television commercials, packaging, and printed advertisements.

Because learning to read for many children has become associated with starting kindergarten or first grade, it is important for teachers to bring environmental print into the classroom and leave no doubt among the children that it, too, involves "real" reading. Effective teachers have found many ways to highlight environmental print in their classrooms, including the construction of units entitled, "Reading Is All Around Us" or "Things We Can Read." A popular activity is to have children bring in labels, wrappers, boxes, and ads clipped from the newspaper and display them in the room.

While constructing a bulletin board of familiar wrappers that the children had brought to school for their "I Can Read" unit, one little girl made a discovery. "This one has my name in it," she said, as she pointed to the *M* on the Milky Way candy wrapper. The teacher immediately confirmed the child's observation by saying, "Melinda, you're right, the letter *M* is at the beginning of your name and at the beginning of 'Milky Way.'" The teacher then wrote "Melinda" on an index card, attached it to the candy wrapper, and placed the two print pieces on the bulletin board. Of course, within a few days, all the children's names were printed on index cards and attached to wrappers.

As a part of the environmental print unit, the teacher might also use some environmental print in her own writing. For example, advertisement logos and even small packages could be used in a dictated group experience chart as shown in Figure 6.2. The children dictated the sentence, "We buy pizza at Pizza Hut." The teacher wrote the first four words, then let the children paste on a cut-out logo from an advertisement to complete the sentence. Using the same pattern, other sentences were added as shown in the figure. The products

Figure 6.2   Sample Environmental Print Experience Chart

could be localized and community store names added to the sentences.

To make further connections between environmental print and beginning reading and writing, the children can paste logos into books (Allen & Canady, 1979). They can browse through newspapers and catalogs to find and cut out logos they can read. When each child has a few items, they can paste the logos into blank books. The children can either write their own captions or sentences, or the teacher can take dictation for a sentence or two, then invite the children to write on their own.

In an interesting study of children's attitudes about environmental print, a group of five-year-olds who had told their teachers they could not read were shown a display of miniature cereal boxes (Canady, 1982a). As the teacher pointed to the boxes, the children easily identified the name of the cereal. Then the teacher asked, "Isn't that reading?" The children shook their heads and said "No." Next the teacher showed the children just the fronts of the cereal boxes, which had been cut out and were displayed on the table. The children "read" all of the box covers, but when asked if that was reading, they again shook their heads. Then the teacher showed the children a book that she had bound, complete with cover, title page, and library card. On each page she had glued the cover of a miniature cereal box. She read the cover of the book, pointed to the title page and the library card, and then let the children read the pages. When asked if they were now reading, the children all agreed that, yes, they were reading. To most young children who have limited preschool reading experience, reading is associated with reading from books. Units like "Things We Can Read" help children view themselves as readers and learn important sound–symbol relationships while building instruction on what they already know.

One teacher reported that the activities in the environmental print unit were so successful that the children had to be reminded not to remove the labels from food cans at home until *after* the can had been opened. Another teacher, whose children came from low-income homes where many of the parents thought of themselves as nonreaders, said that the environmental print unit provided the parents with a way to help their children. In some cases, the parents also saw themselves as readers for the first time.

ENCOURAGING LITERACY PLAY

Kindergarten teachers are aware of young children's need for adult readers as role models; however, studies also show that children emulate each other in reading. In an attempt to understand better the process of emerging literacy, early childhood educators are taking a closer look at children's social interactions during periods of play. In ethnographic studies of home and school, it has been observed that children often become involved in literacy play as they emulate adults and other children in simulated reading behaviors (Isenberg & Jacob, 1983; Taylor, 1983).

An example of literacy play was observed in a kindergarten cooking center (Raines & Isbell, 1989), where two children were pretending to cook together. One was pretending to read the directions from the cookbook while adding the ingredients. When that child put down the cookbook to stir the mixture, the second child picked up the cookbook and pretended to read the directions. Teachers and parents have observed their children pretending to read to a sibling or a child in the classroom, and it is important to realize that emulating each other is an essential part of the emergent literacy process. Time must be scheduled for children to play and to allow these processes to take place within a play environment.

To plan a developmentally appropriate environment for literacy development, Whole Language kindergarten teachers are taking a closer look at the home environments of children who are already reading fluently when they come to school. In their book, *Learning to Read Naturally*, Jewell and Zintz (1986) point out that "natural" readers are ones who have been read to, not only by their parents, but by an older sibling or playmate. These natural readers then read or pretend to read to their younger siblings and friends. Whole Language kindergarten teachers believe that reading should be part of the natural development of young children, and they attempt to create learning activities that allow children to explore all types of printed language in a meaningful, "natural" manner.

In a Whole Language kindergarten, teachers often observe proficient readers pairing themselves with children who are just beginning to read from books. In one situation, Patrick, who had become particularly attached to *The Very Hungry Caterpillar* (Carle, 1981), was reading the book to Emily. Upon finishing it, he handed it to Emily and said, "Now you read it." After listening to Emily struggle through a few pages, Patrick grew a little impatient and with a sigh said, "No, Emily, you have to look at the next page to know what this page says." Children modeling what they have learned for other children is a common occurrence in the Whole Language classroom.

As teachers observe children engaged in this social interaction called "literacy play"—listening, modeling, and reflecting on what they are learning about the reading and writing processes—it becomes obvious that the process of literacy development is much too complex to be captured in a group of skills or the pages of a workbook. There are no shortcuts in the process. If children have not had the opportunities to explore printed materials at home with an adult and other children mediating, then the kindergarten teacher must provide those opportunities in the classroom. Whole Language kindergarten teachers know that reading and writing should develop as easily and as naturally as listening and speaking, through active, purposeful interaction among children and between children and adults.

Whole Language kindergarten teachers have learned that children's errors or "miscues" in their early attempts to read and write should be interpreted as positive indications of their progress. Literacy play in the kindergarten classroom provides opportunities for children to read on their own, engaging in pretend or simulated reading behaviors in a nonthreatening environment. Kindergarten teachers can take seriously the old adage, "Riding a bicycle is learned by riding a bicycle." There is no significant difference between reading and learning to read (Smith, 1983). Reading and learning to read involve risk taking. As children progress toward adultlike reading behaviors, using the reading cues they have learned from adults and other children, they will sometimes "miscue"; but, with the support of an understanding teacher, they will "get back on the bicycle" and try again. It is with this understanding of the reading and learning processes that the IRA suggests that kindergarten teachers "encourage risk taking in first attempts at reading and writing, and accept what appear to be errors as part of children's natural growth and development" (Early Childhood, 1988, p. 6).

IMPROVING THE LIBRARY CORNER

It is unfortunate that many kindergarten teachers who are new to a Whole Language interpretation of reading development are concerned that reading is not actually taught in a Whole Language kindergarten. It is true that it is sometimes difficult to identify a particular lesson as a reading lesson, because reading is an ongoing part of the program; however, there are times during the day when reading is emphasized. Teachers read to and with their children during group- or circletime and interact with the children as they explore books on their own in the library corner during freeplay or center activities.

It is a common practice for kindergarten teachers to read aloud to their children at least once a day (Nurss & Hough, 1986), but in most kindergartens children do not participate in the library corner every day. Morrow and Weinstein (1982), in a study of freeplay in kindergarten, found the mean number of children voluntarily using the library per day was .94, or an average of less than one child per day. After redesigning the library center to create a more inviting atmosphere and encouraging more literature-related activities, the choice of the library for a freeplay activity increased significantly, to an average of over five children per day.

A variety of reasons for the children's disinterest in the library center have been suggested by researchers (Martinez & Teale, 1988; Morrow, 1989). Many kindergarten library centers are poorly arranged and contain a poor quality and variety of books. A most serious shortcoming in many kindergarten programs is the teacher's failure to connect library books with the other activities offered in the classroom. The studies of library-center usage verify what seems to be a concern voiced by many kindergarten teachers: "My children like to have me read to them every day, but they don't seem interested in books at other times." Teachers who recognize the value of reading aloud to their children in grouptime, as well as of pretend and simulated reading behaviors, must view the library corner as an integral part of the total kindergarten program and select the proper books, materials, equipment, and activities that will support children's emerging literacy.

In a Whole Language kindergarten, the library center supports emerging literacy by

1. Connecting books and reading with other areas of the curriculum, including the communication and creative arts;
2. Providing a place for children to explore books and other literature materials in much the same way they use other areas of the classroom, through active participation and social interaction;
3. Stimulating the child's interest in books and literature as a freeplay choice.

Connecting the Library with the Curriculum

Although the library corner is the place where most of the classroom books are kept, the library center is not the only reading area. Just as listening, speaking, and writing occur throughout the room, in the Whole Language kindergarten, reading occurs spontaneously throughout the various areas of the room.

Most Whole Language kindergarten teachers organize the curriculum around themes or units of study, such as community helpers, friendship, families, nutrition, simple machines, and transportation. One way the teacher connects these themes with the library corner is by providing reference books, pleasure-reading books, and special displays that are manipulative as well as visual. For example, when the theme was transportation, one kindergarten teacher had a parent set up a "please touch" model train display (Raines & Canady, 1989). Then factual picture books and fictional stories about trains were placed in prominent view on the open bookshelves. After reading *The Train to Lulu's* (Howard, 1988) in grouptime, where much of the theme teaching takes place, the teacher announced that the book and a tape recording of the book would be displayed in the library corner.

Kindergarten teachers who are already aware of the importance of unit teaching will have little difficulty in redesigning their library corners to make more effective connections between the library books and materials and the unit being taught.

Encouraging Active Participation in the Library Corner

Open bookshelves and comfortable seating are two necessities for encouraging active participation in the library corner (Morrow & Weinstein, 1982). The open shelving allows the covers of the books to be exposed so young children can make their selections visually. Comfortable chairs or cushions are needed so children can relax while reading. The physical arrangement of the library center and the equipment and materials must reflect that this area of the classroom is designed for both independent reading and also as a place where small groups and individuals can be active and social learners. To encourage active participation, teachers should

1. Include a listening station;
2. Have a signal for inviting more participants, such as a reading lamp;
3. Encourage storytelling and retelling;
4. Introduce wordless picture books;
5. Incorporate role playing and puppetry in the library as extensions of the literature.

The listening station.   The library corner should be well stocked with a variety of books that relate to the current unit of study or theme, and it also must include tape recordings of many of the children's favorite books. One Whole Language kindergarten teacher makes a point of stating that after each book is read at grouptime it will be available in the library corner. Then she gives the book to a child who has shown little interest in books and asks that child to place it in the library corner (Raines & Isbell, 1989). Many teachers find it effective to make a tape of the book, either while reading it aloud during grouptime or at some other time. This tape can be placed in the library corner (Raines & Canady, 1989). This practice becomes so routine in some Whole Language kindergartens that the children expect to find each grouptime book at the listening station in the library corner. While many kindergartens include listening stations that have a cassette tape player with jacks for a number of headphones, this equipment is not always used by the children because they tire of the same commercial tapes and stories. Teachers can use the listening station to personalize the reading materials through recordings of stories read by teachers, children, or parent volunteers; and they can also use puppets or pantomime to accompany a tape. The listening station provides an opportunity for the child to hold the actual book, turn the pages at the prerecorded signals, and hear the stories read again.

The reading lamp.   On a daily basis, the teacher must spend time in the library corner reading to individual children or small groups. Mary Montebello suggests that a particularly successful approach is to use a "reading lamp" to signal when the teacher is in the library (workshop, 1988). An attractive lamp is placed in the library corner, and it is turned on whenever the teacher or another adult is in the area reading. More children will choose the library corner when there is an adult available to read to them individually or in small groups, which allows more active participation and interaction with the adult while the book is being read.

Rereading children's favorite books provides students the pleasure of enjoying a story again, but it also encourages a deeper understanding of the story. In studies of books that are repeatedly read aloud to the same class, researchers have found that children ask more involved questions, point out different story and illustration features, and increase their comprehension of the story each time the book is read (Martinez & Roser, 1985; Schickedanz, 1978; Yaden, 1988). Kindergarten teachers need to recognize the value of repeated readings and encourage children to select their favorite books for rereading when the story lamp is on. This also is a good time to encourage children to read books on their own. The use of a familiar story in a nonthreatening environment allows the children to move into independent reading.

The kind of environment the teacher creates when the "story lamp" is on allows children to experience reading in an atmosphere much like the home reading environment of natural readers.

Storytelling and retelling.   Storytelling is an art form at which many kindergarten teachers excel. While teachers often tell stories at grouptime, turning the library corner into a storytelling corner can also make it a livelier place. Teachers who are good storytellers advise others who want to develop these skills to practice a few stories they know well. The children will enjoy hearing them more than once. Direct eye contact and an expressive voice, the predictableness of old favorite stories, and the introduction of some surprising new ones all invite children to come to the area. Group-participation stories, where children are asked to repeat phrases or count wishes or recall all the characters who are repeated, will help the children begin to predict the next scene.

Story retelling also allows children to understand the story through active participation (Hornsby, Sukarna, & Parry, 1986; Morrow, 1985) and helps connect the library corner to the communication and creative arts. As the children become involved in telling and retelling stories, they function as speakers and as an audience of listeners. Children listen and interact verbally, sometimes correcting, sometimes suggesting, often interjecting themselves at whatever point they know the story. Retelling can use various media, such as flannel boards, cassette tapes, drawing, and writing; and it can take the form of oral presentation to a classroom audience.

The flannel board, a favorite teacher's aid for grouptime presentations of stories, can also become a favorite children's activity in the library corner. Whenever the teacher reads a book or tells a story using the flannel board, the felt pieces and flannel board should be placed in the library corner for the children to use while they retell the story on their own, using the book as a reference if needed. Predictable books, folktales, and even songs and fingerplays can be illustrated with flannel-board pieces. To make the story retelling more of a social interaction, one child can be encouraged to tell or read the story while another places the felt pieces on the flannel board.

Wordless picture books.   Library-corner time is also an excellent time for introducing children to wordless picture books. These allow children to become authors without actually writing the story. The teacher needs to prepare children for reading wordless books by first serving as a reading role model for several books and then having the children tell (read) other wordless books (Raines & Isbell, 1988). "Story" wordless books are preferable to "concept" books, which are collections of pictures organized around a theme. The teacher can begin by informing the child that there is a story in the pictures of the book. After looking at the pictures with the child, the teacher can ask the youngster to tell about the actions of the main character. Focusing on the actions helps the reader identify the story problem. The session can conclude with the teacher asking the child to tell the story while reading the pictures. The teacher should listen for story language, such as "once upon a time," dialogue between characters, and a clear development of the plot and the climax.

Author–illustrators whose concept-type wordless books kindergartners enjoy are Mitsumasa Anno's *Anno's Counting Book* (1975), Tana Hoban's *Is it Red? Is it Yellow? Is it Blue?* (1978), and Brian Wildsmith's *Circus* (1970). Several of the children's favorite wordless story-type books include Emily McCully's *Picnic* (1984), Jan Omerod's *Moonlight* (1982), and Mercer Mayer's *Frog Goes to Dinner* (1974).

Role playing and puppetry in the library corner.   Another way Whole Language kindergarten teachers extend literature awareness through active participation is by providing role-playing props and puppets in the library corner. With the teacher's guidance and the support of a few props and costumes, children enjoy dramatizing a story while the teacher reads it. After acting out familiar stories using costumes or puppets, children will soon begin role playing stories without the teacher's assistance. Role playing and puppetry are such popular activities with kindergarten children that the teacher will probably want to add a puppet stage with a few favorite story puppets and include costumes in both the library corner and in the dress-up area. Role playing as a form of story retelling, whether dramatizing with props and costumes or acting out scenes with puppets, promotes children's concepts of story structure, character development, vocabulary expansion, and understanding of authorship.

Promoting the Library Corner As a Freeplay Choice

If the library corner is a place where the teacher is routinely available and where materials and activities are organized in a way that encourages children to interact freely with books, it also will be a place children choose to be during freeplay. Children must view the library corner as a place they can go for meaningful interaction with their friends and where they can center their play around books and other forms of literature.

In order to understand better how children's literacy develops through freeplay, early childhood educators must observe literacy play in real classroom situations. The following scene was observed as several children interacted with books on their own in the library corner. One child, pretending to be the librarian, checked out several books to the other children. Then the children took their books to a table, and one child pretended to be the teacher and read the books to the children. During this encounter with some of their favorite books, the children demonstrated their knowledge of prediction, story structure, and story-reading inflection.

Through their sociodramatic play involving the roles of librarian and teacher, these children interacted with books they knew well, such as *I Love Ladybugs* (Allen, 1985) and *Jamberry* (Degen, 1983). Both are predictable books containing patterned language, interesting repetitions of phrases, cumulative patterns, and language that has an easy rhythm or rhyme (Lynch, 1986; Rhodes, 1981). In addition, they retold two familiar books—*Corduroy* (Freeman, 1968) and *Curious George* (Rey, 1941)—repeating some of the dialogue exactly as it was written and occasionally referring to the books to check the accuracy of the story sequence. Finally, they also took turns "reading" books that were less familiar—*A Baby Sister for Frances* (Hoban, 1964) and *Five Minutes' Peace* (Murphy, 1986)—by looking at the pictures and telling the story using expressive gestures and story-reading inflection.

The observations of the two children pretending to be the librarian and the teacher (Raines & Isbell, 1989) correlate closely with the findings of Martinez and Teale (1988), whose study revealed that young children most often choose familiar and predictable books when in the library corner. Also, the children's use of story-reading inflection in their talk about pictures indicates story awareness, an important characteristic of emergent literacy (Harste et al., 1984; Jensen, 1985).

The high level of social interaction and purposeful reading behavior observed during the literacy play of these two kindergarten children was a result of the teacher's careful preparation of the library corner and the reading role model the teacher provided for the children. This level of literacy play and reading behavior was possible because the teacher connected the library corner with the curriculum and because the materials, equipment, and activities in the library corner were active and social in nature.

SUMMARY

Teachers' complaints that their children show little interest in books except at grouptime indicate a need to improve the kindergarten to make it a rich reading environment—a Whole Language kindergarten. Children's interest in books will increase when teachers use the read-aloud times at grouptime and in the library corner more effectively by

1. Reading quality selections that have a "good" story,
2. Having the children "think with the author,"
3. Having children predict story events or recurring patterns in the language,
4. Incorporating shared reading experiences using big books.

Whole Language teachers also increase children's interest in books by recognizing that the children are already readers. They use children's knowledge of environmental print and help their students to realize that they are indeed reading. A natural extension for using environmental print is to bring that print into the kindergarten. Teachers help children make associations between the functional print in their environment and other things they know about print by

1. Using environmental print in their own writing,
2. Developing "I Can Read" units,
3. Connecting meaningful environmental print and print as children know it in their names,
4. Associating children's knowledge of print with reading in books.

In addition, Whole Language kindergarten teachers recognize the value of literacy play and provide a supportive play environment. When literacy materials are available in play areas, children

1. Engage in literacy play that emulates adults' and other children's reading behaviors;
2. Adopt "story-reading" voices;
3. Learn to use opportunities to try out reading behaviors, to be risk takers without concern for exact reading.

The library corner in a Whole Language kindergarten is a place where children can explore reading materials and extend their literature awareness, on their own or with the assistance of a teacher.

Whole Language kindergarten teachers use the library corner to

1. Connect books and reading with other areas of the curriculum,

2. Provide a place for the child to explore books and other literature materials through active participation and social interaction,
3. Stimulate the child's interest in books and literature as a free-play choice.

Whole Language kindergarten teachers have found numerous ways to increase children's interest in books. Teachers begin with themselves and practice reading aloud more effectively. As they recognize that children already know a great deal about print from reading signs and logos in their environment, teachers find ways to help children realize they are already reading. When teachers recognize the benefits of literacy play, they place reading and writing materials throughout the classroom centers. Teachers also can support young children's exploration of reading materials in the library corner by making it an inviting, lively, social place for interacting with books and stories.

✳ 7 ✳

Thematic Units in the Whole Language Kindergarten

Kindergarten teachers are accustomed to teaching units of study centered around a specific theme from social studies or science. The topics for the units of study that make up the kindergarten curriculum are based on children's needs, interests, and developmental levels (Bredekamp, 1987). They may include the seasons, holidays, families, friends, pets, transportation, simple machines, or plant and animal life; and they are integrated into as many activities as possible throughout the schedule. Kindergarten teachers who redesign their classrooms into Whole Language environments find the thematic unit approach to curriculum planning a valuable asset because the nature of Whole Language is to integrate information and learning processes.

APPROPRIATE PRACTICES FOR THE CHILD-CENTERED AND EXPERIENCE-CENTERED CURRICULUM

Thematic units of study provide the mechanism whereby teachers can plan a kindergarten curriculum that can best be described as child-centered and experience-centered. It is true that the early childhood curriculum has been reshaped over the years due to changing social forces, new information about child growth and development, and expanding general knowledge and information. Nonetheless, the curriculum foundations of the position papers from three major professional organizations—the ACEI, NAEYC, and IRA—have remained child-centered and experience-centered (see Bredekamp, 1987; Early Childhood, 1988; Moyer et al., 1987).

Closely related, both the experience-centered and child-centered curricula can trace their legacy of belief about the nature of the children as active, sensory-perception learners to the 1700s philosopher Rousseau and later to pedagogists Pestalozzi and Froebel in the early 1800s (Ornstein & Hunkins, 1988). With major interpretive changes from the early philosophers and pedagogists, the belief that the curriculum should be child-centered and experience-centered remained evident in the curriculum designs of the progressive educators, Francis Parker (1894), John Dewey (1902), and Anna Bryan and Patty Smith Hill (Snyder, 1972). They, among others, organized model schools and kindergarten teacher-training programs. The curricula in these early laboratory schools were planned around what Dewey (1902) called "the [human] impulses to socialize, to construct, to inquire, to question, to experiment, and to express or to create artistically" (Smith, Stanley, & Shores, 1957, p. 265).

Human Impulses

The reshaped child-centered and experience-centered kindergarten of today continues to emphasize the children's interests and to plan activities that are designed around the "human impulses." For example, from the NAEYC guidelines, concern for the human impulse to socialize is evident in the following appropriate-practice statement: "Children are provided many opportunities to develop social skills such as cooperating, helping, negotiating, and talking with the person involved to solve interpersonal problems" (Bredekamp, 1987, p. 51).

According to the ACEI, early childhood educators are recognizing young children's "impulse to construct" when they "provide multiple opportunities for learning with concrete, manipulative materials" (Moyer et al., 1987, pp. 238–239). Quality early education programs are founded on providing an environment where the young child is free to inquire, question, and experiment. Quoting Ballenger, the same authors describe good kindergarten programs as places for "experimenting, exploring, discovering, trying out, restructuring, speaking and listening" (p. 242). Similarly, one of the recommendations for improvement of prefirst-grade reading instruction is to "encourage children to be active participants in the learning process rather than passive recipients, but using activities that allow for experimentation with talking, listening, writing and reading" (Early Childhood, 1988, p. 7). In kindergarten, perhaps more than in any other year of schooling, teachers provide materials, activities, time, space, and the affective environment that allow the young child to act out the human impulse to express or to create artistically. In addition to children's creative expression through play, appropriate practice includes children having "daily opportunities for aesthetic expression and appreciation through art and music" (Bredekamp, 1987, p. 52).

Developmental Issues

The concept of "developmental levels," which early childhood educators believe should govern appropriate practice and the kindergarten curriculum, is by its nature child-centered and experience-centered. Developmental appropriateness has "two dimensions, age appropriateness and individual appropriateness" (Bredekamp, 1987, p. 2). Developmental appropriateness refers to the "universal, predictable sequences of growth and change" (p. 2) that occur in children as they age. Individual appropriateness refers to the uniqueness of each person in "timing of growth, individual personality, learning styles, and family background" (p. 2). Therefore, some activities are developmentally appropriate for one age but not for another. Concern for developmental and individual appropriateness in curricular activities is congruent with Dewey's basic "human impulses." Educators must plan curricula to meet individual appropriateness, while retaining expectations and practices that allow the children to function fully at their age-appropriate levels.

GUIDANCE FOR DEVELOPING THE SOCIAL STUDIES CURRICULUM

Kindergarten teachers can use the following statement from *Developmentally Appropriate Practice* (Bredekamp, 1987) to guide their decisions about what young children should study.

> Children develop understanding of concepts about themselves, others, and the world around them through observation, interacting with people and real objects, and seeking solutions to concrete problems. Learnings about math, science, social studies, health, and other content areas are all integrated through meaningful activities such as those when children build with blocks; measure sand, water, or ingredients for cooking; observe changes in the environment; work with wood and tools; sort objects for a purpose; explore animals, plants, water, wheels and gears; sing and listen to music from various cultures; and draw, paint and work with clay. Routines are followed that help children keep themselves healthy and safe. [p. 52]

Few kindergarten teachers would argue that the curriculum begins with the child. Teachers enhance young children's self-concepts by providing a wide variety of experiences and activities that lead to a sense of accomplishment. They create an affective atmosphere where learners are free to take risks, and they interact with children in a genuinely open and honest relationship where the learners are appreciated for who they are by virtue of their developmental style and for who they are as individuals.

Young children, by their cognitive nature, are egocentric. They perceive their world, including the social and emotional realms, from a viewpoint that centers on themselves. Piaget (1965) explained this egocentrism as follows:

> In his manner of reasoning, equally, the child is only concerned with himself, and ignores more or less completely the view of others. But, in logic also, if the child sees everything from his own point of view, it is because he believes all the world to think like himself. [p. 167]

Egocentrism is perfectly natural for children from ages two through seven. It is precisely because of this learning characteristic that teachers begin the social studies curriculum with the child. For many teachers, the beginning unit of study each fall is, "I Am Me and I Am Special" or, "Getting to Know You" or, "I Like Me and I Like You" or other similar titles meant to convey to the child that each person is important.

Normally the social studies curriculum also includes units on families, friends, neighborhoods, community helpers, rules for living, feelings, holidays, and celebrations. As the children share information about themselves and learn about each other, including other families' traditions and cultures, they begin to understand the similarities between themselves and others. Of course, this awareness will increase over time, as children grow in their ability to relate to others and to understand at a deeper level. However, the significance of the early childhood social studies curriculum should not be underestimated. Perhaps the most important factor in the success of the social studies curriculum is learning to work and play in the cooperative learning environment of the kindergarten classroom.

A fundamental of both the Whole Language kindergarten and the social studies curriculum is communication. When teachers lead children through activities or provide sets of experiences that begin to build an understanding of how the social world is organized, they are transmitting the culture. The passing on or the communication, from one generation to its young, about how knowledge, information, and systems are organized is social studies. Whether children are composing their own class rules (beginning to understand civics and government), celebrating a holiday (beginning to understand historical significance), shopping for picnic supplies (getting an early economics lesson), or creating a model neighborhood from blocks (learning about geography), they and their teachers are communicating. While kindergarten teachers seldom think of whether they have taught the traditional content areas of social studies (i.e., civics and government, economics, history, geography, and cultural understanding), the units taught in kindergarten often reflect these subject areas (Raines, 1982).

Many of the enduring conceptual underpinnings of the kindergarten are social studies concepts. The nursery school and kindergarten movement was predicated on the value of community experiences in the socialization of the young child (Spodek et al., 1987). Now as in the past, many of the reasons for sending young children to schooling outside of the family are for youngsters to learn to establish relationships, to cooperate, and to respond as individuals and as part of a group.

INTEGRATING THE THEME THROUGHOUT THE CURRICULUM

The integrated unit of study provides the structure for organizing the kindergarten curriculum around Dewey's (1902) concept of "human impulses" and around developmentally appropriate practices (Smith, Stanley, & Shores, 1957). Units of study are composed of "activities, experiences, and goals . . . organized around a theme" (Seefeldt & Barbour, 1986, p. 146). The learning experiences in such a unit of study allow children the opportunity to learn concepts as parts of an integrated whole, rather than isolated bits and pieces of information under a particular content area (Dewey, 1902, 1916; Seefeldt & Barbour, 1986). Jarolimek and Foster (1989) describe the term *unit teaching,* as it is used with the social studies program, as a "coordinated series of learning activities planned around a broad topic that will involve the whole class in a comprehensive study" (p. 54). The importance early childhood educators place on unit planning and theme integration is reflected in the ACEI position paper, which describes the child-centered kindergarten as one that "embraces the teaching of all content areas, presented as integrated experiences that develop and extend concepts, strengthen skills and provide a solid foundation for learning in language, literacy, math, science, health, art and music" (Moyer et al., 1987, p. 239).

In addition to the value of a thematic curriculum, integration occurs when children assimilate new information into existing knowledge structures. It also occurs when children use new information to reorganize or accommodate their thinking. Taba (1962), another advocate of the integrated curriculum unit, implies the constructivist position when she says, "The organization of these experiences should be such that they help the student increasingly to get a unified view and to unify his behavior in relation to the elements dealt with" (p. 298).

The integrated curriculum in a Whole Language kindergarten is organized so that children not only learn the specific information of that particular unit of study, but also how to use that information to develop the concepts and generalizations that will give meaning to the future units of study and learning experiences. In a unit on "Taking Care of Pets," for example, the teacher felt that it was important that children know certain specifics, such as how much food was needed for the fish in the two classroom aquariums. In the discussion that followed, the children wanted to learn the types of fish in the two aquariums, the steps for cleaning the tanks, and why certain species could not be placed together. The factual information of the unit of study was learned by the children as it related to the main concept the teacher wanted the children to learn—that pets have needs that their owners are responsible for meeting.

Each unit of study is planned so that children will be able to build on their prior knowledge, relate personally to the experiences provided, retain the main concept of the unit, and generalize the information to new situations.

SCHEDULING AND PLANNING FOR AN INTEGRATED CURRICULUM THEME

To achieve integration of both content materials and new information into the child's existing knowledge of the unit topic, teachers plan units of study they know will be of interest to the children in their particular classrooms. The children then explore the theme throughout their day. The schedule in Table 7.1 gives an example of how a theme can be woven into the class activities, materials, room arrangement, and interactions. In this section we will discuss in detail how one teacher and a teacher's aide integrated a theme throughout the

Table 7.1   Schedule for Thematic Teaching During
a Half-Day Kindergarten

8:30-9:00	*Arrival time—individual greetings, tabletop activities, or centers; tabletop art activity is related to theme
9:00-9:30	Circletime or grouptime; literature selection, teacher's and children's interactions, song, or fingerplay is related to theme
9:30-10:30	*Freeplay inside, often labeled centertime; special thematic center is one of the freeplay choices
10:30-10:40	Snacktime; when possible, a snack related to theme is served
10:40-10:45	Preparations for outside play
10:45-11:15	*Outside play; depending on the theme, an outside thematic center may be designed
11:15-11:25	Toileting, washing hands, browsing through books while waiting for others
11:25-11:50	Storytime, music, drama; main literature selection relates to theme
11:50-12:00	Departure; children may take home a newsletter informing parents of the theme of the unit of study

*Designated for play activities.

different areas of the curriculum as they carried out one day's plan from their two-week unit of study, "Taking Care of Pets."

Before the children arrived in the morning, the teacher's aide placed manipulative materials on the three tables used for tabletop activities, the first scheduled event of the day (refer to Table 7.1). On the first table, the aide placed Play-Doh; on the second, puzzles, including several of pets, along with some small connecting blocks. The third table was reserved for an art or craft activity that related to the theme. On this particular day, old magazines and cat-picture calendars, scissors, glue, and construction paper were on the table, for making cut-and-paste collages of cats. The plan was for each of the children to make a cat collage, at some time over the next two days. The cat-collage materials stayed on the table during arrival time and throughout freeplay for two days.

The children, who arrived a few at a time, were greeted by the teacher and were free to move to any of the three tabletop activities. The aide, seated at the cat-collage table, conversed with the children about any topic they chose, but the pictures of the cats captured their interest and the conversation naturally turned to cats and other pets. After about 25 minutes, the teacher and aide reminded the children that it was time to finish or reach a stopping point with their Play-Doh sculptures, puzzles, and cat collages, because in a few minutes it would be grouptime.

At nine o'clock the teacher called the children to grouptime by singing a fingerplay song about a cat, which had been taught on the previous day. The children moved to the carpeted grouptime area, joining in the singing. Then the teacher commented on the nice variety of pictures of cats the children had found for their collages. Using one child's collage, the teacher pointed out several different types of cats, which prompted some of the cat owners in the class to tell about their pets. While listening and extending the discussion to include more children, the teacher skillfully solicited comments about how to care for cats. Recognizing that some of the children did not have pets, the teacher asked the children to tell about their friends' or relatives' cats.

After the children had been given the opportunity to participate in the discussion, the teacher introduced the story for the day, *Amelia's Nine Lives* (Balian, 1986), which ended with the mother cat having nine kittens. The teacher selected the book because the next day one of the children, assisted by his grandmother, was going to bring kittens to school for the children to see. After the book was read, the discussion continued with a comparison of how kittens have to be cared for differently from a cat. When one child explained that her family's cat was "fixed" so she could not have kittens, a discussion followed concerning the meaning of the term "fixed." After clarifying a few of the comments, the teacher told the children that next week a veterinarian's assistant would come to class to talk with them about caring for kittens and what happens when there are not enough owners for all of the kittens that are born. The discussion ended as the teacher re-established the theme of the unit, "Taking Care of Pets," and connected it to the family in the story who had to find homes for Amelia's kittens.

After the discussion, the teacher suggested some special theme-related possibilities for children's freeplay activities. These included making more cat collages or using Play-Doh to make cat sculptures. While handing one of the children a stethoscope, the teacher mentioned that for a few days the housekeeping corner had been turned into a veterinarian's office. At the close of grouptime, the teacher led the children in singing the fingerplay song again. Then, in keeping with the unit on pets, children were allowed to move to freeplay centers according to the pets they owned. Cat owners went first, followed by children who had fish, then all children who had friends with cats as pets, and finally all the dog owners. Using such a procedure for dispersing children to centers retains their attention and results in more relaxed movement to the centers.

During the freeplay time, the teacher and the aide interacted with the children, allowing them to reflect on their experiences through conversation. Freeplay time is an excellent opportunity to observe the children as they pursue whatever interests them at the moment, and it is a good time to evaluate the effectiveness of the particular unit of study. Montessori (1964), an astute observer of young children, repeatedly advised early childhood educators to look to the child. Goodman (1978) likewise insists that teachers of young children must become "kidwatchers." It is only through close observation of children in an interesting, nonthreatening environment that teachers can determine the individual needs of children, plan for future learning activities, and know when to offer assistance to children and when not to intervene.

Near the end of the freeplay hour, rather than making a disturbing general announcement, the teacher and the aide went to each area of the classroom and mentioned quietly that in a few minutes it would be time to clean up for snacktime. Then the teacher played a tape of one of the children's favorite songs, as the children cleaned up the room. The children took turns washing their hands while the teacher's aide and helpers prepared the snack. After the helpers determined who would pour refills of the apple juice, the teacher and aide sat with the children and enjoyed a snack of juice, cheese, and crackers. Then the children went outside to play. There had been no theme-related activity planned, but the teacher noticed that some of the conversation centered around pets and one child was overheard singing the fingerplay song from grouptime. The teacher used this opportunity to talk with the child who planned to bring the kittens to school.

Near the end of the outside play period, the teacher and the aide again prepared the children for changing activities, by reminding them that in a few minutes it would be time to go inside. By remaining attentive to children's need for time to make gradual transitions from one activity to another, the adults showed respect for the children's involvement in their activities.

After the outside play period, the teacher's aide assisted with toileting and handwashing, while the teacher placed a collection of children's books about cats on the grouptime rug. As the children finished toileting, they came to the rug and sat, exploring books until their other classmates arrived. The books included *Millions of Cats*

(Gag, 1923); *Hi, Cat* (Keats, 1970); *Where Does My Cat Sleep?* and *Cats Do, Dogs Don't* (Simon, 1982, 1986); and the book read at grouptime, *Amelia's Nine Lives*. Books on other pets were also available, as were some of the children's favorites from other units of study.

After the children spent a few minutes browsing through the books, the teacher asked them to tell about their pets at home. After summarizing what they said, the teacher introduced Nora Simon's book, *Cats Do, Dogs Don't*. The teacher read the book to the children, listened to a few spontaneous comments, and then shared a newsletter about pets for them to take home to their parents.

The power of integrated units of study is not new to kindergarten teachers. The extensive work of preparation and implementation is rewarded as the teacher and aide observe children exploring the materials and equipment, conversing about the theme, learning to connect prior knowledge to new information, building associations, exploring new processes, solving related problems, and creatively constructing representations of what they have learned.

Children construct representations of what they learn through their language, their drawings and sculptures, their role playing, and their uses of materials and equipment. A kindergarten program that is replete with opportunities for hands-on manipulative experiences, artistic expression, and verbal interaction encourages discovery and inquiry. It provides opportunities for young children to become representationally competent. Copple and colleagues (1979) have stated that "representational competence develops fully only in response to interactions with the appropriate physical and social environments" (p. 24). The kindergarten classroom must be a language-rich environment where children are encouraged to explore, inquire, and recall what they have learned through making representations. Integrated thematic units help children gain confidence in their abilities to use language both orally and graphically through drawings and to construct representations of models as they recreate roles they have experienced and imagined. They seek to answer the problems posed, as well as to pose new problems of their own (Raines, 1990).

ADDING MORE WHOLE LANGUAGE EMPHASIS TO THE PETS UNIT

The kindergarten teacher and teacher's aide who planned the day's activities for the pets unit provided many rich experiences through which the children could represent their knowledge related to the topics; however, a Whole Language kindergarten teacher might also include the following activities.

As the children arrive in the morning and are greeted by the teacher, a quick inventory of who has pets and of what types can provide valuable interaction possibilities throughout the day. At the tabletop activities, a writing activity can be added to the listening and speaking interactions that emerged from the children's reactions to the cat pictures. The teacher's aide might suggest that children add captions to their collages, indicate the breeds of cats represented in their pictures, dictate a sentence, or use invented spelling to write a sentence about their own pets. A writing extension to the cat collage could provide the possibility for representing new information or related information already known. Cat-shaped writing booklets, a chart of cat words, and a reminder to the artists that they can write more about cats in the writing center can provide the incentive for some children to represent their new learning about cats through writing.

The well-planned grouptime interaction, which balanced teacher talk and children's interaction, can be made even more effective by three additions: (1) incorporating a printed version of the cat fingerplay song; (2) extending the teacher's reading aloud of the story; and (3) making a better connection between the featured book and the library collection. The excellent idea of singing the fingerplay to signal the start of grouptime can be extended by displaying a printed version of the song. The children had been taught the fingerplay song on a previous day, so they were at least familiar with the words. By adding a printed version on a chart tablet for the children to see, the teacher can read the words, then sing them while pointing to the lines of the fingerplay song, then sing the fingerplay song again with the actions. This creates another opportunity for the children to associate written and spoken words.

While reading the picture book aloud, a Whole Language kindergarten teacher can make an association between the title of the book and its eventual meaning, revealed at the end of the story. The teacher can model important story information needed for comprehension by having the children predict what the story might be about, based on its title and cover, and then allowing them to confirm or change their predictions as the story unfolded. (See Chapter 6 for a more detailed review of this process.)

The high-interest picture book was an excellent choice, but it could have been more effectively connected to the library corner.

This is a good opportunity to indicate that the teacher will be in the library area when the "reading lamp" is on, to reread the book. Also, some children might like to listen to a cassette tape the teacher has made of the story.

In addition to the library corner possibilities, during freeplay or center time the teacher and aide can help the children be more specific in their representations of what they have learned about cats. For example, the cat collage was an appropriate activity because it involved children's fine motor skills, their aesthetic expressions, and a great deal of language. As they cut the pictures from magazines, several children began grouping cats that looked alike, sorting the pictures by sizes and comparing the attributes of the cats by color and length of hair and by whether or not they had ever seen cats like the ones in the picture. The grouping, sorting, comparing and classifying activities were representations of prenumber concepts. The thinking that evolves from this activity can provide the teacher with an excellent opportunity to introduce numeration or for the children to represent numerically what they already know, as well as to add another symbol system to the children's repertoire of representational possibilities. By having the children count, write numerals, or use numeration in their descriptions, the Whole Language teacher encourages more specific spoken and written language. (See Chapter 12 for a fuller discussion of prenumber concepts and representations.)

The second grouptime of the day, which also included an excellent book about comparisons told in story form, *Cats Do, Dogs Don't* (Simon, 1986), presented a variety of comparative possibilities. These make the content easier for the children to remember. One comprehension strategy that Whole Language teachers use is a three-step "K-W-L" chart. First the teacher constructs a chart of what the children already know (K) about cats and dogs, before the book is read. The second step is to add a section for what the children want to know (W). Finally, after the book is read, the children state what they have learned (L). While not all young children's picture books are appropriate for this comprehension strategy, stories that include factual information and make comparisons are excellent material for K-W-L charts.

The kindergarten teacher's unit of study about pets and the activities provided were well planned and reflected a concern for integrated learning; however, more opportunities, such as those discussed, can be provided for the children, individually and collectively, to help them represent what they have learned. Children are more likely to grow in their representational competence when they observe their teachers constructing representations, such as the K-W-L chart, and when they are encouraged to use their personal language as they participate in the construction of representations.

OBSERVING CHILDREN

As stated earlier, in order to create a Whole Language kindergarten, the teacher must become a "kidwatcher," an "astute observer" of young children's needs. One way Whole Language kindergarten teachers evaluate the actual listening, speaking, reading, and writing activities as they occur during the course of a unit of study is by focusing on two children as they engage in the day's activities. By observing a student who reads and writes independently and one who needs encouragement to read and write, the teacher can determine whether the curriculum is meeting the children's needs. Since many units of study last for two weeks (10 school days) and most kindergartens have approximately 20 children, systematic observations of two students per day would mean observations could be collected on each child during each unit. Whenever possible, the teacher should include detailed observations, using narratives, anecdotal notes, time sampling, and other observational tools. However, for the purposes of determining the value of activities and experiences for the two particular children, simple devices often work best.

Some teachers carry notepads in their pockets and jot notes about the two selected children. They observe the students during center time and ask the aide to make notes on the children's participation during grouptime. The notes need not be detailed to be effective. In addition, they collect samples of the children's work throughout the day, examine the pieces more thoroughly after the children leave, and assemble the materials in a portfolio to be shared with parents during conferences. Other teachers prefer to construct simple yes-or-no checklists that correlate with their daily schedule, such as the one shown in Figure 7.1. Of course, checklists by their nature are interpretive. The teacher and teacher's aide will need to discuss the meaning of each item and the types of extra notes that will make the observations more helpful. Often this general checklist will indicate the need for a more detailed observation of some areas of development.

Figure 7.1 Activities and Interactions Observational Checklist

Child's name_____Date_____

Y = yes; N = no

8:30 - 9:00 Arrival and Table-top Notes
~~~~~~
_____ Interacted warmly at greeting
_____ Conversed with adults during table-top activities
_____ Conversed with children during table-top activities
_____ Added captions, labels to pictures or structures,
_____   writing independently; _____ asked for assistance;
_____   asked teacher to write or read print
_____ Child's choice of table-top activity or activities

_____ _____

9:00 - 9:30 Grouptime
~~~~~~
_____ Participated in music; _____ knew song or fingerplay
_____ Volunteered statements; _____ related to topic
_____ Listened attentively to literature presentation
_____ Responded as a member of group at teacher's signal
_____ Responded when questioned or given directions

9:30 - 10:30 Freeplay (Observe in at least three centers)
~~~~~~
First choice of centers _____
_____ Sustained time at center
_____ Play or activity related to theme of unit
_____ Changed activities within center often
_____ Interacted with other children at the center;
_____ Was a leader
_____ Pretend reading; _____ actual reading;
_____ Pretend writing; _____ actual writing
Literacy props _____
Other participants at first center_____

Second center visited_____
_____ Sustained time at center
_____ Play or activity related to theme of unit
_____ Changed activities within center often
_____ Interacted with other children at the center;
_____ Was a leader
_____ Pretend reading; _____ actual reading;
_____ Pretend writing; _____ actual writing
Literacy props _____
Other participants at second center_____

Third center visited_____
_____ Sustained time at center
_____ Play or activity related to theme of unit
_____ Changed activities within center often
_____ Interacted with other children at the center;
_____ Was a leader

Figure 7.1 (*Continued*)

_____ Pretend reading; _____ actual reading;
_____ Pretend writing; _____ actual writing
Literacy props _____
Other participants at third center_____

_____ Participated in clean-up time willingly

10:30 - 10:40 Snack time

_____ Enjoyed snack;
_____ Conversed with children;
_____ Conversed with teacher

10:40 - 10:45 Preparations for Outside Play

_____ Takes care of own clothing;
_____ Asks for equipment

10:45 - 11:15 Outside play (Observe at least two activities)

First activity _____
_____ Sustained activity; _____ leader
_____ Effective use of equipment or materials
Other participants _____

Second activity _____
_____ Sustained activity; _____ leader
_____ Effective use of equipment or materials
Other participants _____

11:15 - 11:25 Toileting, transition to grouptime

First grouptime - books at circle
_____ Took care of own needs;
_____ Browsed through book; _____ number of books
_____ Pretend reading; _____ actual reading
_____ Pointed out illustrations, made comments to others
_____ Pointed out illustrations, made comments to teacher

11:25 - 11:50 Second grouptime

_____ Participated in music; _____ knew song or fingerplay
_____ Volunteered statements; _____ related to topic
_____ Listened attentively to literature presentation
_____ Responded as a member of group at teacher's signal
_____ Responded when questioned or given directions

11:50 - 12:00 Departure

Additional Comments/Expressions of Child's Knowledge of Theme
_____
_____

Topics:_____
_____
_____

In addition to information about whether or not the child engaged in activities related to the theme of the unit of study, the direct observations throughout the day and the completed checklist give the Whole Language kindergarten teacher descriptions of the child as a listener, speaker, reader, and writer. When the checklists of activities and interactions are collected for each unit, the chronology of the child's participation, along with samples of the child's work, provide an excellent set of documents for parent conferences. The compilation of all the students' checklists provides indicators of how effective the theme activities and centers were in capturing the interests of the students.

SUMMARY

Theme teaching is a common structure for organizing the curriculum, and it is one that fits well into the Whole Language view of literacy development, because units are developed around the children's interests and allow for integration across subject areas. Integration of a topic or theme across the curriculum provides multiple opportunities for the child to learn about the topic from a variety of experiences. When children are provided multiple opportunities for their interactions to focus on the theme, they are more likely to integrate new information into their existing ways of thinking about the topic (assimilation) or to form new ways of organizing their thoughts about the topic (accommodation). As children interact with the teacher, their peers, and materials, they have many oppportunities to develop their competence in representing what they have learned.

Thematic units of study are developed around guidelines proposed by the NAEYC (Bredekamp, 1987), the ACEI (Moyer et al., 1987), and the IRA (Early Childhood, 1988), all of which value a child-centered and experience-centered view of the curriculum. Inherent within this view is Dewey's (1902) conceptualization of the human impulses to socialize, construct, inquire, and express or create artistically.

Whole Language kindergarten teachers plan their schedules around the theme of the unit and integrate the topic into as many times of the day and types of activities as possible. In addition, the Whole Language kindergarten teacher incorporates as many opportunities as possible for the children to listen, speak, read, and write about the theme.

Whole Language kindergarten teachers recognize the value of observing children, and they need to develop a clear plan for making systematic observations of all the children in their classrooms. This includes collecting samples of each child's work and completing a checklist of activities and interactions. This should be done regularly, so that observations are made of each child over the course of a two-week thematic unit.

Science in the Whole Language Kindergarten

Studies of plant and animal life, observations of seasonal changes, construction of simple machines, care of classroom pets, and displays of natural specimens are major components of the kindergarten science curriculum and are retained as areas of emphasis in a Whole Language classroom. Many kindergarten teachers already support young children's natural curiosity about their physical world by providing science centers and units of study that have a scientific theme; by collecting the materials and equipment for hands-on science experiences, by displaying objects that invite exploration, by provoking problem solving, by guiding children in the steps of the scientific process, and by helping students devise ways to represent their findings. In addition to the many ways kindergarten teachers already provide science experiences, Whole Language kindergarten teachers provide literacy activities that encourage the children to speak and write about their scientific observations, to use reference materials, and to become more representationally competent when expressing their scientific understandings.

GUIDANCE FOR DEVELOPMENTALLY APPROPRIATE PRACTICES

Early childhood educators who focus on a process approach to science experiences in the kindergarten can find support for developing units of study in the position statements from the NAEYC, ACEI, and IRA. The NAEYC states that "children develop understanding of concepts about themselves, others, and the world around them through observation, interacting with people and real objects, and seeking solutions to concrete problems" (Bredekamp, 1987, p. 52). The ACEI describes the child-centered kindergarten as "emphasizing the processes of learning rather than focusing on finished products" (Moyer et al., 1987, p. 236). In keeping with the IRA position statement (Early Childhood and Literacy Development Committee, 1988), the Whole Language kindergarten teacher realizes the importance of children developing vocabulary specific to each science unit: "For optimal learning, teachers should involve children actively in many meaningful, functional language experiences, including speaking, listening, writing, and reading" (p. 3). Process learning places the emphasis on observing, interacting, and seeking solutions through active involvement in meaningful learning experiences and through the use of listening, speaking, reading, and writing.

GOALS OF THE KINDERGARTEN SCIENCE CURRICULUM

Kindergarten teachers who plan activities that reflect the Piagetian (1974) view of cognitive development (whereby children construct meaning based on their prior knowledge, through the processes of assimilation and accommodation) recognize children as being "young scientists" at the time they enter school. Adults tell children that a dog is a dog and a cat is a cat, but it is up to the child to determine "why" it is so. As each child constructs new categories of knowledge, or schemata, based on her prior knowledge, she alone must choose the criteria for establishing that category which will be used to construct future categories. Whole Language teachers who understand learning as a process of construction can plan activities to encourage and enhance scientific exploration, knowing that kindergarten children are already experienced scientific and language problem solvers.

The science curriculum in a Whole Language kindergarten is thus viewed as a continuation of a process already being used by all young children, and science activities are planned in a way to encourage children to relate new experiences to existing knowledge, make adjustments to existing categories, and establish new categories through careful observation and direction from the teacher. The characteristics of a kindergarten science program which establish it as a Whole Language science program are:

1. The teacher's understanding of the role language plays in learning,
2. The emphasis the teacher places on language while planning and guiding the activities, and

3. The integration of the particular science theme or concept with other curricular and communication activities throughout the day.

Whole Language kindergarten teachers are aware of the long-standing controversy over the role language plays in learning. Some learning theorists believe that children use language to establish categories of knowledge (Vygotsky, 1962), while others believe that language is used more to reflect on learning and to communicate knowledge to others (Piaget, 1926). In a Whole Language kindergarten, there is no controversy. All science activities are planned to encourage children to explore and discover new information, as well as to use the new language they learn to categorize new information and to communicate that new information through oral and written language. The concepts learned during a science activity are then integrated into the other activities throughout the day, allowing the children to establish new relationships among categories and new language to express those relationships.

The kindergarten science curriculum is designed to help young children:

1. To develop an appreciation of living things,
2. To improve their observation skills,
3. To discover properties,
4. To acquire the language of science,
5. To conduct simple investigations.

To reach these goals, teachers organize the science curriculum into units of study with three major components:

1. A science display area, often called the science center,
2. Grouptime presentations related to the theme,
3. Extensions of the theme into other centers of the classroom and other activities scheduled throughout the day.

THE SCIENCE CENTER AND THE UNIT THEME

In most kindergarten classrooms, a major means of delivering instruction related to the theme of the science unit of study is the science center display area. Teachers often refer to this area as the science table. As teachers plan their units of study, they arrange a center where children expect to find materials and equipment related to the theme of the unit. For example, for the unit on nutrition (described in Chapter 4), a variety of berries were available to taste, and there was a display of some strawberry plants and pictures of other plants that supply fruits. For a unit on fish, a teacher moved the class aquarium next to the science center, and a dry display of all the parts of the aquarium was arranged on the science table. For the unit on plants, teachers often turn the science center into a potting area for planting seeds and propagating cuttings.

Whatever the unit of study, the science display table should invite exploration. Children should manipulate the objects, observe them more closely, compare real objects to pictures in reference materials, rearrange the items by classifying them according to attributes, or conduct simple investigations. The purpose of the science center will change depending on the possibilities each theme presents. Whatever the focus, the children should be involved in helping the teacher arrange each display. The displays should promote active learning and invite the children, "Please touch."

CREATING A LEAF DISPLAY
FOR A UNIT ON FALL

Teachers find clues for possible scientific inquiries by listening to children as they help arrange display items in the classroom. For example, in one kindergarten classroom, after the children returned from a nature walk where they collected leaves in their individual grocery bags, the teacher asked the students to select five leaves each from their collection, to place on the display table. As the children made their selections, the teacher heard comments like, "I like this one. I have three of these just alike." "I found five big ones." "Mine are like yours."

The teacher expanded on these comments by having the children begin their scientific investigations of the leaves by comparing them. The teacher chose first to ask the children to find leaves that looked alike or similar. After comparing their leaves and discussing the similarities and differences, the children's leaves were placed on the table. The teacher, recognizing their need to identify their own collections, wrote the children's names on index cards to place in front of each stack of five leaves.

The next day during grouptime, the teacher displayed the grocery bags filled with the rest of the leaves that had been collected during the nature walk. She explained that these leaves would be used for the sorting activities she had planned, without the children having to sacrifice their prized five "best" leaves. It is important for teachers to be cognizant of young children's desires to be collectors, to place their claim on their specimens. The excitement of the nature walk, their comparisons, and their new ways of looking at leaves made their individual collections valued possessions.

At center time, nine children rushed to the science display table to "play" with the leaves. The teacher, eager to build on their interest, divided the children into two groups and asked the aide to work with four of the children at another table. The aide began by asking the children, "What can we do with these leaves to make them interesting for other children to look at?" After a few comments, the children decided to place the leaves in rows so that each leaf could be seen. One child suggested arranging the rows by placing leaves that looked alike together, and the other children agreed. Because the large sycamore leaves had been the most popular choice on the nature walk, there were only a few oaks, maples, dogwoods, elms, and smaller leaves.

Faced with the problem of too many of some kinds of leaves and too few of others, the aide asked the children what to do to make them equal in each row. No one wanted to throw away any of the leaves, but they finally decided to make five rows with at least five leaves in each row. After making this array of leaves, they decided to display some of the prettier of the remaining leaves, in baskets at the top of each row.

Two children emerged as leaders in this rather involved problem-solving task. One was quite verbal and offered various solutions to the problem at hand. The other child was action oriented. He stated, "Let's do it like this," and immediately proceeded to arrange the leaves. At one point, he stacked all the big sycamore leaves together and directed another child to stack all the little ones. After the big ones and the little ones were sorted, it became apparent to the children that there were other sizes of leaves that could be used, and they began sorting the in-between sizes as well. The children did not like the idea of using the pine boughs in their collection and decided to give them back to the children at the other science table.

When they finished their arrangement, the aide complimented them on the way they worked together to make the display. But the "action" leader complained that the other children would mess it up. At first, he told one of the other children to help him tape the leaves to the table, to keep them in place, but then he remembered that this table was the snack table, which posed another problem to be solved. Finally, they decided they could tape the leaves onto a sheet of posterboard and tack it onto the bulletin board. They looked for five pieces of posterboard, one for each type of leaf, but only four pieces could be found. Even the leader was ready to give up at this point, but then a child who had participated very little in the initial leaf arrangement said, pointing to the two groups of smaller leaves, "These leaves can all go on the same piece."

While the aide was assisting her group of children with their problem-solving activities, the teacher's group embarked on a different kind of problem. The teacher provided hand-held magnifying glasses, and the children looked at the veins on the back of each leaf. As with the other group, the large sycamore leaves drew their attention first. Then the teacher asked if they thought the other leaves had veins, so they examined those, too, and talked about the purpose of the veins. Then the teacher asked a child to close her eyes, gave her a leaf to feel, moved her hand around the edges, and then took the leaf away and asked the child to find the basket of leaves on the table that had leaves like the one she had felt. The other children were eager to take their turns with the leaf-feeling process. Soon the children had sorted a whole grocery bag full of leaves by touch. When they left the science table, they emptied the basket of leaves back into the grocery bags for other children to start later.

The next day, the children went to the science table and continued the process of sorting leaves by touch, without the teacher's direction. Then they brought their friends to the table and showed them how to sort the leaves, checking closely to see that their eyes were closed. News of the "leaf game," as they called it, spread through the classroom; before the week was over, all the children had sorted leaves at the science display table, had used the magnifying glasses to look at the veins, and had identified the names of leaves from the posterboard displays.

These two activities are excellent examples of how kindergarten teachers can take advantage of children's initial interests. This teacher altered the plan for the morning by creating two groups, so that all nine children could participate at that time. Rather than discourage the children's interest by having some of them come back later, she spontaneously involved the aide with the children, and two successful, thought-provoking science experiences evolved.

The aide in this particular classroom had spent many hours observing the teacher making plans and directing problem-solving activities with the children. Much of the success enjoyed by the children in this room is due to the daily conference between the teacher and the aide, when they evaluate the day's events and review their plans for individual children and for the activities for the following day.

Although the teacher and the aide chose different ways to have the children learn about leaves, their activities had some common features typical of all good science experiences. First, the teacher personalized the experience by drawing upon the children's prior knowledge during the grouptime discussion about leaves. Then the two groups of children were given problems to be solved by scientific investigation. One group was asked to arrange the leaves in an interesting display for other children to see, and the second group separated the leaves by touch with their eyes closed. Both tasks were developmentally appropriate, because they encouraged the children to manipulate the leaves, observe them closely, and classify them by attributes.

LANGUAGE PROBLEM SOLVING AT THE SCIENCE CENTER

Although the leaf-sorting activities are excellent examples of scientific inquiry for kindergarten children, there are some language-oriented problem-solving strategies that the teacher can use to make the activity more of a Whole Language experience. These additions can be made during the activity or as follow-up activities.

Consider, for example, the first day, when the children wanted to keep their individual leaf collections intact. The teacher immediately solved the identification problem for them by writing the children's names on individual index cards. The Whole Language teacher can let the children solve the problem themselves, by asking, "How can we remember whose leaves are whose?" Children who are allowed to be active participants in their own problem-solving activities often produce creative solutions. In fact, in the classroom described here, one child solved the problem by tearing her name from the grocery bag in which she had collected the leaves. She had her brown-paper-bag nametag already on top of her leaves when the teacher arrived with a nicely printed index card.

Other language-based problem-solving strategies can be added to the leaf activities. Both teachers used reference guides to identify the leaves collected by the children, but they neglected to show the children what they were doing. Unfortunately, many teachers of young children fail to share this important step in the scientific inquiry process and leave the children with the impression that "the teacher knows everything." There are some excellent children's field guides to nature study which have colorful pictures given in the approximate sizes of individual leaves. Children can be given the opportunity to identify their leaves by making comparisons between the pictures and their leaves, thus learning a valuable lesson in scientific investigation.

The teacher and aide in the foregoing activity were both excellent listeners and engaged the children in active, hands-on manipulation of the specimens; however, they did not engage the children in personal construction of written language. In the leaf-display activity, written labels could have been added by the aide at the time the children decided to arrange the leaves into rows according to type. During the leaf-sorting activity, each time the children placed the leaves in their appropriate row or basket, the teacher emphasized the names of the leaf: "Look, Michael found a dogwood leaf." And Michael added, "Yeah, it's the little one with the round sides." If the children had seen the word *dogwood* being written as they heard it, it would have helped them to associate the written word with a word they had heard spoken many times.

There are other meaningful language extensions that can be used to supplement the two leaf activities. For example, the teacher can have the children recall some key words that describe each type of leaf, adding these to the printed labels. When children who participate in the sorting-by-touch activity find themselves telling other children what to do, the teacher can seize the opportunity to have the initial leaf sorters make a rebus chart[1] with directions for other children to follow. Then, as the experienced leaf sorters help their friends with the "game," they can also point out each step on the chart.

The intensity of the interest in the leaves also might prompt the teacher to suggest that the children write about their nature walk. They can write a dictated group experience chart composed during grouptime or a small-group dictated story during freeplay. They can write captions for their pictures of themselves on the nature walk or compose their own stories to accompany their illustrations. Whole Language kindergarten teachers have found that activities associated with the science unit produce enthusiastic verbalizations, providing the teacher with numerous opportunities to help the children relate

---

[1] A rebus chart combines pictures and words to express a message. Figure 6.2 is an example of a rebus chart, used for an environmental-print unit.

spoken and written language, at the time the activity is occurring and later in recording and remembering the exciting experiences.

Retelling rich experiences such as a nature walk produces many different versions, because children experience the activity in their own individual ways. Group retelling helps children not only to reflect on what they have learned, but to see that similar experiences can be expressed in many different ways. Even the selection of leaves for the display table can be retold, to allow the children to reflect on the thought processes in which they are involved. Through small-group dictation, the teacher might have children tell about the leaves they selected and then ask them to summarize the experience. For example, Matt, Denise, and Brent each said, "My favorite leaf is the sycamore because it is the biggest." After each child has dictated this sentence, the teacher's response might be to ask, "Is there another way we can say that some children liked the same kind of leaf?" Then, after listening to the teacher reread the entire experience chart, someone will suggest the teacher write, "Matt, Denise, and Brent like the sycamore leaf best because it is the biggest." Or a child might suggest writing, "Three kids like sycamore leaves."

The writing center can be a place for group dictation, but it also should be a place where children write on their own. The nature walk was an exciting experience for the children because many of them had never investigated the woods before. What had begun as a leaf-collecting project turned into an experience that they enjoyed recalling for several days after the walk. They talked about the worms and bugs hiding under piles of leaves on the moist ground. They remembered standing very still, listening to the wind blowing through the trees and crouching under the pine trees when it started to sprinkle. They recalled the funny smell of wet leaves and pine needles, which some children liked and others didn't. The nature walk was not only a successful science experience for each child, but it provided a rich source of material for individual and group dictation, as well as for individual compositions at the writing center.

The particular form chosen for independent writing will depend on the various levels of the children's abilities. Some children who are at the labeling stage in their writing may choose to make their own, smaller versions of the leaf displays from the science table, writing name labels for the leaves they have taped onto pieces of construction paper. Others will choose to record their experience through pictures they draw of themselves walking in the woods. Some will use invented spelling to label certain objects on their pictures, while others will use their pictures as a basis for a longer composition. It is important to remember that drawing and talking represent the first stages of composing for young children (Raines, 1986).

Kindergarten children can be heard rehearsing their compositions as they draw pictures of particular events: "I'm going to write about almost getting rained on." "I'm going to write about what happened when we looked under the leaves and all the bugs and worms were running around and going into the little holes in the ground." "I'm going to write about how pine trees have needles, but not sewing needles, and they smell good, too." When they do begin writing, some children will be content to use invented spellings for their entire compositions, while others will take their papers over to the leaf displays and copy the correct spelling of the leaves from the labels. Rich science experiences provide the possibilities for rich re-telling and writing experiences.

GROUPTIME AND THE THEME OF THE UNIT

For children to grasp the concept of scientific problem solving pre-sented in the activities of the science unit, they must also have the opportunity to reflect on the oral presentations and the manipulations of the materials. Personal reading and writing provide reflection possi-bilities. In a Whole Language kindergarten, using one's own oral and written expression is an integral part of solving the scientific problem.

Grouptime provides an excellent opportunity for science and language problem solving. When children attempt to associate with, clarify, or communicate new information through the use of personal language, they are using language problem solving. When kinder-garten teachers introduce a new book with a science theme at group-time, they should use the opportunity to make sure each child relates both the science concepts of the unit and the reading concepts inher-ent in the experience.

The book the teacher selects to read at grouptime helps to integrate reading and science, as well as relate the science concepts in a form the children enjoy. For example, science concepts can be found for a unit on fall in many books the children will enjoy, includ-ing *Chipmunk Song* (Ryder, 1987), *The Seasons of Arnold's Apple Tree* (Gibbons, 1984), and *Leaves* (Testa, 1980). Most kindergarten teachers are already doing an excellent job of teaching the content or major concepts of a science unit when they engage children in a problem-solving activity, such as classifying leaves, but they may not see the potential for read-aloud time as a time of language problem solving.

By finding ways to have the children interact more with the text of the story, the children will learn to construct meaning from the print and become language problem solvers, just as they have become scientific problem solvers, when they sort and classify the leaves for a display table. For example, when one teacher read *Chipmunk Song*, she correlated the tunnel illustrations in the book with the children's observations of the bugs and worms tunneling into the topsoil when the children lifted the shelter of leaves. The association was very successful and caused the children to recall the nature walk experience and relate it to the book. However, if the teacher had introduced the book using the strategies for interacting with the author, as mentioned in Chapter 6, the children could have become more involved with language problem solving.

A Whole Language kindergarten teacher, using the same book, used a prediction strategy and asked the children to tell what signs of fall they saw on the cover of the book. Then, after reading the title and the names of the author and illustrator, she asked the children to predict what they thought the author, Joanne Ryder, would write in the story. Then she proceeded to read, but paused after each of the first few pages of illustrations for the children to notice additional signs of fall, as well as to confirm or reject their predictions. The artist's underground and aboveground illustrations helped the children visualize the tunnels and animal life found on the floor of the forest, but they also imagined what the life of a chipmunk might be like. The main character in the story imagines being a chipmunk, and the children related well to pretending to be a chipmunk. After a few scenes in the book, the children became so engrossed in the story it was not necessary to stop for predictions and confirmations. Many of the children leaned forward while listening intently, thoroughly captivated by the illustrations and the text.

After the teacher finished reading the story, the children were eager to discuss the story. Without the teacher suggesting it, several children made the associations between the tunnels in the pictures and the tunnels they observed on their nature walk. The Whole Language kindergarten teacher allows children to use their experience and their language to integrate their real-life experiences with the information in a book. In this case, the children could relate to an important scientific concept without the teacher constructing the association for them.

Several listeners identified so well with the child in the story that, when the main character imagined being a chipmunk and was burrowing in the ground, the children began to make burrowing movements with their hands and arms as the teacher read. One child wiggled with his body and told the teacher, "He crawled like this." Some children commented that the chipmunk looked like the gerbil in their class. Others mentioned the acorns, the brown leaves, the trees, and the dried grass in the illustrations and associated them with the class nature walk. Since the name of the child is not mentioned in the story, the girls thought the main character was a girl in bluejeans, but the boys argued that it was a boy. The children seemed to have placed themselves in the story and imagined playing in the woods; thus, they were thinking with the author and constructing the story for themselves. Their interactions with the main character and the illustrations, and the associations they made with their nature walk, allowed the children to use both language and science problem-solving strategies.

STRETCHING THE THEME AND STORY
INTO THE LEARNING CENTERS

The teacher related the fall theme and *Chipmunk Song* throughout the day by planning activities based on the story and stretching the ideas into many areas of the classroom. Along with the leaf displays for the science center, there was a table for counting, weighing, and measuring scoops of acorns; leaf rubbings for the art center; a recording of the song "Autumn Leaves" for the movement activity; and a collection of books about fall for the library corner (Raines & Canady, 1989). The science theme was integrated into all of the curriculum areas, as well as being integrated conceptually into the associations the children constructed based on their prior knowledge about fall and their new knowledge gained from new experiences.

An integrated unit of study allows the children to encounter the main ideas or major concepts of the theme throughout the classroom. Most kindergarten teachers already use science activities to encourage problem solving. Whole Language kindergarten teachers have added various language problem-solving activities to integrate the science unit further into a total learning process. In the fall unit, the children not only heard the names of the trees, but saw the names written in print, which helped build an association between meaningful spoken and written language, an important ingredient for emerging literacy. As the children classified the leaves, they made keen observations, discovered the properties of the specimens, and heard and used new descriptive language. With the addition of writing, the descriptive language became visible in print, as they labeled the leaves and wrote about their collections. By talking about the insects and worms they observed tunneling in the ground, the children were able to associate the concept of tunneling with the illustrations and print in the story the teacher read to them. They also wrote about their inquiries and discoveries and in the process became more competent at using language in both its spoken and written forms. They were able to solve the problem of communicating, through language and actions, what they had learned about the theme of the science unit.

ENJOYING THE NATURE EXPERIENCE
FOR ITS OWN SAKE

Not every nature experience needs to be extended. Some should simply be enjoyed for their own sake. One teacher shared the following event, which occurred during a field trip to the beach. Her school was located within walking distance of the ocean, and the teacher often took the class on walking field trips to search for shells and to investigate the sea life that washed ashore. One day, as the teacher strolled along the beach with the children, she noticed that three boys who had gone ahead had stopped and were staring down at something. As the teacher quickened her pace to share in the excitement of their discovery, she heard one little boy say, "Let's show it to the teacher!" Then another boy interjected quickly, "No, let's don't. If we show it to her, we have to weigh it, measure, it, draw it, paint it, and write about it." "Yeah," they all agreed and kicked sand over the dead fish. The teacher learned a valuable lesson that day: Not every experience needs to be extended. Some nature studies are best enjoyed as natural happenings and need no follow-up lessons to be recalled or appreciated.

AIMS OF THE KINDERGARTEN SCIENCE CURRICULUM

The kindergarten teacher's unit on fall helped the children to develop an appreciation of living things, improve their observation skills, discover properties, acquire the language of science, conduct simple investigations, and represent their findings.

Appreciation of Living Things

There are many ways that children can develop an appreciation of living things as part of a science unit. One way is through caring for pets and growing plants in the classroom.

Selecting an appropriate classroom pet is an important decision. Teachers must consider the expense involved and who will care for the pet during school-year and summer vacations and on holidays. But the benefits of having a classroom pet far outweigh the expense and care concerns. Young children learn that living things have special needs, including attention and a habitat that fits the environmental and nutritional needs of the animal. Mistreatment of animals has become a national concern. Many children who have pets at home have never received instruction on how to handle animals and how to care for their needs. Teachers of young children have a responsibility to teach proper care and respect for all living things. The unit of study on pets should include special instruction about the children's own classroom pet.

The following are a few tips kindergarten teachers have found to be effective:

1. Instruct the children by demonstrating how to handle the animal, then allow small groups of children to take turns practicing.
2. Assign helpers to be responsible for the pet, but refresh their memories periodically about the care, feeding, and handling of the animal.
3. Rather than changing pet helpers each day, assign the duties for a week so that the children learn to do their jobs well.
4. Involve young children in both the pleasant tasks, such as handling and feeding the pet, and in the not-so-pleasant ones of cleaning cages or tanks.
5. If a classroom pet becomes ill, have a veterinarian visit the classroom and tell the children about the special care the pet will need.
6. If the animal should die, use the incident as a positive learning experience, and allow the children to relate the death to their own losses of household pets.
7. Later, solicit the children's assistance in selecting a new pet. Teachers usually find it is best to get a different kind of pet than the one that died.

The instructions for caring for classroom pets as well as children's affection for the animal in their classroom have long been favorite sources for dictated stories, experience charts, and language activities in the kindergarten classroom. After the teacher has established the rules for the handling and care of the animal, the children may put the rules into their own words and, with or without the teacher's assistance, construct a poster of the rules to be placed near the animal's cage. This activity helps children confirm that print is used in various ways, depending on the function.

In addition, the children can compare the classroom pet to ones they have at home. One five-year-old, who was obviously concerned about animals in cages, wrote, "Jrbls hs ta sa in kjs. Cats dnt." (Gerbils has to stay in cages. Cats don't.) After sharing her writing with the teacher, she decided to add, "I lk my cat kz he cm an plas with me." (I like my cat 'cause he comes and plays with me.) She read what she had written and added in print, "I dnt tatk hm owt a kj." (I don't take him out of a cage.) Although this five-year-old was involved in many discussions about pets and different kinds of animals during the unit on pets, her personal writing always focused on her own experiences with animals, which she will use later when her writing expands to other kinds of animals.

The unit on classroom pets, which included the study of household pets, prepared the children for future units on farm animals and wild animals. The Whole Language kindergarten teacher should always emphasize the similarities and differences among classroom pets, home pets, farm animals, zoo animals, and wild animals, as well as the variations in the language used to discuss these animals. Young children's intense interest in animals of all kinds invites many possibilities for science and language learning.

While the experience of caring for plants is not quite as emotional as caring for a classroom pet, many lessons about appreciation for growing things can be learned from having plants in the classroom. The traditional planting of seeds in spring has great value to young children and offers many possibilities for expansion into other areas of the classroom. The science center can be turned into a potting shed, with pots, different mixtures of soil and sand, and a variety of plants. If the teacher feels insecure about teaching potting procedures, a kindergarten parent or grandparent who knows a great deal about plants is usually eager to help.

In addition to the science center as a place to plant and sprout seeds, to make cuttings, to watch the root systems form, and to care for the growing sepcimens, the study of plants has possibilities for every area of the classroom. For example, gardening clothes can be placed in the housekeeping and creative dramatics area. The block area can be supplemented with several clay pots, stackable potting containers, and sturdy bags of mulch, bark, and pebbles, which the toy truck drivers can load and unload for several days. An array of beautiful blooming plants can be placed in the art area, to inspire artwork and so children can mix paints to achieve the colors of the blossoms. Charting plant growth can be a part of the mathematics and manipulatives center (Raines & Canady, 1989).

The classroom library can be filled with both fiction and non-fiction selections about plant life, and the teacher can use the opportunity to point out the differences between what is true and what is not. For example, a teacher might read the classic fiction book, *The Carrot Seed* (Krauss, 1945), a tale of a little boy whose mother, father, and brother have no faith in his gardening ability, and who repeatedly tell him, "It won't come up!" The child perseveres, however, and waters the seed, pulls up the weeds that grow around the spot where he planted the seed, and, much to everyone's surprise, he harvests a carrot so huge it takes a wheelbarrow to carry it from the garden. The teacher might also read *Growing Vegetable Soup* (Ehlert, 1987), a colorful nonfiction story of planting, caring for, harvesting, and cooking the vegetables that make a soup. Both fiction and nonfiction books are excellent resources for the plant-life unit of study.

Like all units of study, the plants unit should be connected to other areas of the curriculum, and the Whole Language teacher will quickly begin to see the many listening, speaking, reading, and writing possibilities. Books from the plants unit can be recorded by the teacher on cassette tapes for a listening extension. *The Carrot Seed* also makes an excellent flannel board activity for story retelling.

A natural extension after reading *Growing Vegetable Soup* is actually preparing some soup for lunch. A rebus chart of the recipe will help children learn the importance of reading directions carefully. Numerous writing extensions also are possible, as the children record the growth of their plants for factual information, write about their own cooking and gardening experiences at home, or imagine their bean seeds are magic and develop some modified "Jack and the Beanstalk" tales.

As has been said repeatedly throughout this book, Whole Language is not a step-by-step program, but rather an attitude about child development and literacy acquisition. Once teachers realize the importance of a language-centered curriculum, the possibilities for language expansion during daily classroom activities are limited only to the imaginations of the teacher and children.

Whether conducting an extensive study of fall, learning to handle a class pet, or studying plant life, the underlying reason for a science unit is for young children to develop an understanding and appreciation of living things. As they hear the teacher's enthusiastic comments about their physical world; as they exercise the caution and restraint necesary when caring for a living, breathing pet which responds to their handling; and as they learn to observe more closely and become excited about their discoveries, the children will grow to appreciate living things.

Improvement of Observation Skills

A basic aim of the kindergarten science curriculum is to improve observation skills. These, like listening skills, must be taught to young children. It is not enough simply to tell children to look or to listen; in addition, teachers or adult leaders must model effective observation skills, verbalize what they are doing, and encourage the children to do the same. Collecting leaf specimens for the science display table is one of the many activities through which children can improve their skills of observation. Teachers should instruct adult volunteers who assist during the nature walk to help the children observe the leaves in their natural state, observe what happens when the leaves have been walked on, and observe the changes when leaves are removed from the surroundings. Through close observations, the children will make some interesting discoveries and will verbalize those observations in response to the leaders' inquiries. Verbalizing at the time of discovery helps the children to recall the experience when they go back in the classroom.

Whole Language kindergarten teachers have found that taking notes of observations and verbal interactions during nature walks and then creating a "talking mural" of the experience when they return to the classroom helps the children remember the experience. The talking mural is simply a story that the children paint about their nature walk. Then the teacher can add "dialogue balloons" over the heads of the pictured children, noting inside them what each said during the walk. Nature walks and the language activities that follow them emphasize the three basic strategies for scientific investigations: (1) to observe closely; (2) to record observations accurately; and (3) to analyze the information that has been collected.

Observation skills are necessary for field studies in the natural world, but close observation is also important for specimens that are brought back to the classroom. As children use simple scientific tools such as magnifying glasses and simple balances for making weight comparisons, their findings can be added to the mural, to create a permanent record of their discoveries.

Discovery of Properties

When children engage in field studies, examine specimens in their science-center laboratory, and conduct simple investigations, they begin to discover properties. As they search for new ways to make comparisons and associations, they discover ways to describe what they see, hear, feel, and touch. These descriptions are statements of attributes. During initial observations, the children focus on the most prominent attributes of a material, such as the large size of the sycamore leaves, the heavy weight of the bottle filled with pebbles, the rough textures of the sandpaper, the musty aroma of the decaying leaves, and the sound of wind blowing through the trees. They first classify their observations according to characteristics that are the same or similar, using the process of assimilation. As they gather more information, they find it necessary to modify their classification categories or create new categories and language to accommodate the new information. It is important for teachers of young children to remember as they plan science activities that "scientific" investigation and discovery are not new to young children. Classroom activities should be planned with the attitude of continuing and expanding on the processes children have already been using to gain the knowledge they bring to school.

Kindergarten teachers who are "kidwatchers" are aware of their children's prior knowledge and are able to help them accommodate new information and make meaningful associations. For example, during the fall leaf study, many children collected acorns along with leaves on their nature walk. Later, the teacher related the acorns to the leaves, dissected some acorns to see what was inside, read about squirrels and acorns, and set up a weighing activity where the children filled various-sized containers and attempted to balance the weights. On their own, the children put the acorns in the water table, to test their buoyancy. After several experiences with the acorns, the teacher asked the children who were weighing them, "What can you tell me about acorns?" Some of the children associated the information with a particular learning activity, the walk in the woods, while others recalled information according to a sequence of events: "We get them in the woods" (nature walk). "They grow on trees like leaves do, and squirrels eat acorns" (teacher's discussion at grouptime). "Acorns floated in the water" (water-table discovery). "They smell funny when you open them" (teacher dissecting acorns). "They're heavy" (referring to the entire pail of acorns the child was weighing).

From many observations, the children will begin to construct verbal comparisons, make associations, and describe the properties across attributes. However, each of these levels of thinking must grow from hands-on experiences in the presence of a teacher who is able to ask thought-provoking questions and is not eager to give children the answers.

Acquisition of Science Vocabulary

Children are exposed to new words and phrases within the context of the nature walk, through grouptime presentations, and through the extensions into the learning centers during freeplay. As with any discipline, science has its own vocabulary and terminology. Teachers who work with young children have found that, when the terms are introduced through meaningful experiences, children are not only capable of learning proper scientific terminology, but they are fascinated with words like *biodegradable* and *metamorphosis*. They take pride in using phrases, such as *conducting an experiment* or *collecting specimens*. During the leaf-collecting and classifying activity, one teacher observed that, after labeling the leaves that had been sorted and placed on charts, most of the children could remember the names of the leaves the following days, and they could tell where they were collected as well as why they placed them on a particular chart.

When science vocabulary is learned through meaningful activities that encourage children's natural curiosity and desire to group and classify things, children learn the scientific principles and terminology, as well as the various forms and functions of language itself. Children in a Whole Language kindergarten also use language to reflect on their scientific investigations and to share those findings with their teachers and the other children.

Conducting Simple Investigations

Many simple investigations can be found in science curriculum guides for kindergarten, such as sink-and-float comparisons, magnetic property tests, comparing weights, charting the growth of plants, and constructing simple machines. While each of these investigations may capture the interests of young children, many teachers are beginning to realize that their students are also capable of more extensive field investigations. For instance, one kindergarten teacher roped off a section of a wooded area near the school so she and the children could inventory the trees and bushes that grew there. Later they conducted a broader ecosystem investigation by studying the birds, insects, and small animals they observed in the area.

It is important for the kindergarten teacher to remember that young children have been making close observations all of their lives and that they are also capable of sustained interest in a topic, when the field-study site has many learning possibilities. Kindergarten teachers should plan on-site science experiences as often as possible. Most simple investigations, however, will be conducted in the laboratory of the kindergarten classroom, where the young scientists can control their experiments, observe the interactions that occur, and record their observations and summarize them in some manner.

It is a common occurrence for kindergarten teachers to plan interesting activities that encourage children to solve problems by exploring various materials, but too many times the children are not assisted in how to observe closely and record their findings. For example, the activity of having children place a variety of objects in water to observe whether the objects sink or float is a popular one. Kindergarten teachers usually provide time for the children to explore the materials and experience the sinking and floating on their own, but many teachers fail to take advantage of the opportunities this activity offers for close observation and language development. In one kindergarten class, two children had played at the water table for several days, and, although they enjoyed watching the different objects float and sink, their activity and verbal interaction seemed to wane. When the teacher asked, "Which of these objects float and which ones sink?" the children were quick to respond and even added that some of the floating things sink when you fill them with pebbles or water. Then the teacher asked, "How much water do you have to put in this bottle before it will sink to the bottom of the water table?" The children looked at each other and shrugged, "I don't know." After the teacher left, the children quickly put the bottle into the water and started filling it with water until it sank. They did the same thing with the other containers. Then they lined all of the containers up on the shelf near the water table with the amount of water in each that it took to make it sink and ran to the teacher with their findings. With just one question, the teacher had given purpose to the children's investigations, and the children had created their own way of organizing and reporting the information.

Many kindergarten classrooms are equipped with a table that can be used for sand and water play, as well as weight, volume, mass, and buoyancy investigations. While the aim of the simple investigations will be for young children to make observations, state their discoveries, and record their findings, the first step remains that the children must explore the materials with their senses and with ample time to manipulate the items without an adult's guidance. Then the sensory impressions necessary for the close observations will already be a part of the learner's experience. It would be a mistake for the teacher to move too quickly to the stage of recording observations and summarizing findings. The children engaged in the sink-and-float activity were able to make the comparisons and generalize their findings to new materials because they had thoroughly explored the materials for several days in their own way.

A Whole Language kindergarten teacher might encourage the sink-and-float investigators to represent their new learnings beyond the initial sorting and lining up of the items. The teacher can ask the children to invite two friends over and tell them about their observations. The teacher might make a chart, listing all the items that float under one column and the ones that sink under another. Then, as the children tested new items for their sink or float capabilities, they could add these objects to the chart, either by writing the names or by drawing an outline picture of the items, to represent them visually. As children find ways to represent their learnings, they are able to reconstruct them to share with others. They become more representationally competent as they talk about or find ways to record their findings (Raines, 1990).

SUMMARY

When kindergarten teachers consider becoming Whole Language teachers, they often ask about specific changes in their classrooms. The teachers who ask whether they will still have a science center in their classroom if they become Whole Language teachers are often the educators who value and appreciate how very much young children can learn about their physical world from manipulating interesting objects, collecting specimens for display, and solving simple but interesting problems. Teachers who are enthusiastic about helping children observe, describe, investigate, and record findings about the physical world are excellent candidates for a Whole Language emphasis. In the process of observing, describing, investigating, and recording, children are listening, speaking, reading, and writing. Moreover, the teacher who is interested in young children as science problem solvers also sees them as language problem solvers. The problems of science provide children with something interesting to talk about and to listen for new information about. They motivate children to read or listen to fiction and nonfiction books with data that the child can associate with the physical world.

The teacher interested in science must allow the child to construct ways to represent what has been learned, through words both spoken and written. In the process of solving the science problem, the child solves the language problem by hearing and speaking new words, phrases, terms, and understandings uttered within the context of the real or remembered experience. Children also are language problem solvers when they figure out how to draw, graph, and write representations of what they have experienced, and how to use those representations to recall the experience long after it is over.

The science curriculum for the Whole Language kindergarten becomes much more than a science center. It is a collection of integrated science themes that use, as their major instructional components, the science displays created with the children; the teacher-led grouptime presentations, including good children's literature; and the multiple extensions of the theme into each area of the classroom. For the Whole Language kindergarten teacher, the science curriculum provides the opportunities for young children to develop their appreciation of living things, to become better observers of their physical world, to use the vocabulary of science, to conduct simple investigations, and to discover properties. In the process of their development as young scientists, they communicate their appreciations, observations, investigative findings, and descriptions by using the vocabulary of science. They represent their questions, answers, uncertainties, misunderstandings, and wonderings and curiosities as they find ways to listen, speak, read, and write about their world.

Art in the
Whole Language Kindergarten

Throughout this book, an emphasis has been placed on children as constructors of language and of other representations of what they know, feel, and desire to express. Teachers concerned about the role of the visual arts in the Whole Language classroom can rest assured that there are numerous connections they can build between children's drawing, painting, and three-dimensional artwork and a Whole Language emphasis. Teachers who understand the importance of art in the curriculum and who know how to provide the classroom climate where art flourishes are better able to see the extensive connections between art as creative problem solving and the various forms of Whole Language communication.

IMPORTANCE OF ART

Art meets one of the basic needs inherent in the development of young children, the human urge for expression (Rudolph & Cohen, 1984). For art to flourish in the kindergarten classroom, it is the teacher's responsibility to create a climate where children are able to explore various media in multiple ways to achieve expressions that are truly their own. If teachers are to provide such a climate, they will need to respect children as individuals and therefore support artistic expressions that are highly individualized. In addition, they must recognize the truth of Victor Lowenfeld's (1957) belief that every child is creative. He has called creativity an instinct we are born with, and he relates it to the basic ability of all human beings to express and solve problems. Borrowing from Lowenfeld, the underlying question connecting artistic expression and Whole Language becomes, "What are the developmentally appropriate practices for arts instruction, and what are the teacher's roles in fostering individual children's expressions of creative problem solving?"

GUIDELINES FOR DEVELOPMENTALLY APPROPRIATE PRACTICES

Early childhood educators can find guidelines for appropriate practices in the three position papers mentioned throughout this book. The ACEI (Moyer et al., 1987) describes the child-centered kindergarten as

1. Emphasizing the processes of learning rather than focusing on finished products . . . ;
2. Embracing the teaching of all content areas, presented as integrated experiences that develop and extend concepts, strengthen skills and provide a solid foundation for learning . . . ;
3. Allowing children to make choices and decisions within the limits of the materials provided, resulting in increased independence, attention, joy in learning and feelings of success necessary for growth and development. [pp. 236, 239]

The NAEYC emphasizes the importance of daily art expressions and the use of a variety of media: "Children have daily opportunities for aesthetic expression and appreciation through art and music. A variety of art media are available for creative expression, such as easel and finger painting and clay" (Bredekamp, 1987, p. 52).

In the IRA position paper, the communication value of art is stressed. It is recommended that teachers "provide reading experiences as an integrated part of the broader communication process, which includes speaking, listening, and writing, as well as other communication systems such as art, math, and music" (Early Childhood, 1988, p. 8). From these three position papers, the major points are that art for young children means

1. Cultivating a process orientation rather than product orientation,
2. Integrating art with other areas of the curriculum,
3. Allowing for independent choices of materials,
4. Providing daily opportunities for expression,
5. Developing the arts as a communication system.

Each of the major points is consistent with the assumption that the art curriculum satisfies a basic human urge for expression.

CREATING A CLASSROOM ENVIRONMENT
FOR ARTISTIC EXPRESSION

As designers of developmentally appropriate practices, teachers realize that they are managing an environment for creative expression, rather than isolated sets of visual arts activities. Therefore, creating the classroom environment for creative expression through art is contingent upon teachers

1. Knowing the characteristics of young children as artists (Brittain, 1979);
2. Understanding the artistic process (Chapman, 1978);
3. Providing the positive classroom atmosphere in which children feel free to express themselves;
4. Supplying the time, materials, and background experiences that best enable the child to engage in the art process;
5. Knowing the basic elements of art (Chapman, 1978);
6. Teaching creatively through deliberate preparation, dedication to the value of what is being taught, and expression of themselves as creative and adaptive persons capable of enthusiastic involvement (Wachowiak, 1985).

Characteristics of Young Children As Artists

In addition to knowing the general developmental characteristics of the five-year-old, the kindergarten teacher also needs to know the individual characteristics of the children. The teacher must recognize that Jennifer needs more encouragement than Lucinda to explore a new medium, that Steven is afraid of getting messy and will need some reassurance, that Betsy needs attention to sustain her project. However, knowledge of individual children's behavioral needs, while important, is insufficient if the teacher is not also cognizant of young children's development as artists.

Brittain (1979) has described five-year-olds as being in the stage of "preschematic" drawing, where they anchor their objects to the ground; develop more size proportion; and represent a human by drawing a head, body, arms, fingers, legs, and sometimes feet or shoes. As children gain more control of brush and paint their works begin to look more like illustrations. The colors they select have less to do with the actual colors of the objects being painted than they do with what colors are available to them at a given time. Likewise, children manipulating clay and other three-dimensional media tend to follow a similar sequence of gradually refining their human figures and developing more size proportions as they gain experience with and control of their medium.

Creative Problem Solving and the Artistic Process

Early childhood educators recognize that the process is more important than the product. Problem solving in art is a process through which children select a medium of expression, manipulate the materials, explore the possibilities, extend and adapt previous ways of working with the medium, and create a representation of a thought or feeling. Kindergarten teachers seeking to understand young children's creative problem solving in art can compare the process to the child constructing meaning through print when learning to write. When young children begin writing, they use what they know about print at that moment. Kindergartners who only know the letters of their first names manipulate those letters and explore the possibilities by arranging and rearranging them to represent different meanings.

Similarly, kindergartners who only know a little about how to paint on an easel with a long-handled brush will dip the brush in the paint and manipulate it in a variety of ways, arranging and rearranging the colors on the paper. As they gain control of the painting process, they will explore the wider possibilities of the paints, such as mixing colors on the paper, letting paint drip from the brush, exerting varying amounts of pressure on the brush, overloading the brush with paint, and using only a little paint on the brush. As these young painters learn more ways to control the medium, they will begin to adapt and use the materials more flexibly, purposefully manipulating the medium for expression.

Often in these stages of creative problem solving, the finished product may lose its interest. This of course depends on the developmental stage of each child, but, in general, in the early stages of learning, the process is more important than the product. This becomes quite evident when young children fail to recognize their own finished pieces only a few minutes after painting them. For instance, while observing a classroom of four- and five-year-olds, we noted that the older fives, who painted representative pictures with identifiable houses, pets, and people, tended to value their artwork more. They often sought the teacher's approval when a painting was finished. The younger fives and the fours, meanwhile, tended to seek assistance with getting their wet paintings onto the drying shelf or pinned to the clothesline to dry, but at the end of the day did not recognize their paintings.

Affective Aspects of the Classroom Environment

In creating their classroom environment, the issue that is perhaps of most concern to teachers is how to create an affective climate that will free children to express themselves creatively. Schools have been accused of stifling children's creativity, and kindergarten teachers are particularly concerned that young children continue to develop their ability for artistic, creative expression. While time, a variety of art materials, and multiple experiences are necessary elements for the creative classroom, whether or not children feel free to express themselves depends on the teacher's attitude toward them as learners and toward art as creative problem solving.

For example, in an observation of a kindergarten classroom during freeplay or learning-center activity time, five children were participating in art activities. Joseph and Lindsey were painting at the easels with tempera paints, using long-handled brushes. Ti was drawing with crayons and colored pencils. Shannon and Monica were cutting and pasting bits of construction paper to make a collage. They were at varying levels of completion of their projects. A comparison of the teacher's and the aide's responses to the children provides some insights into the need for a positive attitudinal climate where the adults respect the children's engagement in the process.

The teacher walked by the easels, observed Joseph and Lindsey engrossed in their painting, glanced at Ti who was drawing, and joined Shannon and Monica who were chattering back and forth over their collages. The teacher's decision of whether to interact or not with the artists was predicated upon the level of the children's involvement with their work. The two painters and one sketcher were deeply engrossed in their activity, while the two collage makers were enjoying talking to each other and occasionally discussing what they were making. After a few minutes, one of the easel painters looked around for some assistance to get his painting onto the drying line. The teacher, sensitive to his need, helped him attach the painting to the drying line, then commented, "Joseph, you worked for a very long time on your painting. I see you used a lot of the orange paint. I mixed a lot of orange paint for the easels today." The exchange with Joseph took only a minute, because he was looking around, spotting the next activity he wanted to do. The teacher read Joseph's and the other artists' verbal and nonverbal signals as cues for appropriate adult interaction.

Later, the aide, a less experienced assistant, interacted with the remaining artists in an entirely different manner. Being a quite verbal person, the aide immediately interrupted the remaining child at the easel and said, "Oh, Lindsey, that is a beautiful picture. Tell me all about it." While normally this open-ended request to talk about a painting is an appropriate one, it was inappropriate at this time because it interrupted the child in the process of creating the painting. This question would have been appropriate once the child had finished the artwork, provided she seemed to want to discuss the piece.

The aide also interfered needlessly with the child who was sketching. Ti was adding an illustration to a series of drawings about his dog's disappearance. He was standing up and leaning over the table, drawing with crayons and colored pencils. He was talking to himself and appeared to be telling the story. The aide came over and suggested that he draw a picture about fall for the bulletin board the teacher wanted to have assembled. While it certainly is appropriate to ask children to contribute artwork to a group project for the class, Ti took the aide's suggestion as something he was required to do and immediately put away his drawing and began a new picture.

There are few kindergarten teachers who make the blatant mistakes of criticizing children's artwork when they choose to color the grass purple or draw humans without hair or feet, but many teachers fail to be sensitive to the depth of engagement of children involved in the process of creating as they paint and draw. There is a tendency to interrupt and to question and talk too much about the drawing or the painting.

Children's and adults' drawings, paintings, and sculptures often change during the process. What starts out to be a scene of two friends playing frisbee may change into an entirely different drawing because, as the child draws the frisbee, it reminds him of airplanes, and he proceeds to draw a series of planes.

Observing children manipulating clay, Play-Doh, and other three-dimensional media also provides teachers the opportunity to notice how many times the children change what they are making within any one session. A group of three children were observed working with clay, a medium they had not used often. They had Play-Doh available almost every day, but the natural clay was a relatively new experience for them. The teacher gave each child a lump of clay about the size of a small orange, showed them how to pat just a little water onto the surface if it became too dry, then left the clay players to experiment. One child came immediately to the teacher and told her that it was "slappy," and demonstrated the sound her hand made when patting the water onto the clay. She continued to experiment with making sounds, rather than making things, until her final decision to make a mud pie. Another child, who declared at the beginning, "I'm gonna make a monster," proceeded to pinch off bits of the clay and lay them on the newspaper covering the table, making more of a collage figure than a sculpture. The monster became a man and then a wrestler. When one long arm became disconnected, the child made it into a boat. The third child used the clay like Play-Doh and began rolling it into coil "hot dogs," pretending to bite one. This child next made cookies, then a bird's nest and eggs, and then went back to making flat cookies again. At the end of the session, the three sculptors collected their pieces of clay, shaped them back into a ball, and happily deposited them in the earthen jar for storage. The process ebbed and flowed with the changing characteristics of the wet and drying clay. As the three children manipulated the clay, their products changed, depending on what appeared from their manipulation. The only product verbalized ahead of time was the monster, but when the process took too long to look like a monster, the child relabeled the various products along the way.

These three children's interactions with a new medium are typical. They manipulated the medium; they began exploring the possibilities; and, as their manipulations produced different shapes, sizes, and textures, they labeled what they were making, rather than deciding on an end product at the onset. Over time, as children gain more control of a medium and learn to use it flexibly in a variety of ways, they begin to designate an end product and proceed to construct what they plan. However, this doesn't preclude still more trial-and-error experimenting along the way and enjoying the happenstance creations that the shapes infer. For example, when the bird's nest begins to look like a saucer, the experienced sculptor may make a cup and enjoy seeing it take shape, but will return to making the originally stated product of a condor's nest.

Most important, teachers must realize that youngsters take varying amounts of time in each of the stages of the creative problem-solving process and should not be encouraged to "make" something while they are still in the manipulation, exploration, and experimentation stages. Even in the later product-oriented stage, the artists will continue to explore and experiment on their way to a finished product.

The teacher who understands the process of creating and who understands children's characteristics as learners and artists is more likely to follow their leads, to read their signals and nonverbal cues, and to allow them the latitude to work without adult interference. Yet, when a child wants a response or when an adult's interaction can provide encouragement and support to a frustrated artist, the teacher will read those signals as well and will intervene positively. The child who is eager to talk about her painting needs a good listener. The child who is exasperated because he wants to draw a horse may ask for the adult to draw it for him. Of course, the teacher will refrain and continue to encourage the child to draw.

Providing Time, Materials, and Background Experiences

The climate or atmosphere for creative problem solving is also dependent upon the resources of time, materials, and background experiences of the students. There are two major time periods in the schedule when art activities are planned, during tabletop activities as children are arriving in the morning and during freeplay time when the students may choose the art center. Tabletop art activities often accompany the theme of the unit of study. Each child will be encouraged to complete the special art project within a day or two. For example, the unit on fall may include using crayons to make leaf rubbings on manila paper.

Choosing the art center during freeplay is the second time kindergartners usually are involved in art. In classrooms where creative expression is encouraged, the easels—equipped with a variety of sizes of brushes, tempera paints, and paper—are available every day. Watercolors and fingerpaints require more supervision and are incorporated into the schedule less frequently. Crayons, markers, chalks, charcoals, and colored pencils are available daily in abundance, for use with a variety of sizes, colors, and textures of papers. In addition, collage materials, scissors, glue, and a wealth of construction paper also are routinely used for many cut-and-paste activities. Supplies for constructing and sculpting three-dimensional works are often a part of the center, as are clay, Play-Doh, and cardboard.

It is recommended that as the year begins, the teacher plan special art activities that build up the background experiences the children need to have in order to use each medium productively. The children need to become acquainted with the materials and tools, and the procedures for their use, so that they feel free to go through the steps of manipulating the medium, exploring the possibilities of the materials, experimenting and using the medium in new and flexible ways, and finally creating a finished product. It is imperative that teachers leave the materials out and accessible so that the children feel comfortable with continuing in a medium until they reach the stage of creating a product.

One teacher said she used natural potter's clay with the children about one day a month. The infrequency of use made it impossible for the children to go any further in the creative problem-solving process than simply manipulating the medium and beginning to explore the possibilities. The clay, a medium not usually found in the children's background experiences, needed to remain out for at least a week at a time. The variety of materials, their easy availability on low storage shelves, and the teacher's instruction in their care and use will result in kindergartners feeling free to express themselves through painting, drawing, and sculpting or devising three-dimensional constructions.

Knowing the Basic Elements of Art

Teachers who have a degree in child development or early childhood education usually have at least one course in art. Those who are successful art teachers within their classrooms know how to use the basic elements of art and a visual-arts vocabulary in their teaching and in their conversations with children.

Chapman (1978) reminds teachers that art is categorized by "dimension and sensory appeal. The three-dimensional arts include products with height, width, and depth, while two-dimensional are essentially flat" (pp. 22–23). Sensory appeal is determined by whether the products appeal mostly to the eye or to the kinesthetic or tactile senses. Materials and tools have specific names—including tempera paints, watercolors, charcoals, and chalks—and should be called by their proper names. Similarly, teachers should introduce art concepts such as primary and secondary colors, shape and volume, proportion, depth, value, and texture. There is a tendency to talk down to children, especially among teachers who have not continued to talk about and think about art as a major curricular area. This should be avoided.

While it is not recommended that formal lessons be given to kindergartners in drawing, painting, or constructing, children should live in a classroom where their art is connected to a descriptive vocabulary used in the field. For example, when the color of the construction paper is magenta, it should not be called purple. When the class experiments with painting over crayons and then scraping off the paints to reveal the crayon beneath, the term *etching* should be used. When a group of children plan how their finished box sculpture will look, the teacher should inform them they are "designing" a product. When a child draws her baby sister smaller than herself, the teacher should compliment the child on the proportion and size of the subjects in the drawing. When a child paints a rainbow over a house and says, "It means they lived happily ever after," the teacher should use the term *symbol* when discussing the significance of the rainbow.

Early childhood educators tend to focus on two-dimensional art and to supply mostly paint, crayons, and chalk. Given the infinite array of possible materials, such a narrow focus is inexcusable. Teachers need to expand their horizons and thus the horizons of their students. To illustrate, after visiting an art exhibit at a college, one kindergarten teacher returned to the classroom quite enthused about using ordinary materials in extraordinary ways. She had seen an unusual exhibit of sculptures made of cardboard. Immediately she envisioned her kindergartners capable of constructing these designs, because she had seen them build extraordinary constructions with the hollow blocks in the classroom. She was correct. Supplied with boxes of many different sizes and shapes, the children began first to make the usual buildings—doll houses from stacks of shoe boxes, garages from partitioned boxes, and a fire station by joining one large square box to a smaller one.

Initially, the teacher was disappointed with these structures, until she experimented by making a mobile she designed by stringing colorful boxes at strange angles onto some fishing line. She simply hung the mobile over the art area, without making any comments. She inferred that, just as she had been inspired by the art exhibit, the children might be inspired by her creation. Of course, it received immediate attention and the children began designing their own mobiles. But there were some huge boxes left over, and the children wanted to do something with them. They had already played in them, pretending they were elevators and spaceships; however, after their very successful individual box mobiles, they decided to build a huge mobile. Later they decided to keep it on the ground, so they could look at the top and all the sides, which they had decorated in different pictorial and graphic designs. It then became a box sculpture rather than a mobile.

The kindergarten teacher who kept her own interest in art alive and who felt free to use a familiar material in an unfamiliar way taught the children a far greater lesson than how to make mobiles. She demonstrated one of the hallmarks of artistic expression. As Marshall McLuhan (1967) says, "The medium is the message." The materials we use remind us first of the things we know; hence, the children's awareness of boxes as squares and rectangles reminded them of the squares and rectangles of houses and fire stations. Later, as their imaginations took over, the boxes became elevators to the moon or spaceships for travel to faraway planets. Inspired by seeing boxes hanging from their corners, painted unusual colors on the inside, and printed with graphic designs on the outside, the children's imaginations soared again, and the young artists wanted to try their hands at inventive new ways to use an old, familiar product—the cardboard box.

Teaching Creatively

The teacher who experimented with the cardboard-box sculpture exemplified a creative teacher, one who expresses himself by adapting ideas. Some kindergarten teachers who are good art teachers find inspiration for materials and techniques from the world of art, and others find it in nature. One teacher who was a wonderful gardener routinely brought flowers, fruits, and vegetables into the classroom and displayed them as objects for the science table. She also used them as inspirational materials for the art area. She displayed the assorted fruits, vegetables, flowers, and even some weeds and grasses in beautiful baskets with contrasting swatches of fabric. She also used seeds, buds, blossoms, and dried flowers.

The fruits and vegetables for the science table were for cutting apart, observing, tasting, and cooking; but in the art area she encouraged the children to arrange and rearrange them to create still-lifes like the famous ones in the prints of masterpieces she placed on display. They also made centerpieces for the snack table, and she discussed the beautiful forms, colors, and textures in conversation with the children over snacks. Obviously the colors, forms, and arrangements appeared in the children's drawings and paintings. But, most important, the teacher capitalized on her own interest in providing nature's harvest as a source of inspiration for her young artists' expressions.

In addition to the usual preparation good teachers make to supply their classrooms with materials, teachers who value art also make deliberate preparation for children to feel connected to other artists. The teacher who incorporated the famous still-life prints and the teacher who introduced cardboard-box sculptures connected the young artists with art professionals whose work the teacher had seen at the exhibit. These works of art were not models for the children, but inspirations. Even though children recognize that exact replications of the paintings and sculptures are not within their range, they are nonetheless inspired.

Coloring-book art, dittoes, and other prefabricated drawing activities for children provide artificial models that are not even good adult art and therefore should be avoided. To illustrate, soon after seeing a volunteer in a classroom draw "lollipop" trees, many of the children's trees became the lollipop variety. This was in contrast to a few days earlier when, after a nature walk where the children had stood under tall trees and looked up through the branches, their drawn trees had been an elaborate maze of lines. Deliberate classroom preparation thus means not only deciding about materials and designing the space for their use and storage, but also deciding what is to be excluded.

Kindergarten teachers can value art as a means for human expression; as a means of feeling connected to the beauty in nature and in great masterpieces; and as a means of inventing new, creative uses of the ordinary to make it extraordinary. Likewise, teachers who view themselves as creative and as connected to the beauty and value of art are most likely to transmit those sensibilities to the children they teach.

INCORPORATING WHOLE LANGUAGE CONCEPTS IN THE TEACHING OF ART

Young children are eager artists. They solve problems creatively when teachers provide materials and guidance in an atmosphere that encourages manipulation, exploration, and experimentation. Children present their feelings and ideas, as well as make representations of concepts they have learned. The Whole Language kindergarten teacher can use many opportunities to connect the children's creative problem solving in art with the children's development as communicators.

Speech As an Organizing Vehicle

Kindergartners also are eager language users, and teachers respect the formal and informal language that accompanies the creative process. This use of language can be observed on a daily basis. Even when drawing and painting alone, children can be heard "muttering" to themselves, making commentary to accompany their action. One lone crayon drawer was heard saying in a quiet voice, "Now, I need a yellow one. Come here, yellow, where are you?" as he scratched around in the crayon box.

The language that accompanies art activities should be allowed to continue. Children should not be "shushed"; rather, teachers must accept the children's mutterings and talking among themselves as perfectly normal. In fact, teachers can identify with the children by recalling how they themselves go about planning and cooking dinner for a large number of people. If tape recorders were placed in their kitchens, no doubt they would record a great deal of "talking to oneself" as these cooks tried to keep on schedule and remember all the details of the food preparation.

All forms of talk that children use while they work are respected by Whole Language kindergarten teachers, because they realize that language is an organizing vehicle. Teachers also value their own use of explicit language to help children know how to proceed. They use it to give more meaning to instruction, to teach the use of materials, and to create a "community of artists" who appreciate each other's uniqueness as creative problem solvers. For example, Alicia took a wooden spool and wound it with yarn to represent a hose, and then combined it with her crayon drawing of a fire and fire truck. When she searched for glitter to sprinkle on the crayon fire to represent sparks, the teacher noted her inventive combination of materials and at grouptime showed Alicia's creation to the class. The teacher used her own speech to communicate to the class that Alicia's use of the materials in unusual ways was a creative expression.

Written Language As an Organizing Vehicle

At the beginning of the year and whenever the teacher introduces new materials and tools, the instruction in their use is given aloud and with a great deal of hands-on manipulation of the materials. This instruction is also saved for future reference, through writing and pictures. For example, if the teacher introduces roller printmaking, the step-by-step instructions will be stored with the supplies, so children can use the materials more independently in the future. The most helpful is a combination of pictures and printed words—a rebus chart for directions.

While teachers in many classrooms use these prepared sets of instructions to accompany tasks, Whole Language kindergarten teachers often involve the children in making the instructions after the task is completed. The teacher may ask, "How can we remember all the steps we went through to make our roller prints?" The children will dictate the steps, check for correct sequencing, and then try following their own written directions to decide if they are adequate. They learn to use writing for directions in a most functional way.

In addition to the writing to remember instructions, writing also accompanies artwork related to the theme of the unit of study and to the children's choice of art activities. For example, when leaf rubbings, which are a part of the fall unit, are completed, the teacher or aide can suggest that the children label the rubbings so they can look up the names of the leaves in the future.

Similarly, writing also accompanies artwork that is of the child's own choosing. The teacher can decide whether to extend an art activity by conversing with the children or by encouraging them to write about the subjects they chose or the processes they used in their creations. For example, Ti, the child who was drawing a series of three pictures about his pet, was actually rehearsing his story as he drew. He eventually wrote a story about his dog who disappeared, including how he felt at first and how happy he was when the pet was later found by a neighbor.

Teachers who encourage their children as writers often find them moving back and forth between drawing and writing, as both are a part of the composing process. Kindergartners' oral presentations about the story they are making in their pictures are usually a great deal longer than their written versions of the same story. This is perfectly natural, because their spoken vocabularies far outdistance their writing and reading vocabularies.

Whole Language teachers find that writing also is often incorporated into the very artwork itself. For instance, after reading *This Is the Bear* (Hayes, 1986), which is illustrated with cartoons and dialogue enclosed in "bubbles," one kindergarten teacher noticed the children incorporating conversation bubbles into their own artwork, to tell of the conversations their subjects were having. The teacher had called attention to the cartoonist's bubbles in the comic strips as an introduction to the book and had showed how the illustrator added them to the story of the lost bear. Because almost all young children have experienced a lost toy, the book was particularly endearing to them, and they borrowed the bubbles as a way to express their feelings in their subsequent "lost-toy" series of drawings.

Teachers often see children using print to add detail to a picture. Figure 9.1 shows the printing of a kindergartner who had dictated a sentence about his picture and had dutifully copied the teacher's printing. Of more interest, however, is the writing the child printed on his own; "Christ Chu rch of." The child started in the middle of the steeple, but when he ran out of space he went back to the top and finished his sign, meaning it to read, "Church of Christ."

Taking dictation from a child and having children write their own captions are certainly excellent ways to have children associate spoken and written language. As already stated, Whole Language kindergarten teachers prefer to have children use whatever print

Figure 9.1   Drawing with Child's Writing

they know to construct their meaning in print. It is important to remember, however, that using one's limited knowledge of print is a taxing job and young children are sometimes eager to see their complete stories in print. One Whole Language teacher tells of a child who came back from a camping trip to Canada and was quite eager to tell the whole story to the class. Each day for a week she brought in mementoes and photos of the trip. Every day her artwork related to this wonderful camping trip. The Whole Language kindergarten teacher, eager to capture the child's intense interest, asked the child to write the story of her camping trip, which she agreed to do.

Later her mother recalled the child declaring that night that she would never go back to kindergarten. After hours of moping around the house, suddenly the child stopped crying and the mother asked if she was feeling better. She was. Her mother asked, "Why, just a few minutes ago you were terribly upset. What made you feel better?" The child answered, "I just know what I'm going to say. I'm going to write, 'We went camping and we had fun. The end.'"

Sometimes kindergartners' struggling writing is simply no match for the lively spoken language they use to retell an event or story. In an instance such as this, the lively retelling of the camping trip is an excellent choice for a dictated story, with the child contributing her own writing in the form of captions for the illustrations.

Artwork to Accompany Listening and Speaking

Whole Language kindergartens often used puppetry as a mainstay of the language arts curriculum because it promotes active, hands-on learning and provides the opportunity for children to use their rich speaking and listening vocabularies (Bromley, 1988). While commercial puppets certainly prompt a great deal of role playing, Whole Language kindergarten teachers encourage their children to make their own puppets to represent the characters of their favorite stories or of the best stories they have written. They can also use their puppets for improvisations for an audience or for enjoyable play with a partner. The art and construction work in designing a puppet need not be complicated to be effective. Paper-bag puppets and stick puppets can be works of art.

Amy decided to make the story of *The Three Billy Goats Gruff* (Asbjornsen & Moe, 1981) by using stick puppets. First she drew and colored the scenes, then cut out the subjects and glued them onto popsicle sticks, and finally proceeded to act out the entire story. Lauren and Jeff, after having been taught how to make paper-bag puppets, decided to make two puppets of the main character of *Dandelion* (Freeman, 1964), one when he had his hair curled to go to the party and one when his hair was rained on and he was not a dandy lion any more. The two "Dandelions" were an instant success, and soon other children constructed their own versions. There was no pattern for these puppets; if there had been, this would no longer have been an art project. The teacher had taught the children how to make stick puppets and paper-bag puppets, and the kindergartners applied their new knowledge and constructed their own artwork— their own versions of the story—to make their communication of the story more effective.

Combining Reading and Artwork

Illustrations in children's books are often as inspiring as the story told by the author. The illustrations provide many young children with their first art appreciation lessons. Some even begin looking for certain artists, because they like Eric Carle's bold colors, or Leo Lionni's stylized animals, or Susan Jeffers's line drawings. Many children who are eager to "own" a story will redraw the illustrations and try reprinting all the words. Purposely using story retelling through artwork is one way to help children comprehend the story, retell it at home without the book, or simply to savor their favorite parts.

Dictated stories, language experience charts, and story retellings, as well as having children read each other's writing, provide some of the meaningful reading materials in the Whole Language kindergarten. Children almost always want to add illustrations to accompany the stories and charts which they write to record their experiences. Adding the illustrations to their individual and group compositions is a natural response because the young child thinks of reading materials as both print and illustrations.

When teachers work with their young writers, they find them capable of composing elaborate stories that are interesting enough to be bound into books for other children to read. And because the children view reading as both print and illustrations, they spend a great deal of time and effort drawing and painting to enhance their print. In the beginning, the writing will grow out of the drawing; a story will emerge as the artwork evolves. Then, as children plan with their teacher how to page the story and bind it into a book, they may add more illustrations. This is one of the many reasons that the art center is stationed near the writing and library centers, because children move back and forth among these areas as they read, write, and draw.

Whole Language kindergarten teachers seek to free children to express themselves artistically in a variety of media; therefore, art is not simply the two-dimensional type connecting illustrations and print to create a story. Children can also use three-dimensional art media to express their responses to literature, as they use puppets to tell favorite folktales such as *The Three Billy Goats Gruff* (Asbjornsen & Moe, 1981), or sculpt in clay to depict the various scenes from *Jack and the Beanstalk* (Jacobs, 1982), or to construct a village for the *Teeny, Tiny Woman* (Bennett, 1986). When the children are free to express themselves artistically, they begin to associate art with recalling important information, with writing and reading, and with telling and retelling their favorite stories until they become their own.

SUMMARY

When kindergarten teachers recognize the children's drawing, painting, and construction of three-dimensional artwork as a part of the human urge for expression, then art becomes one of many communication processes in a Whole Language kindergarten. When teachers view art and language as creative problem solving, they will appreciate the significance of the process and not just focus on the finished product. Children will reach the point of creating products after they have manipulated the materials and explored the possibilities of the medium, and when they have experimented by using the materials in new and flexible ways.

For the visual arts to thrive in a kindergarten classroom, teachers need to know the characteristics of young children as artists, and they must understand that creating art is creative problem solving. They also must insure that the affective climate will free children to express themselves. Kindergarten teachers must provide the time, materials, and background experiences that enable young artists to go through the stages of creative problem solving, and, of course, teachers must be well prepared themselves by knowing the basic elements of art. In addition, kindergarten teachers must plan adequately for art in the classroom, value the children as creative thinkers, and value the role of art as a vehicle for the basic human urge for self-expression.

Whole Language kindergarten teachers connect young children's creative problem solving in the visual arts with the communication arts of speaking, listening, reading, and writing. They respect the young child's "self-chatter" and talking with others, recognizing speech as an organizing vehicle for the thoughts that accompany problem solving. Whole Language kindergarten teachers also use speech to make explicit the use and care instructions necessary for children to learn how to handle the various media. When the students want to use the materials, the children in a Whole Language kindergarten can refer to written and pictorial directions which they helped to write.

In addition, Whole Language kindergarten teachers build upon the connections young children already make between print and illustrations. A great deal of young children's first writing is found incorporated in drawings—as captions for pictures and as early attempts to capture a story they want to "own." As the children become more proficient as writers, many of their most meaningful reading materials will be their own stories and those of their classmates. The Whole Language kindergarten teacher demonstrates the valuing of these efforts by binding them into homemade books. Similarly, the teacher encourages the children to use a variety of art forms, both two-dimensional and three-dimensional, to tell and retell commercially published stories and to create stories of their own.

❋ 10 ❋

Music and Movement Activities in the Whole Language Kindergarten

The kindergarten classroom that is alive with music and movement activities is a fertile environment from which a Whole Language focus can grow. The seeds of Whole Language have already been planted in the kindergarten where children are enjoying music and movement and where they are already connecting spoken and written language with meaningful activity. When they sing along with the Hap Palmer (1969) record, "Red stand up, Green stand up, Red and Green stand up and sit down," they are learning to listen to the words, interpret them, and follow the sequence of directions. When they, along with their teacher, read the words to the fingerplay song "Five Little Monkeys" (Bayless & Ramsey, 1978) and learn the accompanying motions, they are associating the written words with the spoken words, and they are seeing an adult use print to remember lines. When they compose a new version of "Five Little Monkeys" and create "Five Little Pumpkins," or "Five Little Scarecrows," they are learning to tell a different story while retaining the underlying structure of the song. These are just a few examples of how the connections between music and movement already being made in many kindergarten programs create endless possibilities for a Whole Language emphasis through music and movement.

TEACHERS' TALENTS AND INHIBITIONS

Kindergarten teachers who use music and movement most effectively are people who enjoy music and do not feel inhibited about movement. Some teachers have had special training in music, dance, and dramatics and can assist others on the faculty. Other teachers may have had little specialized training, but seem to have a natural talent for teaching music and movement. When asked about how she developed her talents in these areas, one teacher shrugged her shoulders and said,

> Some of my earliest memories of family gatherings were of my parents and aunts and uncles "making music." Each Sunday, after the dinner dishes were done, a variety of musical instruments would appear and one of my uncles would say, "Everybody ready? Okay, let's make some music." We would sing and the adults would play everything from pop songs, hymns, and mountain ballads, and childhood ditties. I was raised by a musical family to think of music as fun, relaxation, and a way to express feelings. Later, I learned to play the piano, sang in choirs, and enjoyed the classics, but when I think of what I want my children to remember about music, it is the same feeling I had on those Sunday evenings. I want my children to enjoy "making some music."

But what about the teachers who have no specialized training, or the persons who lack the benefits of family who expressed themselves through music? While most teacher preparation programs in early childhood education contain courses in basic music and movement, the actual emphasis placed on music and movement activities in the kindergarten program is usually determined by the individual teachers after they have their own classrooms. Kindergarten teachers are aware of the importance of music and movement in the classroom, and most find that, even though they may have felt inhibited about expressing their limited abilities with adults in teacher preparation classes, they become much more free to express themselves as they experience music and movement with their children. Fortunately, most kindergarten teachers feel teaching music and movement is one of their responsibilities, even if the children also have a special music teacher who comes in once a week. Music and movement are integral parts of the total kindergarten curriculum; regardless of the teacher's level of knowledge and particular talents in the music and movement activities, they must be a part of the daily schedule in a Whole Language kindergarten.

PURPOSES OF MUSIC AND MOVEMENT IN THE CURRICULUM

The songs, chants, and rhythms of childhood found in various cultures play a significant role in childhood development and help to connect one generation to the next. Whether signing a lullaby, saying a jump-rope chant, coordinating movements and lyrics for a finger-play, or even humming a popular jingle from television, the shared enjoyment of the lyrics, melodies, and movements are expressions of who we are as a particular group of people. In this day of multicultural classrooms, rich musical and movement possibilities abound if members of various cultures are invited to share their musical and movement heritage.

Some children come to kindergarten from families where music accompanies many of their daily activities and is the focus of celebrations, and where the child is an active participant. Other children may equate music with background noise from a radio or television left on continually at home, rather than as an opportunity to participate in a creative process. It is the kindergarten teacher's responsibility to build an appreciation for music and movement from whatever level of experience the young child brings to school.

Appreciation of Music and Movement

Kindergarten teachers who weave music and movement into daily activities find that an appreciation for music and movement comes easily for young children, because both are highly social and interactive endeavors. Fortunately most teachers treat music and movement not as a special talent given to a few select children, but as a natural means of personal and social communication. Young children naturally join in when they hear singing. Because five-year-olds are "movers," music and movement seem to fit their needs for expression. But helping children to grow from their often limited early exposure and to develop a broad-based appreciation of music and movement takes careful planning.

Dorman and Alvarez (1989) describe the teacher's responsibility as one of "becoming more musical" (p. 53). They advise teachers to "listen to a variety of musical styles . . . [and] go to children's concerts where conductors talk about music in laymen's language" (p. 59). In addition, they suggest teachers collect a variety of music aimed at the child audience. Many teachers admit that their own understanding and appreciation of music and movement was increased significantly by exposure to programs designed for children. Teachers who use commercial children's recordings find that they are soon able to adapt the music for their own use. It is equally important that teachers learn about and experience a variety of types of movement expressions for the sake of movement, as well as in response to music.

Learning the Languages of Music and Movement

Successful kindergarten teachers must be performers. It is essential that they become comfortable enough with music and movement to perform as a means of instruction. Dorman and Alvarez (1989) suggest that there are two key elements to successful music lessons: "moving from a warm-up activity to a creative activity" and "pinpoint-[ing] the key musical concept" (p. 56). A good warm-up activity is one that the children already know how to do. The second element, pinpointing the key musical concept, requires teachers to be knowledgeable about the basic elements of music. Dorman and Alvarez suggest the basics are rhythm, melody, harmony, form, dynamics, tempo, articulation, and timbre, as well as the style of the musical selection.

Music has a vocabulary that the children can learn to understand. Teachers need to use the terms that express rhythm, melody, harmony, dynamics, and stops, as well as the words for mood and style. The simple vocabulary of musical directions provides the student with a basic understanding of the expressive elements of music. Loud, soft, fast, and slow sounds, as well as smooth and connected sounds versus staccato or quick and disconnected sounds, are easy to teach young children, as they can express them through the sounds they make by singing, clapping, and stamping and by using other parts of their bodies, as well as the sounds from rhythm band instruments.

Traditional Songs and Chants As Expressions of Childhood

It has been said that there is a secret society of childhood. Songs, chants, jokes, riddles, and some forms of teasing are passed on from older children to younger children in a ritual reserved for them and to which adults are relegated to the limited roles of observing and remembering their own experiences as children. While there are certain songs, chants, and jokes that are identified with particular cultures or areas of the country, there remains a vast number of traditional songs, chants, and rhythms that teachers find popular with all children.

The variety of possibilities for children's songs ranges from the traditional, such as "Here We Go 'Round the Mulberry Bush," to the more recent "The Wheels on the Bus Go Round and Round" (Bayless & Ramsey, 1978). New songs are introduced daily, for example, on television programs such as "Sesame Street" and "Mr. Rogers' Neighborhood." A variety of songs and styles of music is important, but the types of songs that children seem to enjoy most are the movement and fingerplay songs. One teacher beamed with delight as she told of a child with a learning disability who spent months learning the lengthy "Bear Hunt" song. Once she had learned it, she performed it for each guest who came to the classroom. The complementary rhythms and movements of fingerplays and action songs incorporate language, symbolism, and perception, which help children to remember them.

Using Music to Improve Coordination

The expressive elements and rhythm of music help the young child control movement, and learning to control one's movement is a developmental task for the kindergartner. Jacques D'Amboise (1989), the former ballet dancer who founded the National Dance Institute, says, "I can use dance to help a child discover that he can control the way he moves. . . . When a youngster learns how to dance [move], he learns he can control his life" (p. 4). Teachers who are fortunate enough to have a movement, dance, or physical education teacher to assist with their program should make certain those professionals understand about developmentally appropriate practices for the young child. They should accompany their children to the sessions with the special teacher, repeat some of the activities in the regular classroom, and build a rapport with the teacher that invites collaboration in planning for individual kindergartners' needs.

Five-year-olds are movers; they are impulsive, natural, and energetic but often out-of-control movers. Carefully planned music and movement activities that draw upon the strengths of young children can help them develop their own inner sense of control through a pleasantly imposed structure. Through movement that is a response to music, through following directions that build body awareness, and through interpreting music as dramatic movement, youngsters learn to control their body movements. Children are fortunate if they have a teacher who will lead them and move with them, and who seeks to expand their repertoire of ways of moving. Such a teacher undoubtedly will contribute to the children's sense of enjoyment of themselves, of their creative expressions, and of their physical capabilities.

Responsive Listening and Movement

The once-popular activity of having young children stand up, turn on the music, then move any way they choose has been replaced by helping the children to feel the music and then encouraging them to move in response. Bayless and Ramsey (1978) suggest that young children must be led to feel the music. Teachers need to listen with the children, helping them first to hear the beat and to respond rhythmically by tapping a drum or patting a knee until they feel the music. After much practice of hearing, feeling, and keeping time to the beat, the children can then begin to move with their whole bodies as the music makes them feel.

Another popular listening and movement activity some teachers use is to have the children move like a certain animal. However, if the children have not seen a bear, or an elephant, or a giraffe, except in pictures or on television, they have little sense of how the animal actually moves. Before asking for interpretive movements, the teacher should discuss the mood of the music and talk about the animal (how large it is, how slowly or quickly it moves), asking the children to describe verbally how they think the animal might move. They could make comparisons, such as between a huge elephant and a tiny mouse. Once the children have a sense of the music and the interpretive possibilities, they are better able to symbolize the movement.

Moomaw (1984) suggests that props can aid in movement and responses to music. Scarves, ribbons, and crepe-paper strips have a nice way of flowing through the air and so lend themselves to interpretations of some movements from classical and popular music. Similarly, props can be used to help children recall the sequences of fingerplays, such as flannel board pieces or stick puppets of "Over in the Meadow" (Bayless & Ramsey, 1978, p. 148).

One particularly inventive teacher used flashlights as props to emphasize tempo. She darkened the room, helped the children establish the beat of the music, then gave three children flashlights which they used to create beams of light that moved across the ceiling in time with the music. After experimenting with a variety of tempos, the class decided they liked the slow, "flowy" music best (Raines, 1982).

Instruments to Use with Young Children

Before anyone can use an instrument, she needs to learn about it, and this is certainly true of children. Dorman (1989) points out that rhythm band instruments can be used to make noise or to make music and that teachers should help children to distinguish between the two. It is necessary to introduce the instruments, instruct children in how to play them, and let children experience the instruments one at a time. Dorman suggests working with children first in small groups and finally as a part of a whole-class rhythm band. Children should be helped to get the beat of the music, to express the beat on their instrument, and to follow their teacher's directions. The emphasis on playing the instrument is not on performing, but on experiencing the instrument and its possibilities, on responding to and accompanying the music.

In addition, while homemade instruments serve a definite purpose, children need to develop an appreciation of quality rhythm and classroom instruments and the sounds each makes. Parents, grandparents, older children, and community volunteers should be invited to play their musical instruments for the class or to demonstrate a movement or dance interpretation to music. It is important to warn the visitors that young children will need to "experience" the instrument. They will want to strum the guitar, move the bow over the strings of the violin, and feel the instrument in their hands as they try to make the sounds. Children need to be taught to respect the quality of the professional musician's instrument, but, for the children to learn about the instrument, they must experience it.

One father of a kindergartner, an accomplished classical guitarist, agreed to bring an old guitar to the classroom and leave it for a week. The teacher who was simply demonstrating how to hold the guitar received enthusiastic applause from the children the first time she strummed it. To her surprise, the children were delighted and thought her an accomplished musician.

Music and movement provide the kindergarten teacher with an opportunity to involve the parents and the community, whatever the musical heritage. From bluegrass to classical, the children need to hear the sounds, experience the instruments, appreciate the music, and learn to respond with their rhythm instruments in the kindergarten classroom.

GUIDELINES FOR DEVELOPMENTALLY APPROPRIATE PRACTICE

The NAEYC's description of developmentally appropriate practice contains several references to music and movement in the kindergarten curriculum (Bredekamp, 1987). It recommends that "children have daily opportunities for aesthetic expression and appreciation through art and music," and that they "experiment [with] and enjoy various forms of music" (p. 52). The ACEI's position paper also contains references to music and movement as vital to the child-centered kindergarten (Moyer et al., 1987). While emphasizing the need for integrated experiences, the paper reminds teachers to "develop and extend concepts, strengthen skills and provide a solid foundation for learning" (Moyer et al., 1987, p. 239) in music, as well as in other subject areas. Obviously what is needed to accomplish these goals are daily opportunities for music and movement, as well as careful planning by the teacher.

MUSIC, MOVEMENT, AND THE WHOLE CHILD

Early childhood educators who understand the underlying principles put forth by the NAEYC (Bredekamp, 1987) and the ACEI (Moyer et al., 1987) evaluate activities for the different curricular areas in light of their effects on the whole child. Kindergarten teachers may select activities that have the potential to enable children to develop in the four major areas of cognitive, language, social/emotional, and physical growth and development. Many music and movement activities are excellent whole-child development activities. For example, remembering musical phrases and keeping a beat by controlling the playing of a rhythm instrument are cognitive functions. The language involved in the melody, in the musical terms, in following directions, and in using one's voice provides numerous receptive and expressive language development possibilities. In addition, music and movement by their very nature are social. Controlling one's voice, instrument, or movements to blend in with the group, or to participate at the teacher's cue requires an awareness of others and their contributions to "making the music." The shared joy, delight, pleasure, and eagerness with which children participate with each other and the teacher during music and movement also indicate social and emotional values of music and movement.

One teacher told us about how she uses music to change moods. When the weather is dreary, she sings her way into a cheerful mood by letting the children sing their happiest songs. Likewise, on exuberant days when the children get overstimulated, she chooses slower, gentler tunes to soothe and relax. Certainly learning to express emotion and moods as they are conveyed in songs, music, or movement aids in the young child's emotional development. Inherent in music and movement are numerous possibilities for children's physical development. As they learn to use their voices, coordinate their fine and large muscles in playing instruments, control their movements, move expressively in conveying a dramatic meaning, and move responsively to the music, they are practicing the skillful use of their bodies. They are becoming more agile, more controlled, more graceful, and more expressive. Children delight in their physical accomplishments, and music and movement by their very nature are physical and have many possibilities for developing a sense of confidence.

SCHEDULING MUSIC AND MOVEMENT ACTIVITIES

There are two major times when kindergarten teachers can engage their children in daily planned music and movement activities—at grouptime and in the music center. Some teachers plan a separate grouptime centered around music and movement, while others incorporate music and movement into each grouptime presentation. (See the sample schedule in Chapter 3 for variations.)

In addition to the music and movement activities for grouptime, some teachers arrange a special music center in their classrooms, for working with individuals and small groups and as a center children can choose during freeplay. They place the listening station, record player, cassette player, xylophone, and tonal bells together, for ease of use. Most prefer to have the children play the rhythm band instruments with teacher assistance. Records and tapes of the children's favorite commercially recorded musicians are selected for active and passive listening. It should be remembered that the tapes the children most often request are the ones of themselves singing as a group, so there should be plenty of these. Parents, grandparents, and community volunteers can also use their talents to record tapes for children's listening. The children can savor again a live performance from a musical guest or enjoy hearing themselves sing their favorite grouptime fingerplays and songs.

GROUPTIME AND CENTER ACTIVITIES

To appreciate fully the possibilities for incorporating music and movement into grouptimes, let's refer back to our earlier discussion of one teacher's grouptime presentation about nutrition. She brought a basket of fruit to the circle, led a discussion of fruits as snacks, and concluded by reading Bruce Degen's humorous book, *Jamberry*.

The reading of this book can easily be stretched into a musical and movement activity. The central character, Jamberry Bear, loves berries and sings about them, marches in a parade about them, and chants his way from page to page, shouting about wonderful berries to eat. The children pick up the cadence and are already chanting along before the teacher finishes reading the book aloud. In addition to emphasizing how the repeated phrases are like a song, the teacher can play a marching record and the children can parade like Jamberry Bear (Raines & Canady, 1989). Experienced rhythm band players may even contrive a "Jamberry Bear March." The rhythm and rhyme of the book are musical and infer several interpretive movement possibilities.

After thinking of ways to stretch the musical and movement ideas from *Jamberry*, the kindergarten teacher in our example did in fact invite a few children over to try chanting the phrases and tapping out a beat on the rhythm band drum. Several children then tried playing the melody of the repeated phrase, "One berry, two berry, pick me a blueberry," on the xylophone. Few children needed assistance in remembering the repeated phrases, but they needed assistance in exploring the musical instruments. The exploration time for learning about and experimenting with the instruments required some teacher modeling, but, as with all early childhood activities, the students also needed to experience the instruments on their own terms. After a few attempts, the teacher recorded the children playing their instruments and singing what they called "Jamberry's Song."

ANALYSIS FOR A WHOLE LANGUAGE EMPHASIS

The multitude of activities connected to the *Jamberry* book, the repeated phrases, the tapping out of the rhythm, the melody the children composed, and the interpretations of the scenes as they marched like Jamberry Bear are just a few examples of the endless variety of Whole Language activities that are possible through music and movement. Every five-year-old in that particular kindergarten classroom could read the phrase, "One berry, two berry, pick me a blueberry." Every child could recall all the different types of berries Jamberry liked. Every child wanted to read the book again, with the teacher and on his own. As the children listened, spoke, sang, and marched, they made the character, the story, and the repeated phrases their own. There was listening, speaking, reading, and even composing, as the children wrote a melody to accompany the words. When children interact with a text enough and begin to "own" the meaning and the words, it is a Whole Language activity.

As has been emphasized throughout this book, teachers who wish to develop Whole Language kindergartens need to become familiar with the International Reading Association's recommendations in *Literacy Development and Prefirst Grade* (Early Childhood, 1988). It is recommended there that teachers "provide reading experiences as an integrated part of the communication process, which includes speaking, listening and writing" (p. 6). The nutrition lesson and the additional Jamberry music and movement activities are excellent examples of integrating the communication process.

To strengthen the writing process in this case, the teacher can model how to write the music for the melody the children composed on the xylophone. Another possibility is to write a song about another kind of snack, such as, "One crunch, two cruch, bring me a carrot and celery munch." Some children might try rewriting the book in dialogue form, rather than the rhyming scheme the author chose. More personal writing can be elicited by asking the children to write about themselves enjoying their favorite nutritious snacks. After preparing nutritious snacks, they could also write functional recipes or directions for others to follow.

Certainly the *Jamberry* book fits well with the IRA recommendation that teachers use reading materials that are predictable, as the main character communicates via repeated phrases and rhyme throughout the book. As mentioned in the IRA position statement, predictable materials "provide children with a sense of control and confidence in their ability to learn" (Early Childhood, 1988, p. 6). Similarly, the highly active experiences during grouptime and the following center time allow the children to be "active participants in the learning process rather than passive recipients, by using activities that allow for experimentation with talking, listening, writing and reading" (p. 7).

SUMMARY

The kindergarten teacher who has a strong music and movement component in the curriculum is well on the way to a Whole Language emphasis. Music and movement are both means of communication. Young children are developing cognitively, linguistically, socially, emotionally, and physically, as they experience the moods of the music, interpret movements, decide how and when to respond with their voices and body movements, and as they play instruments. When teachers recognize the inherent value of music and movement to five-year-olds as learners, they can design ways to incorporate them into the schedule.

Music and movement activities provide the opportunities for young children to develop a broader appreciation of these two aesthetic expressions. Through them, children learn new vocabulary as well as the traditional songs and chants and the modern expressions of children. They improve their ability to control their own movements. They learn to listen and respond with their voices and bodies and with musical instruments.

Teachers can be assured that they are following the recommendations of professionals when they incorporate music and movement into the curriculum, because the position papers from the NAEYC, ACEI, and IRA refer to the value of these activities. By their nature music and movement are active communication processes and therefore fit the Whole Language approach. Kindergarten teachers can strengthen their presentations at grouptime and in follow-up center activities by examining their lessons in light of emergent literacy recommendations. The proof of the value of music and movement activities in the curriculum rests with the fact that teachers and children not only enjoy these two aesthetic expressions, but feel a sense of "ownership" of the experience, with all its rich language and communication possibilities.

* $\boxed{11}$ *

Housekeeping and Blocks in the Whole Language Kindergarten

Susan Isaacs' (1948, 1977) observations of play, first published in the 1930s, helped educators see the benefits of play in all areas of child growth and development. And Patty Smith Hill, another play advocate of the period, helped teachers structure the curriculum for the large blocks of time needed for uninterrupted play in the housekeeping and blocks areas (Hill, 1923). Although the value of play as a theme in early education goes back to Rousseau and Pestalozzi, the current emphasis on early mastery of skills makes it necessary for teachers to express continually the value of play to parents and to other educators (Arnaud, 1971). This is especially evident in the noticeable decrease in space and time allowed for housekeeping and blocks in many kindergarten classrooms (Isenberg & Quisenberry, 1988).

The teacher who comments that her students love to play in the housekeeping corner and with the blocks knows the value of play as an important developmental activity. Even when such a teacher begins including more Whole Language activities in the program, this does not have to take away from the housekeeping and blocks centers. Whole Language kindergarten teachers also recognize that allowing for freeplay and for children to select their own centers is a developmentally appropriate practice. They are aware of the unlimited potential the housekeeping and blocks areas have for language growth and development. Freeplay in the housekeeping corner and the blocks areas is not only encouraged in the Whole Language kindergarten, it is an essential part of the program.

"MISEDUCATION" OF THE KINDERGARTNER

As some kindergarten teachers have attempted to continue to provide a variety of activities and also find time for the "skills" lessons that are a part of the "push-down" curriculum, they have shortened or eliminated the amount of time devoted to play (Elkind, 1987). Concern about the harmful effects of "academic" preschools and kindergartens, and thus the "miseducation" of young children, has led the NAEYC to delineate what is meant by "developmentally appropriate practices" (Bredekamp, 1987). It has likewise led the ACEI to characterize the "child-centered kindergarten" (Moyer et al., 1987). As Elkind (1987) has stated, "When we instruct children in academic subjects . . . at too early an age, we miseducate them; we put them at risk for short-term stress and long-term personality damage for no useful purpose" (pp. 3–4).

In addition to these voices and those of numerous other experts in early childhood education, concern over the miseducation of the young is expressed in the IRA's *Literacy Development and Prefirst Grade* (Early Childhood, 1988). A major concern is teaching "isolated skills" rather than integrated programs that take place in a supportive environment where "children can build a positive attitude toward themselves and toward language and literacy" (p. 3). It is particularly important that IRA is raising these concerns and making recommendations about the education of young children, because many parents' major educational concern is whether the kindergarten is providing the appropriate "reading readiness skills."

In kindergarten programs where parental and administrative concerns over "skills" have influenced teachers, there is a tendency to insert more sit-down paper-and-pencil tasks into the curriculum. This has often resulted in time being taken away from freeplay and the children's selection of centers. In many cases, the materials in these centers have actually been removed from the classroom, to make room for more tables and chairs for group paper-and-pencil tasks. Even though for many years early childhood educators have been concerned about the decline of play in kindergartens (Robison, 1971), the tendency continues today. Some teachers have attempted to keep a freeplay period while adding on "readiness skills centers," so children spend part of the period at freeplay and the rest of the time on readiness worksheets. The effect is the same. The children are robbed of valuable freeplay time to engage in "developmentally appropriate activities."

Some teachers, however, have taken the time to inform parents about the value of the housekeeping and blocks centers and have not succumbed to the "scheduling" pressures. They have likewise judiciously informed their school directors and principals of the benefits of these play environments. These teachers have chosen to stay true to their own professional standards while addressing parental and administrative concerns. A large number of these teachers who chose "developmentally appropriate" activities for their classrooms, instead of skills-and-drills worksheets, were among the first kindergarten teachers to recognize themselves as Whole Language teachers.

PURPOSES OF HOUSEKEEPING AND BLOCKS CENTERS

To many teachers and children, the housekeeping and blocks centers are the areas of the classroom most associated with play. A general discussion of the benefits of play is presented in Chapter 3; however, the uniqueness of these two play centers necessitates a more thorough examination of their roles in the Whole Language kindergarten.

Rudolph and Cohen (1984) describe play as "reflecting the dimensions of experience" (p. 108). Because the housekeeping corner represents family life, which is common to all children, it helps them relate to each other through their shared experiences. The block center also has curricular and developmental benefits, which have been thoroughly described in what has now become a modern classic in early education, *The Block Book* (Hirsch, 1974). Winsor (1974), writing about the use of blocks as a learning material, says that the "development of play requires adaptable materials which can serve fantasy as well as reality experience" (p. 8).

THE HOUSEKEEPING CENTER

In some early childhood classrooms, the housekeeping corner is called the family living area. In others, it is the kitchen and bedroom, and some also include a living room with child-sized furniture. Children often call the area the playhouse or the dress-up corner because the costumes and other dress-up clothes are kept there. Some catalog suppliers of kindergarten equipment label the center the dramatic play center, as if this were the only area where dramatic play is expected. Whatever the title, the area of the classroom where children find model appliances and cooking utensils, a child-sized table and chairs, model bedroom furnishings and dolls, and in some classrooms model living room pieces, is usually called the housekeeping center or corner.

Changes in the Housekeeping Corner

Children of today play in much the same way as those in Susan Isaacs' era. They continue to reflect their own living experiences and their parents' roles, but today the roles for both genders are represented both within and outside the home. Over the years, the equipment in the housekeeping corner has been expanded to include props that indicate the roles of adults working outside of the home (Isbell, Floyd, Peters, & Raines, 1988).[1] Teachers may occasionally include office equipment, dress-up clothes for work, typewriters, and computers; a variety of plumbing or carpentry tools also may be added. Some teachers have updated the model home environment by adding exercise equipment and at-home workstations (Isbell & Raines, 1989). Others routinely change the housekeeping corner to match the community helper roles they are studying (Hudson, Speight, & Salisbury, 1988). The housekeeping corner may become a fire station, a post office, a pediatrician's office, or a veterinarian's clinic, as well as a community retail business, such as a grocery store, a florist shop, a bakery, or a fast-food restaurant.

In one classroom, two players who were observed in the housekeeping area and an adjacent office area turned the bedroom part of the housekeeping corner into a babysitter's home. The children who were playing the mother and father dropped off their infant at the sitter's and proceeded to their office.[2] Even though the housekeeping corner had been updated to represent offices, stores, and community helpers' workplaces, the play emanated from the setting that represented the home.

Aside from the obvious benefits of children recalling their own experiences and acting out roles they have seen, when other props are added to the housekeeping corner, new roles and play themes are created. Kindergartners become veterinarians, florists, customers, waiters, and clerks. For example, the two players who left their infant at the babysitter's house imitated their own parents' morning activi-

---

[1]The authors are indebted to Dr. Rebecca Isbell, Associate Professor, East Tennessee State University in Johnson City, for her suggestions and insights about young children's play, and for some of the examples from the housekeeping and blocks centers.

[2]The play episodes were observed during a research study of the effects of literacy materials in play centers, conducted by Raines at George Mason University's Project for the Study of Young Children, for a joint project of the Children's Literature Workshop and the Center for Applied Research and Development.

ties of preparing to leave for work by dressing, packing lunches, checking briefcases, and dropping the baby off, but they also had to imagine the roles of office workers. For one of the children, who had visited her mother at her real estate office, the transition from mother to office worker was an easy one. But the other child became confused and thought the office was a doctor's office. Only after the first child explained the setting several times was the second child able to pretend to type on the computer and make his "boss" happy. The confused role player eventually found a way to get out of that scene and returned to the housekeeping corner, where he was more comfortable and more verbal.

There are times when the children transform the housekeeping area into a different imaginary space by the clothes they choose for dress-up. For example, one five-year-old was observed wearing a housecoat while playing her mother role of singing a baby doll to sleep. That done, she put on a white coat, hung a stethoscope around her neck, and announced quite authoritatively, "Michael, you can bring Jasper the dog in now." Her actions, language, posture, and dress were convincing to Michael, who was holding a stuffed tiger but put it down and brought in a toy dog for the veterinarian to examine. She continued her exaggerated rendition of this role through a lengthy play session which she ended by scribbling a prescription for heartworm medicine for Michael's stuffed dog.

Adding Thematic Centers

Some kindergarten teachers choose to replace the housekeeping center periodically with play materials for a particular thematic unit. Griffing (1983) recommends two or three thematic centers, as well as a housekeeping corner. Most Whole Language kindergarten teachers would agree with Griffing that the housekeeping corner should act as a "homebase" from which children can initiate their role playing and explore the special thematic centers and workplace, and to which they can return if they choose. If space does not permit this extensive an expansion of housekeeping, teachers may want to alternate house-keeping and thematic centers.

THE BLOCKS CENTER

Aside from the blocks themselves, the most obvious resource needed for a good block center is space for the children to build. Sets of low open shelves with large compartments for the children to store blocks of similar size and shape are also important. A good kindergarten blocks center will include large hollow blocks, an extensive collection of unit blocks, accessories such as animal figures and family and community-helper figures, and an assortment of vehicles (Stanton et al., 1974). Pulleys and short lengths of rope can add to the possibilities for play and physical science discoveries.

Curricular Benefits

All parents and teachers of young children are aware of the fascination five-year-olds have for block play, but many parents and some teachers are not fully aware of the role blocks play as children begin to internalize the physical foundation of all mathematical and scientific concepts. By physically manipulating blocks, young children learn the meaning of size, shape, length, weight, volume, capacity, and balance. Even before they can label or describe the blocks, they have internalized their physical attributes and established important relationships between the objects.

Moffitt (1974) has said that blocks are important for scientific understanding because building with blocks focuses on answering the basic question of science: "What will happen if . . . ?" She also points out that blocks allow the child to create a system that operates by controlling the interactions of the parts, another important scientific understanding. Likewise, as children build with the blocks, they must balance each piece, and in so doing they are internalizing cause and effect.

Like Moffitt, Leeb-Lundberg (1974) also recommends blocks as a means for acquiring both scientific and mathematical understanding. As children experiment with the use of space and with various sizes and shapes of blocks, and as they manipulate the blocks to form enclosures and open forms, they intuitively learn the fundamentals of geometry. As they observe similarities and differences, they create sets and associate equivalencies. As they build architectural forms, they are dealing with area, volume, foundations, and balance.

Young block builders, however, are not concerned about the mathematical and scientific values of blocks. They are concerned with playing, with creating their structures. Five-year-olds, who are usually beyond the stage of simple manipulation of the blocks, also use them as part of their cooperative play ventures, which form the foundation of the social studies curriculum. When the children play with trucks, cars, and blocks to create an elaborate "interstate highway," they are relating to the social studies unit of transportation. They must cooperate to finish their road-building project and play out the roles they have chosen for themselves, usually designated by virtue of the vehicle they have chosen to drive.

Beginning geography concepts are involved when the moving van comes to a house that has been built of blocks. The players use their houses on an imaginary street to play out their roles as family members and friends, as an emotional drama unfolds when one of the families leaves the neighborhood. When the children build the fire station and respond quickly to save a burning building, they are representing one of the many community helpers they will play in the days to come. The interdependence among members of society and the roles they play for the emotional and physical well-being of the community are foundational understandings of the social studies curriculum.

Developmental Benefits

The curricular goals of blocks in the kindergarten program are usually concerned with the child's growth in mathematics, science, social studies, and motor abilities. Whole Language teachers add cognitive and language development to these goals and plan activities that encourage children to use oral and written language during block play and as extensions of it.

Physical development. A boy shouted over his shoulder to his friends, "I'll get 'em," pointing to the long hollow blocks. Then he stacked up four blocks, started to lift them, and was confronted with a physical problem to be solved. He couldn't budge the stack of heavy blocks. He had to make a decision. He knew he could take one at a time and run back and forth to the construction site, but that would take a lot of time. Experienced teachers are familiar with this scene and would not be surprised to learn that the child's solution to the problem was to pick up two blocks, hug them lengthwise, and stagger over to the building site, bragging about how strong he was. Later, after many building experiences, the child will learn to have another child stack the blocks in his arms like logs of wood, so he can carry more of them at once. The potential for gross motor development is apparent in the bending, lifting, stacking, carrying, pushing, and pulling required as children play with the heavy blocks. Fine muscle development and eye–hand coordination are also promoted as the players gingerly balance small unit blocks at the top of their structures by using the small muscles in their hands and fingers.

Social and emotional development. Play is a social and emotional event. The term *sociodramatic play* reflects the social and emotional nature of play as children interact with their environment and with each other. When two or more children engage in related behaviors in a progression of steps where communication is necessary in order to keep the play going, they are developing important social skills and relationships. As they play out the roles of a chosen theme, they experience the drama of a variety of emotions. Drama is evident when the excited fire fighters rush off to rescue a burning building, or when family members wave goodbye to their neighbors while the moving van pulls away. The children feel free to exaggerate their excitement and their expressions of emotion. In play they are able to try out emotions that may feel less comfortable to them in real-life situations.

Children practice expressing a wide range of emotions, under the security blanket of "pretending," and see the effects their actions have on their fellow players. They are rehearsing the expressions they will eventually use in the real world. While *play therapy* is a term usually reserved for psychologists, kindergarten teachers have long been aware of the therapeutic value of play for children who are dealing with personal problems. The controlled social interactions of a chosen theme of play, the materials, and the supportive climate of the classroom allow the child to interact socially and emotionally to solve problems. The environment provides a sense of safety and security under the guidance of a warm and caring adult.

Cognitive and intellectual development. Blocks provide a learning medium for exploring intuitions and developing foundational learnings, which are acquired through perceptual–motor activity. This "interiorization of actions" is the basis from which thought is constructed (Piaget, Inhelder, & Szeminska, 1964). Therefore, when children are engaged in block-play activities they are building the framework upon which concepts are developed.

Building with blocks also provides children with a format for testing hypotheses and constructing knowledge through a variety of types of problem-solving opportunities. For example, the "strong man" who lifted two hefty long blocks, hugged them to his body, and staggered over to the construction site later tried dragging the blocks, and finally solicited the help of another child who stacked the blocks in his arms like logs of wood. When the other builders demanded speedier delivery of their materials, he found that, by stacking the blocks on an "18-wheeler" toy truck, he was able to transport even more blocks at once.

Discovery learning, which plays an important role in the kindergarten program, is a part of the block-building experience. One teacher who had observed the children struggling to make their buildings more stable decided it was time for a lesson on the importance of firm foundations. Instead of simply telling the children how to build a foundation to stabilize their tall buildings, she employed an excellent early childhood intervention technique. She provided a model and let the children discover its properties. The next day, before the children arrived, she built a very sturdy two-story house on a foundation that was larger than the actual building. In the morning when the children arrived, they looked at the house, which was constructed in the middle of the block center, and wondered who had built it. They decided it must have been the afternoon class who had left it. Attempting to build one just like it, Mark said, "Wow, this house is strong. Look how thick it is." The other children joined in building a series of strong, thick buildings, constructed with wide, firm foundations.

Block builders also learn to design a plan and follow it through, but they are always prepared to change if something else appears more interesting. For example, Leigh Anne, who was directing the construction of a town, suddenly suggested that the children build a shopping mall instead. The builders liked her suggestion and, after pausing for a moment to survey their present arrangement, began a discussion that included "we could" phrases to communicate their ideas. Ty said, "We could take this long block here and put it here to make the 'rage" (garage). Mark then replied, "We could put this one like this for the driveway up" (meaning the ramp leading to the garage). The "we coulds" continued until the town was transformed into an expansive shopping mall. Through observation of the processes involved in block building, teachers can see evidence of hypothesis testing, trial-and-error learning, discovery learning, and designing.

Language development.   The negotiations, transformations, and representations each child must process to engage in play are beneficial to language development because each requires communication. Language development cannot be separated from each of the other areas of development. As young children internalize the physical attributes of the blocks, the activity is usually accompanied by some form of speech, either oral or silent talk to oneself. As they describe the blocks, direct other children to add a certain type of block to a building, or use the blocks to represent a variety of forms, they are continually talking. As the children interact in their sociodramatic play, they use language to explain their actions to others, to solicit another's assistance, and to give directions and sometimes commands. They also use language to keep the momentum of the play alive. Problem solving occurs as they take on the various roles, change roles, and communicate what a particular block or form means. As they redirect their own and others' actions, they communicate both through spoken language and the language of their actions.

The roles children choose to play in representing their social, emotional, and physical activity are often negotiated among the players. Researchers such as Bruner (1976) have been able to verify certain personality types (e.g., leader and negotiator) within the play setting. The players' assertions and rejections and the negotiated balance that allows the play to proceed provide great benefits for children's language development.

As the players transform themselves and the objects they play with into a variety of roles and scenes, they discover new ways to communicate these transformations with their peers. A block may be a brick for constructing a wall, or it may be held in a child's hand and flown like an airplane, or it may represent a loaf of bread for the dinner table. These object transformations are action oriented and usually are accompanied by descriptive language: "We could put this brick on the corner" or, "Zoooommm, the 747 is coming in for a landing" or, "Take the bread out of the oven before it burns."

The children also transform themselves through actions accompanied by supporting language. For example, as Jennie swayed back and forth singing, she held the block up in front of her like a mirror, then said, "I can make my hair look pretty. You like my hair with these bows?" Then, in a split second, she darted across the room, deposited the block into a brown paper grocery bag, and said, "I'll take these to your car." The suprised shopper wanted to put more cans and cereal boxes in the bag, but her groceries were whisked away.

An interesting characteristic of play in the kindergarten setting is that the transformations of objects and of the children themselves into different roles are understood by the children as they play together. The children understand that the block is not a block, but rather bread, or a mirror, or a brick; it is a representation. The drama of the situation elicits language and actions that allow the players to share in the meaning.

The complement of players will continue their transformations of materials, actions, themselves, and their language until their drama is played out. Children are able to read voice inflection in play, so when they change their play voices to their natural voices they are indicating the end of the play. For example, after a lengthy bakery scene where Play-Doh symbolized cookies and unit blocks were loaves of bread and cakes, the clerk announced in her natural voice, "I'm through playing now." Two children then took over the cherished roles of cashier and weigher of the cookies on the scales, and the play continued without the child who had been the originator of the episode.

The children hear each other's language, see the actions, and read the meaning. Successful play is contingent upon the players being able to transfer a shared meaning to the objects, to make the representations, and to designate and change their roles through actions and words that will communicate.

In a study comparing the effects of types of centers on language, the children used a greater diversity of vocabulary words and more words per play period in the block center than in housekeeping or the changing sociodramatic centers (Isbell & Raines, 1989). This finding was true for both boys and girls. Perhaps the reason there was significantly greater use and diversity of language in the blocks area is that the hollow blocks and unit blocks are materials children can transform into a great variety of objects and scenes. The specificity of the contents of housekeeping and sociodramatic centers, such as props for kitchens, grocery stores, florist shops, and spaceships, may limit the children to fewer role alternatives. The open-endedness of building with the hollow blocks and unit blocks provides greater creative possibilities. In creating and negotiating more diverse roles, and thus in making more diverse transformations, the children are able to make a greater variety of representations, which naturally leads them to use more diverse vocabulary.

INVOLVING BOYS IN HOUSEKEEPING AND GIRLS IN BLOCKS

Many teachers express concern that the girls choose to play in the housekeeping corner and the boys most often choose the thematic centers and the blocks area. Researchers have verified that older kindergarten boys spend little time in the housekeeping corner, while they are more apt to be found in the thematic play areas that the teacher has assembled. Meanwhile, girls are less likely than boys to choose the blocks area (Dodge & Frost, 1986; Quay, Weaver, & Neel, 1986). The underlying question, however, is whether the boys are socialized away from housekeeping and girls socialized to avoid the blocks.

The influence of sex-role stereotyping is a significant question for kindergarten teachers. Some researchers point out that the materials in the housekeeping area do not support the fantasy role plays that many boys engage in at this age (Dodge & Frost, 1986; Olszewski & Fuson, 1982). Teachers concerned about sex-role stereotyping can make the play areas more inviting for each gender. For example, both male and female clothing items need to be a part of the housekeeping corner, and other props also should be selected for their appeal to both sexes. Teachers might want to intervene occasionally in the blocks area by suggesting a special construction project and asking for both girls' and boys' assistance. In the end, however, as much as the teacher might like to see girls and boys using both areas, the child's own selection of freeplay centers remains an important practice in a "developmentally appropriate" classroom (Bredekamp, 1987).

MODIFYING HOUSEKEEPING AND BLOCKS TO INCLUDE A WHOLE LANGUAGE EMPHASIS

Much of our awareness of what is and is not Whole Language education has come from studying the nature of the literacy process and the natural learning processes of young children. Play is a vital part of the natural learning process. Kindergarten teachers who have retained their housekeeping and blocks centers are already aware of the value of these centers in the total kindergarten curriculum and are anxious to learn more about the possibilities the centers have for literacy development. As Kenneth Goodman (1986) points out repeatedly in *What's Whole in Whole Language?*, many teachers wishing to stress Whole Language in their classrooms, once they understand the nature of literacy development, may find that their instructional program is already rich with Whole Language activities.

The housekeeping and block centers already foster Whole Language activity, by the nature of the interactions that occur in them. Play in these centers is alive with interaction and accompanying language, which occurs in a meaningful whole. None of the language development programs, designed as they are around selected lists of vocabulary words, can begin to produce the variety and breadth of vocabulary that sociodramatic play elicits naturally.

Through play children construct the foundations necessary for spoken and written communication. They construct meaning from reading each other's body language, symbols, and transformations; by bringing background knowledge to the play scene; by representing real and imagined roles; and by sharing the "whole" of the play episode. The players, in the roles they have assumed for themselves, can make predictions by anticipating their counterparts' next reaction. For example, if two players are mother and father, they are able to play the scene based on their background knowledge of the two roles and likewise predict how the other is to act. If the counterpart player follows the expected pattern, the play continues. If the player does something unexpected, the other player accommodates the action as long as it fits the role. However, if the action does not fit the role, the children correct each other by saying, "You're s'posed to . . ." The counterpart player confirms the intended meaning by clarifying or changing the action. The children's attempts to understand or to clarify can be observed in the inflections of their voices as they ask questions, by the way they look at their peers, and by what they say in the dialogue. Finally, children integrate new information with what is already known by listening and by recognizing the action and language clues. They proceed through the drama of the play episode by using the thought–language processes of sampling, predicting, confirming, and integrating—steps Whole Language teachers know are necessary for constructing meaning.

Encouraging Literacy Play in the Housekeeping Area

While acknowledging that the activities found in the housekeeping area, blocks area, and other sociodramatic play areas are inherently Whole Language, teachers enrich the Whole Language environment by adding materials to the areas, by becoming reading and writing role models, and by connecting the play environment to a story. Literacy materials may include books, newspapers, magazines, pencils, pens, markers, notebooks, note pads, scratch paper, lined writing paper, envelopes, greeting cards, computer paper, and plain paper. Teachers can play an active role in the child's play by modeling adult reading and writing and encouraging the children to include reading and writing in their play. Also, by finding ways to connect the housekeeping corner and block areas to stories that are read aloud at storytime, the teacher can build a more active association between stories and play.

Adding literacy materials. In a study by Raines (1990b), it was found that children changed their play in the housekeeping corner and in an adjacent grocery story when literacy materials were added. The teacher engaged the parents' help in collecting a wide assortment of cans, cereal boxes, plastic containers, and boxes from frozen foods. The teacher and the children worked together to arrange a grocery store. During the first days of playing in the housekeeping center and the grocery store, the children pretended to "go shopping." When a cash register with a bell and pretend money was added, all of the players wanted to be the cashier.

During the following week, the teacher added newspapers, sales flyers from grocery stores, coupons, notepads, paper, pencils, and pens to the housekeeping corner. The children immediately incorporated these environmental literacy materials into their play. They looked at the special flyers and the coupons, wrote pretend grocery lists, and then went shopping. One child attempted to match the picture in the ad to the cans on the shelf, to see which were on sale. Two children were more successful at matching the cents-off coupons for cereals to the cereal boxes than they were at looking at the ads in the flyer.

The next week, the teacher added poster board, markers, paper, and pencils to the grocery store. On the first day, the children made signs with arrows and wrote large numerals for prices, but it was the sign making on the second and third days that proved most inventive. They used the poster board to reorganize the grocery store. They placed all the canned foods together and made a sign that said, "Kns." Then one of the readers corrected the writer by marking through the word and rewriting below, "Can," while reading it "cans." When they grouped all the boxes together, the teacher expected to see the sign maker write the word *boxes*, but instead she wrote "SRL," for *cereal.* There were, after all, more cereal boxes than any other kind. On the third day, they reorganized the food containers again and wrote two new signs. A child asked the teacher how to spell *junk*, then wrote "JUNK FDD" on one sign and "GOODSTF" on the other.

The cash register continued to play an important role in the grocery store scene. It was there that the teacher noticed a certain kind of writing taking place (see Figure 11.1). The children used a combination of scribbles and real and mock writing on rectangular notepads, which they turned sideways to represent checkbooks. They wrote their checks and gave them to the cashier, who put them in the cash drawer of the register.

When the teacher examined the pretend checks, she was puzzled by one of them. At first she thought the child was representing a cash register receipt, but the next day when she observed the play, she noticed the cashier turning the notepad paper over, drawing little boxes, and writing in them. She asked the child what she was doing and she said, "I'm making the back of the check" (see Figure 11.2). While not understanding the reason, she knew the actions of the cashier's role in verifying the check-writer's identification by writing down driver's license and credit card numbers.

The teacher encouraged the children's literacy play by simply

Figure 11.1   Check Written by a Kindergartner

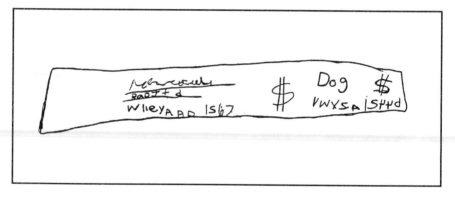

Figure 11.2   Back of Check Written by a Kindergartner

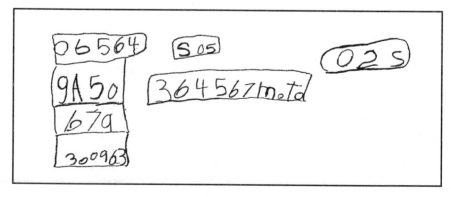

providing the raw materials of literacy. In addition to the materials just mentioned, magazines, cookbooks, newspapers, and letters were added to the housekeeping corner. The children pretended to read, both silently and aloud, and they made comments about the pictures. When writing materials were added, the children also incorporated them. They scribbled notes, pretended to do homework, and made endless lists.

While a variety of reading and writing materials are needed in the housekeeping corner, there appears to be a point at which there can be too many (Raines, 1990b). The children paid attention to the materials when there were just a few, but when a large stack of magazines and books was added, they simply moved them out of the area. Having first a few notepads, pieces of paper, and pencils or pens also appeared to be effective, while too many appeared to distract the play. In one of the classrooms, when the teacher added several notebooks and pads and lots of markers, pencils, and paper, a child stacked up all the paper, collected the markers, and took them over to the art area. Literacy materials are needed to support play, but they should not be in such abundant supply that they overwhelm the players and defeat the purpose of the play center.

Literacy role models.   In addition to adding literacy materials, a second way teachers encourage literacy play is by their interactions with the children while they are playing. It is critical, however, that Whole Language teachers be selective in interjecting themselves in the play setting, choosing only meaningful, natural interactions. For example, in the play episode with the cashier "making the back of the check," the teacher became one of the shoppers, went through the check-out line, and there informally asked the child about her writing.

Whole Language kindergarten teachers whose children come from homes where there are few books, newspapers, and magazines, and where reading and writing are not family priorities, may find that playing with the children helps them incorporate these literacy materials. Teachers should recognize that there are parents in every income bracket who do not read to their children, who do not know the importance of letting children write and scribble, and who are not good reading and writing role models. The old assumption that children who come to school with limited experiences in reading and writing all come from low-income families has been proved false.

Teachers may interject themselves into play by becoming the grandparent who reads to the children, or the mother who writes a letter, or the father who tells his children he will come out and play with them as soon as he finishes reading a particularly exciting book. One Whole Language teacher encourages her students' "pretend reading" by playing the role of a child and then asking one of the kindergartners to be a parent and read to her.

During a study of the effects of literacy materials (Raines, 1990b), one teacher added a cake-decorating book to the housekeeping center. The children looked at the pictures, but soon lost interest in the book until the teacher sat in the center and pretended to decorate a cake. The teacher read the list of ingredients aloud and checked the measurements. For several days after the teacher's presence in the center, the children pretended to decorate cakes and referred back and forth to the cookbook.

Literacy play also can be encouraged by the teacher's reading aloud. For example, Marisa was a young five-year-old who had shown little interest in books in grouptime and never went to the library corner. After the teacher asked the children to hold a doll or a stuffed animal while she read *The Teddy Bears' Picnic* (Kennedy, 1983), Marisa began reading to the teddy bears. The next day, Marisa's friend was observed reading *The Teddy Bears' Picnic* to the dolls and the stuffed animals in the housekeeping corner. Soon Marisa was imitating her friend and her teacher, but with a minor change. Her friend read other books to the pretend listeners, but Marisa reserved the bear book for the teddy bears. She carried the book with her throughout most of the freeplay periods for several days.

Favorite books become as precious to children as favorite toys. For pretend-reading behaviors, it is important that children are also allowed to read for pleasure. Obviously Marisa enjoyed *The Teddy Bears' Picnic* and had developed an attachment to the book. A less sensitive teacher might have insisted that the books stay in the library corner. Fortunately for Marisa, her Whole Language kindergarten teacher recognized how playing at reading and writing is essential for children to build their concepts of themselves as readers. This is especially important for children who have had limited experience with pretend reading and with being read to at home.

Connecting stories with the housekeeping center.   Another effective way to add a Whole Language emphasis is to connect stories with the play environment. For example, at grouptime a teacher read *The Doorbell Rang* (Hutchins, 1986) and then stretched the story into the housekeeping area by having cookie cutters, a rolling pin, a cookie sheet, and Play-Doh there. The children made cookies and pretended to have lots of people dropping by unexpectedly to share the cookies, just as it happened in the book. Good stories for young children are filled with possible play extensions. After playing out the story, they retain it, retell it, and make it their own. Because the stories in so many children's books take place in the home, the housekeeping corner lends itself to building connections between the story read and the story acted out.

Encouraging Literacy Play in the Blocks Area

Environmental print, such as that found on signs, logos, and advertisements, can be added to the blocks area to enhance children's literacy play. Since a great deal of the five-year-old's construction with blocks represents building roadways, houses, towns, cities, and shopping malls, environmental print is a natural addition. Models of traffic signs, a form of environmental print, are already found in many block areas, and more could be added.

Adding literacy materials. One teacher encouraged the children's incorporation of environmental print by decorating the trucks in the blocks area (Raines & Canady, 1989). The teacher cut construction paper into pieces that were the length of the trailers and asked the children to decorate them to make them look like the sides of real trucks. Then they taped their designs onto the trailers. Before they made their designs, they were taken in small groups to a busy street corner, where they watched for trucks with signs. The activity was not only successful as an environmental print activity, but it also captured the girls' interest and got them involved in the blocks area.

The logos and pictures of products cut from magazines and packaging can also entice more meaningful reading. For example, after building a shopping mall, a project that took several days, the children began calling parts of the mall by department store names. The observant teacher brought in ads from the Sunday newspaper, and the children cut out the department store names and taped them onto their block structures. When they could not find names they wanted, some children wrote their own, while others cut out magazine pictures of what was sold there.

Literacy role models. The teacher just described added to the play by providing the newspaper ads, but did not control the activity. In another block-building episode, the teacher helped the children understand the need for giving directions and following directions by engaging in the play with them. While the children were involved in building a rather elaborate zoo for the plastic models of wild animals they had in the classroom, the teacher pretended to be a visitor to the zoo. The teacher picked up a figure of a man and asked, "Which way to the elephants?" The zoo builder stopped, pointed, and said, "Over there, can't you see?" The teacher, moving the figure back and forth as if the man were speaking, said, "No, the wall is too tall. Is it just down this path?" The teacher continued pretending to be the visitor and asked each of the builders for directions to different animals. Finally, confronted with the problem of the visitors not knowing where the animals were, the children decided signs were needed. A combination of signs and drawings provided the directions. After the signs were made, the teacher again walked the figure of the man up and down the paths of the zoo and read the signs aloud.

Connecting stories and the blocks area.   Many of the books with stories about transportation are good ones for building connections between stories and block play, but the illustrations may prompt the connections as well. For example, a teacher read *Truck Song* (Siebert, 1984) during grouptime, showed the children the picture of the docks, and asked a child to build a dock with blocks. Then the teacher asked the truck driver to back up a truck so that it was near the docks. For several days, the block builders concentrated on building docks, backing up their 18-wheelers, and loading them, even though they had never actually seen a dock.

SUMMARY

Whole Language kindergarten teachers recognize the inherent "wholeness" of children's play. They value play because it is a naturally satisfying behavior for young children (Isenberg & Quisenberry, 1988). They protect the time for play in their schedules, and they retain in their classrooms the two centers that the children most associate with play—the housekeeping corner and the blocks area. Whole Language teachers supply the two centers with appropriate equipment and materials, as well as periodically adding other materials that extend these centers to other sociodramatic themes.

Whole Language kindergarten teachers know that blocks require adequate space, storage, and an assortment of accessories. They value block play for its curricular possibilities in science, mathematics, and social studies, but also for its developmental benefits. They are able to articulate to concerned parents and administrators the physical, social, emotional, cognitive, and language development possibilities of block play.

Whole Language kindergarten teachers recognize, as Pellegrini and Galda (1985) point out, that play involving dramatics, social interaction and symbolism has direct connections to the development of children's literate behaviors. However, Whole Language kindergarten teachers highlight these connections in the housekeeping and blocks centers by adding literacy materials, by modeling reading and writing behaviors in the play context, and by connecting the stories in books with the materials and equipment in the centers. Much of the literacy play in housekeeping and blocks is stimulated by the materials that are added. Literacy play can be described as "contagious behavior." From seeing others pretend to read, from watching real reading modeled by adults, and from making connections to stories, the children build concepts of themselves as readers, writers, and enjoyers of stories.

* 12 *

Using Whole Language to Teach Mathematics

David, Marcy, Phillipe, and Jennifer scrambled to return to the table that stood in what the teacher called the small blocks center. Marcy and Phillipe had been building an elaborate two-tower structure before the teacher called them over for grouptime. They had persuaded the teacher to let them leave their blocks intact, rather than picking them up and putting them away. David and Jennifer had also been playing at the table. David, the confident puzzle worker, was trying a difficult new puzzle. Jennifer, who was more an observer than a builder, stood at the end, randomly fingering a bristle block among the Legos. But all the attention was on Phillipe and Marcy, whose precarious structure was made by connecting slotted plastic blocks. David looked up at the tower and warned, "Watch out, it's gonna crash!"

RECOMMENDED CLASSROOM PRACTICES

Kindergartners need the fine muscle activities that small manipulative blocks and puzzles provide. They also enjoy finding solutions to problems, whether they are fitting jigsaw puzzle pieces together to make a picture or seeing how many blocks they can balance when building a tower. While teachers readily recognize the fine motor coordination possibilities of small blocks and manipulatives, many do not think of the language and mathematical possibilities for the materials.

Like all other subject areas of the kindergarten curriculum, mathematics has its own language, one that kindergarten children acquire readily. In the Whole Language kindergarten, an emphasis is placed on the language of mathematics that accompanies the solving of meaningful problems from the child's everyday world and from curricular themes or units of study. For example, math is used throughout the day in the usual classroom activities of taking a lunch count, determining how many people can be in one center at a time, and distributing napkins in a one-to-one correspondence. The Whole Language teacher involves the children in the language and problem solving that make the classroom function. When the unit is on nutrition, a count might be made of the number of different fruits in the basket on the snack table. Or, for the unit on fall, a graph might be constructed comparing leaves found on the nature walk. In addition, when mathematics manipulatives are paired with real problems to be solved, the kindergartners will find numerous ways to solve problems.

According to the appropriate-practice recommendations from the NAEYC, allowing children to select manipulative materials, providing problem-solving opportunities, and integrating learning are the three main points that teachers should keep in mind (Bredekamp, 1987). Specifically, children should "select many of their own activities from among a variety of learning areas the teacher prepares, inlcuding dramatic play, blocks, science, math, games and puzzles, books, recordings, art, and music" (p. 50). Two other recommendations are particularly significant for problem solving. First, "children are provided concrete learning activities with materials and people relevant to their own life experiences" (p. 50). Second, "children develop understanding of concepts about themselves, others, and the world around them through observation, interacting with people and real objects, and seeking solutions to concrete problems" (p. 52). In addition, reference is made to the need for integrating "learnings from math, science, social studies, health and other content areas" (p. 52).

The emphasis on materials, meaningful problem solving, and integrated experiences across subject areas is also found in the ACEI's recommendations (Moyer et al., 1987). An effective environment is described as one that "provides multiple opportunities for learning with concrete, manipulative materials that 1) are relevant to children's experiential background and 2) keep them actively engaged in learning and discovering through use of all the senses, leading to more input upon which thought is constructed" (p. 239). An emphasis on meaningfulness and the process of problem solving is also implied in the statement that an effective program, both in terms of curriculum and learning environment, is one that "responds to the needs of the children as developing, thinking individuals by focusing on the processes of learning rather than disparate skills, content and products" (p. 238). Likewise, IRA's position statement contains references to children as active participants in the learning process and to the need for integrated learnings (Early Childhood, 1988).

Therefore, in addition to insuring that children select their own materials and that opportunities for meaningful problem solving and integration of learnings are provided, the Whole Language kindergarten teacher would emphasize the language of mathematics, the descriptions of the manipulatives, and the representations children construct of their integrated learnings.

SOME OBSERVATIONS OF ACTUAL CLASSROOM PRACTICE

Children's Selection of Materials

David, Marcy, Phillipe, and Jennifer's classroom, referred to at the beginning of this chapter, met several of the criteria for good kindergarten practice. The teacher organized the classroom into learning centers and gathered the manipulatives into one area where the children could select their own materials. There was open shelving for the multitude of puzzles, games, small blocks, and other manipulatives, and space for children to work with them on the table or on the carpet near the center. The materials included those already mentioned—puzzles, Tinker Toys, Legos, connecting blocks, and bristle blocks—plus numerous others, such as small wooden logs, plastic linking blocks, parquetry cards and blocks, attribute blocks, wooden beads and strings, unifix cubes, cuisenaire rods, and one-inch cubes the teacher referred to as counting blocks. The materials were stored in plastic bins and on trays for easy sorting and returning to their appropriate places. While occasionally a puzzle piece was lost or a bristle block was found in the bin with the cuisenaire rods, for the most part the children were able to select, use, and store the materials without assistance from the adults in the classroom.

The manipulatives and mathematics center was often chosen as a tabletop activity as soon as children arrived in the morning. It also was a popular choice during center time or freeplay. Although the children were attracted to the manipulative quality of the materials in the center, there appeared to be very little interaction between the teacher and the children. The children had limited understanding of the mathematical concepts represented by the materials. The teacher seemed content to have the materials used primarily for fine motor development.

Opportunities for Problem Solving

During a week of observations in the classroom, it was noted that the teacher provided many opportunities for meaningful problem solving. At the beginning of circletime, the children looked at their attendance chart and counted how many children were absent. The teacher then generalized their finding by having them tell her how many snacks would be needed, how many chairs should be placed at the snack tables, and how many children's coats were in the closet. Another example of excellent problem solving occurred when the teacher asked a child to bring construction paper for each person at the art table. During the morning group, the child counted five children at the art table, then found five sheets of paper. In the afternoon session, a child in the prenumber stage went back and forth from shelf to table, distributing the paper one piece at a time by making a one-to-one correspondence, one sheet of paper per child.

Integration of Learning Across Subject Areas and Themes

The teacher used mathematical concepts functionally throughout the day to solve routine problems, especially emphasizing mathematical terms during grouptime. For instance, after the children's nature walk (when they collected leaves), the teacher told the children to make stacks of their favorite leaves. During the process, the children made comparisons, formed classifications, and ordered or sequenced by size. Although the activity encouraged the children to use constructive thinking, the teacher seemed more concerned with the end product of each child making a set of favorite leaves for the display table, and so paid little attention to the underlying thought processes. In such a case, the science lesson can also become a mathematics lesson, if the teacher recognizes the constructive thought processes that are occurring, calls attention to them by having the children tell what they were doing, and uses the appropriate mathematical language to describe what is happening.

THINKING PROCESSES

Science and social studies themes, which are the organizational units of the kindergarten classroom, employ the same thinking processes as mathematics. These can occur even before children have clear concepts of numbers. For example, one child who was not yet a "counter" made quite a tall stack of sycamore leaves, which were large and easy to handle. When he made a stack of dogwood leaves, which were actually greater in number but did not stack very tall, he was convinced that he had many more sycamore leaves. Even when the "foster grandparent" volunteer helped him count the two stacks, the child remained unconvinced. He demonstrated, as most preoperational thinkers do, that he was "perception oriented" and so could only center on the attribute that provided the strongest perceptual evidence—the largeness of the sycamore leaves and their greater height when stacked together (Osborn & Osborn, 1983). In addition, even though he counted both stacks with the volunteer, the numbers appeared to have little meaning to him.

The thinking processes of forming sets by sorting the leaves (comparing and then classifying) were evidence of very deliberate, thoughtful examination of the leaves, which were to become the specimens for the science table. Some children were also observed ordering or seriating by arranging leaves according to size. One little girl made an array, a pattern of leaves, which she displayed in groups of threes. The children's thinking, even without the concept of number, was appropriate for their age and their preoperational stage of development. Some preoperational youngsters are able to conserve number, that is, to hold constant in their minds that the quantity remains the same even when the objects are rearranged (Kamii, 1982).

As preoperational thinkers begin to construct number concepts and conserve numbers, they become "counters." This occurs through numerous activities where they actively manipulate objects and participate with their teachers, other adults, and fellow students as they count to express quantities (Osborn & Osborn, 1983). This involves using the same mathematical thinking processes as before, but with the descriptive language of numbers added. Children continue to sort by comparing attributes and to classify, seriate, and form patterns, but now they also count the objects in sets.

Recognizing the Language of Mathematics
As the Descriptive Language of Thinking

Looking back at the scene of the four children who were at the small block table, it is clear the youngsters were developing mathematical understandings. David, the puzzle worker, was learning basic geometric concepts as he examined each shape, determined how much space it would occupy, and tried to figure out where it might fit. Jennifer, who was fingering the bristle blocks among the smooth Legos, was actually sorting by a tactic attribute, and Marcy and Phillipe were involved in a sophisticated physics experiment. They were creating equivalencies to balance their structure. First, Marcy fit a small plastic circle into her tower, then Phillipe added the same-sized circle to his side, and the process continued until there was a problem to be solved. Eventually the remaining pieces were not equivalent in size and weight. When Marcy connected a large plastic square to her side of the structure, it leaned over, but Phillipe added two small round pieces to the slots on his side, and the twin-tower structure seemed balanced again. When Marcy then held onto the structure and attached a large plastic cylinder into the slot, the twin towers topped over with a crash as the connections came apart.

Problems in geometry and physics and in making comparisons of attributes sound like sophisticated mathematics for five-year-olds. In reality, they are not. Some teachers fail to recognize that the every-day manipulative materials that comprise their small-blocks center are really providing children with the sensory and motor input—the foundational experiences—upon which later mathematical under-standings are built. Even many teachers who do see this process, and who have studied young children's development as logico-mathematical thinkers, still grapple with the question of how much to add to the experience by modeling, or by talking with the child about what is occurring, or by asking the child to describe or answer questions about the task.

Early childhood educators vary in the range of language interactions they provide. Some leave the mediation and language associated with the task entirely up to the child, while others place more of an emphasis on enriching the environment through description, question, and dialogue. Teachers who are concerned with the main perceptual task may demonstrate how to build a tower and then ask the child to build a tower just like the one the teacher has built (Montessori, 1964). Other teachers will allow the tower building to continue without any discussion of what has occurred, unless the child initiates the interaction. The children will build and rebuild the tower for as long as the activity sustains their attention. If the activity has captured a great deal of attention, the Whole Language teacher is likely to interact with the children, asking them to describe what happened, or challenging the thinkers to see if they can construct a tower that will not fall over, or suggesting that they reconstruct a fallen tower to see what caused it to fall. In any case, the language used to describe the activity always grows out of the child's own interests, rather than from predetermined outcomes (Copple et al., 1979).

Constructing Mathematical Problems and Solutions

The Whole Language perspective of mathematical problem solving is most like the Piagetian constructivist view. The child develops logical thought from numerous sensory and perceptual encounters and interactions with the physical world. Language then is used by the child as she acts upon the physical world, observes actions, and clarifies reactions. For young thinkers, language naturally accompanies activity; it is used to formulate questions and to reflect upon the actions they have experienced. The Whole Language teacher therefore seeks language interactions that grow out of meaningful, often playful activities, such as those of David, Marcy, Phillipe, and Jennifer. The teacher might ask the children to tell what happened—to describe the physical occurrence—and then pose a stimulating problem based on their answers. "Do you think you could build another tower in the same way, up to the point where it fell over?" or, "Can you build a tower and then show me how to make it topple over?" Obviously, not every physical interaction with the manipulatives needs to be discussed and extended , but the teacher can be sensitive to the challenge the children have created for themselves—in this case, "to build two towers just alike"—and can choose to extend their activity by asking leading questions.

While the teacher's interaction with David, the puzzle builder, might be more casual, the results could be similar. For example, suppose the teacher invited Jennifer, a frustrated puzzle worker, to watch and listen to David as he shared his expertise. Often young children know intuitively what to do, but may not express verbally what they know unless asked. David's teacher might say, "Show Jennifer how you work a puzzle," and David would do just that. He would say, "I do it like this" and proceed to work the puzzle without verbalizing any of his actions. But if the teacher questioned, "David, when you work a puzzle for the first time, what do you do?" he probably would say, "I look at the picture on the front." If the teacher continues to question, "What do you do next?" David might state, "I dump out all the pieces, then I turn them over. I put in the pieces around the edges first."

While David may never have verbalized his puzzle-working strategies before, the questions prompt some reflective thinking on his part and provide concrete suggestions for Jennifer. She can then attempt a difficult puzzle while the teacher asks her what David suggested she do first. With the teacher assisting Jennifer through each step by asking questions, and with David's modeling accompanied by simple verbal instructions, Jennifer can learn a great deal about the theory of puzzle working. For her actually to become a better puzzle worker, however, it is necessary for her to construct the puzzle for herself and verbalize the steps as she goes along. The difference between the Whole Language teacher and many other language-oriented teachers is that the former finds ways for children to construct their own answers, while the latter tend simply to provide the answers—in this case, directions about how to work a puzzle.

Encouraging Descriptive and Specific Language

Perhaps one of the easiest ways for teachers to begin using mathematics language is to begin to be more descriptive about color, shape, size, and quality, as well as about measurements of quantity such as weight, volume, and capacity. It is the position of Whole Language researchers that the language of the adults in the child's environment strongly influences the child's language. If teachers become more specific in their own use of language, as well as ask for more descriptive information from children, then the children's language will become more specific and descriptive. Because the physical world of the well-equipped kindergarten classroom is filled with materials for the child to manipulate, one of the beginning steps toward more descriptive mathematical language is to have children use and describe more specifically the materials in the small-blocks center.

In David, Marcy, Phillipe, and Jennifer's classroom, the construction blocks and puzzles received adequate attention from the children. The one-inch-cube blocks were the ones the teacher referred to as the counting blocks, and she often used those in her functional problem solving for classroom routine activities, but few of the other materials were used for their mathematical purposes. The attribute blocks, the unifix cubes, the parquetry blocks, and the cuisenaire rods received little attention except for their occasional use for building.

Attribute blocks are a set of wooden blocks containing a variety of shapes, with each shape appearing in small and large sizes and in different colors. The blocks can thus be sorted and described by shape, size, and color, as well as by combinations of attributes. For example, one child might place all the red blocks together, while another might place all the square blocks together, and a third child with more advanced thinking might group all the small blocks together regardless of their color or shape. The materials are excellent for children to sort, first by matching blocks to others of like shape, color, or size. Children can also use them to begin to name attributes and then to discriminate or sort according to an attribute the teacher requests. The hierarchy of tasks supports the expansion of the child's specific descriptive language.

Attribute blocks, colored wooden beads and strings, and parquetry blocks can also be used for patterning activities. Following the same sequence of first matching, then labeling, and finally designing or constructing their own patterns, young children gain more control of descriptive language. In addition to the pattern cards that often accompany parquetry blocks, another child can make a pattern of colored wooden beads and then have a friend match it or replicate it. At the labeling stage, the teacher can ask the child to identify the pattern that has been created (e.g., one red bead, one blue bead, two green beads, one yellow bead). Next, the teacher, or children working in pairs, can verbalize a pattern and the child who is stringing the beads will select from an assortment and discriminate which beads fit the pattern. More complicated patterns also can be created, using open, repeated, and closed sequences. The problem solving represented by the attribute blocks, parquetry blocks, and bead stringing can be enhanced by descriptive and specific language.

Using Materials Designed for Mathematical Representations

Mathematical materials can be used to represent solutions to problems. Unifix cubes, often associated with counting, can be used by students in the prenumber stage to establish one-to-one correspondence. Unifix cubes are usually sets of plastic cubes of the same size or unit which can be fixed together by a plastic connector on the ends. As children count, they connect the blocks, so they stay together. A teacher was observed constructing a simple graph using unifix cubes, without using any numbers. She asked the children if there were more girls than boys in the class. Then she gave each girl a blue unifix cube and each boy a red cube. The girls connected their cubes together and the boys connected theirs. When placed at the edge of the table, the blue unifix cube line was longer. The children visually compared the lines, without counting the units, and determined the answer.

Cuisenaire rods are made of wood and are also based on units of measurement. The smallest rod is 1 cm long and is a natural wood color. The other rods increase in length by increments of 1 cm, and each new length is painted another color. Thus the 1-cm length represents 1, the 2-cm length represents 2, the 3-cm length represents 3, and so on, up through 10 cm. Ten of the 10-cm rods make up a flat of 100, and 10 flats make a cube of 1,000. Cuisenaire rods are excellent devices to help children build concrete associations when they count. However, like unifix cubes, they need to be used in the kindergarten classroom to solve meaningful problems. The cuisenaire rods are best used in helping children to see equivalencies, such as that the 5-cm rod is the same length as five of the 1-cm rods. The rods can be used to create graphs as well.

Standard and Nonstandard Measurements

A popular unit that involves young children in nonstandard measurement is a unit called "Sunshine and Shadow." Children created shadows with flashlights, singing about sunshine and shadows, and drawing outlines around shadows they made of different shapes. The activity that captured their attention the most was "string a shadow" (Raines & Canady, 1989). The teacher, an aide, a parent volunteer, and the children stood on the sidewalk that bordered their playground and looked at their shadows, early in the morning, at noon, and just before they left to go home. At the last shadow-viewing time, each child was paired with a friend who stretched a length of string as long as the person's shadow was, cut the string, and placed it in an envelope. The strings were then sent home with the children, for them to tell their parents what they represented (Raines, 1990a).

Strings, yarn, lengths of construction paper, a chain of paper clips, and other nonstandard measurement devices need to be used often to help children learn to represent lengths and heights. Nonstandard measurements are best until the idea of measuring is clearly established and children understand the concept of number (Robinson, Mahaffey, & Nelson, 1975). Then the standard linear devices—rulers, yardsticks, and metersticks—as well as liquid measurement devices can be used. Researchers have found that children's familiarity with standard measuring devices is a product of age, mental ability, and socioeconomic level (Robinson et al., 1975). Some kindergartners may be more ready for experiences with standard devices than others who are just becoming acquainted with the process of measuring.

One exception to this advice is in cooking, where exactness is required for the recipe. When preparing snacks or baking, emphasize the measurements by placing a strip of masking tape around the outside of the measuring cups so that the level can be easily seen by the child making the measurement and by others who are observing. There are numerous cookbooks for young children which provide excellent, meaningful measurement activities.

Sand and Water: Natural Mathematic Materials

While young children are thrilled to find that their teachers actually encourage them to play in sand and water, few teachers think of these natural materials as mathematical manipulatives. Quite aside from the imaginative play that transpires as a child pours water from container to container, or sifts sand or pours it through a funnel, children learn about quantities through the sensorimotor input that results from these activities. Sensory learning about quantities provides a foundation for children to begin to grasp the concepts associated with equivalencies of lengths, weights, and volume.

The sand-and-water table, a long rectangular frame around a fiberglass tub which is elevated on legs to be the correct height for kindergartners, was once a staple in all classrooms for five-year-olds. Unfortunately, as more paper-and-pencil tasks have been included in the curriculum, fewer of these versatile pieces of equipment are found in classrooms. Perhaps if teachers explained their value for teaching mathematics, principals, school directors, and parents could appreciate their significance. Teachers who use the sand-and-water table effectively can alternate filling it with sand for a week or two, then with water. Other materials may also be used, such as rice, unpopped popcorn, beans, and styrofoam pellets. However, many teachers voice concerns that, with so many hungry children in the world, food should not be used for purposes other than eating; and that styrofoam is an environmental problem. So, the best materials continue to be natural sand and water.

Teachers who observe children's activities at the sand-and-water table can see evidence of the children's evolving sense of equivalencies and inequivalencies in length, weight, and volume, among many other comparative types of measurements. To the untrained observer, the children appear simply to be playing in the water as they pour from several small containers into a large pitcher and vice versa, or as they squeeze water from a liquid detergent bottle and from a mustard bottle, or as they drip water from an eyedropper. The children are experiencing, observing, exploring possibilities, and eventually experimenting with and deciding about equivalencies.

During the first few days, the physical activity and coordination of pouring and controlling the water consume the children's attention. Later, after experiencing the water and the containers, the children begin to build certain associations. One child may count the number of plastic cups of water it takes to fill the half-gallon pitcher, then proceed to take the top off the detergent bottle, repeatedly fill it, and empty it into the same pitcher, counting the number of bottles full it takes. The child's sense of equivalent measurement evolves naturally from this activity. One observant teacher who recognized a child's interest in making comparisons said, "Craig, I wonder how many times you would have to fill the mustard bottle and empty it into the pitcher to fill it to the top?" Craig quickly began to solve the problem.

A few days later, during art activities, when the children were using plastic mustard bottles full of paint to create multicolored patterns of lines, Craig said, "It takes longer for this paint to come out." The teacher asked, "Longer than what?" and Craig replied, "It takes longer to get this paint out than it does to get all the water out of the bottle." The teacher complimented the child on his observation and asked him to show the other children what he meant. Craig demonstrated by first squeezing the water from a mustard bottle, then squeezing the paint from a bottle the teacher had filled. While the teacher was sure Craig understood, she wanted to involve the interested onlookers, so she asked the observers to try his experiment. She told Craig it was hard to remember which went faster, and she asked him if he could think of a way to have a race that the children could watch. Craig organized the experiment by having one child squeeze the paint bottle and one squeeze the water bottle. He gave the signal: "One, two, three, go." After the race was over, Li said, "See, Craig was right. The paint is slow," and the other experimenter chimed in, "Yeah, and the water is fast." While no one seemed interested in pursuing why paint takes longer, everyone seemed interested in trying Craig's experiment, so the teacher brought more water bottles and paint for them to use. When more children came to try the squeeze-bottle race, the teacher began counting while the liquids were flowing. The children then had some way of measuring the length of time, or associating the length of time with the counting.

One teacher's favorite extension of water play was a "sink-or-float" experiment, which emphasized several mathematical and scientific understandings. After the children had several days to explore and enjoy the water table, the teacher added new items and simply asked, "Which ones of these sink, and which ones float?" The children proceeded to test the buoyancy of each item, even though they didn't know that term. After their experimenting, the teacher asked them to think of a way to tell the other children which items sink and which ones float. One child said, "Just tell them to watch us at the water table." Another child said, "We can put everything that floats in this dishpan and sinking things in this one." Another one replied, "Make a list." At the next grouptime, the teacher let the three experimenters report their findings in three different ways—demonstrating, sorting into dishpans, and writing a list.

Later the teacher posed another interesting question: "How can we make these containers that float sink to the bottom of the water table?" The experimenters tried filling them with sand, pebbles, and styrofoam pellets. When their results were in, the teacher again extended the hands-on experiment and posed the question of how to tell the other children or how to represent what we know about making the containers sink.

The hands-on water play and water experiments gave the children the sensory input necessary to make comparisons of volume and weights and even the temporal relationship of offering lengths of time needed to empty various squeeze bottles. As the children formed the set of objects that floated and the set of objects that sank (or, as the children often said, "sinked"), some of the children counted the objects and compared, while others simply looked inside the dishpan and perceptually realized there were many more objects that floated. The concept of number could have been added to each experience, but their success in providing both scientific and mathematical understandings was not dependent upon numbers.

There are numerous sand activities that provide children with opportunities for making comparisons of weight and volume, as well as for understanding equivalencies and inequivalencies. After looking at the pictures in Crews's book, *Flying* (1986), the children decided to make a town with a river flowing through it. They used the sand table and with their hands made a squiggley river. When they poured water into the trench, their river kept disappearing. Finally, after deciding the sand was drinking the water, the children put three dishpans end to end and poured water in them to form their river. They still did not seem pleased, as the river looked red like the plastic dishpans, wasn't long enough, and didn't flow. The next day the teacher brought in a long, narrow, blue tray used to wet wallpaper. Even before grouptime, when the teacher planned to have the children brainstorm about what the tray could be used for, one of the children took the tray to the sand table, removed the three dishpans, and inserted and filled the wallpaper tray. Much to the satisfaction of the children, their new river was long and narrow and was blue like the one in their storybook. What's more, they could make it flow, by tipping up one end of the tray.

Noting that these students, like most other five-year-olds, were able to compare lengths more easily than weight or volume, the teacher began using the sand table to encourage perceptual awareness (Raines & Canady, 1989). First the children were asked to fill each hand with dry sand, lift their hands up out of the sand table, and using their hands like the arms of a balance, decide if one hand was heavier than the other or felt the same. Then the teacher had the children wet the sand on one side of the sand table, fill one hand with wet sand and the other with dry sand, and compare the weights as before. Later they compared a handful of sand to a handful of pebbles, and then cotton balls, and then dried beans. The teacher realized that, before the children could use the concept of balance effectively for science and mathematics experiences, they had to have a perception of what balanced weights meant, and that they could use the best perceptual learning device available—their own bodies.

Sand and water are natural mathematical materials because they offer so many comparison possibilities, and this is true whether the children are already conserving number or are in the prenumber stage. The effective kindergarten teacher provides them with these materials for experiencing and exploring, but also provokes the kindergartners into thoughtful problem solving which requires their attention to the perceptions of equivalencies. Whenever possible, the teacher adds number concepts to the experience by using number words, writing the numerals, and supporting and reinforcing the children's counting as it relates to problem solving.

REPRESENTATIONS OF SCIENCE LEARNINGS USING MATHEMATICS MANIPULATIVES

The sand- and water-table activities are indices of young children's evolving understandings of length, weight, and volume, which are measurement terms associated with science. The science area of the classroom also is an appropriate place for small-blocks activities, because the manipulatives can represent number, quality, or quantity.

The science display table is an excellent place for combining scientific understandings, as well as using numbers to represent what one has learned. Teachers can help their children use the counting blocks or unifix cubes to represent one-to-one correspondence and to provide practice in counting. For example, one teacher read *Chickens Aren't the Only Ones* (Heller, 1981) to help the children begin to associate which animals had their babies from laying eggs. Before reading the book, the teacher had the children think of all the animals they knew that laid eggs. The children thought of birds, ducks, and chickens. The teacher printed the words as the children said them. Next they were asked to count the number of items on the list, and the teacher wrote the numbers 1, 2, and 3 beside the items. The teacher and the children then reread the list, but this time, as they said the animals, the teacher placed a unifix cube on the table. The children counted the cubes, and the cubes represented how many they could remember.

After reading *Chickens Aren't the Only Ones*, the teacher asked the children to think of all the animals they knew that were "oviparous," as the book had taught them this scientific term for laying eggs. As they shouted out the long list of 11 others they recalled, the teacher wrote the names of the animals on a chart tablet. As they reread the names, the teacher placed one unifix cube on the table for each egg-layer the children named. One of the children who was already a counter said, "We thought of a whole lot more," then came up and touched each cube and counted to 11. All the children agreed. The teacher then compared how many they said at first. Without extending the problem to subtraction, the teacher graphically represented the 11 and the 3 by placing them side by side on the table. The book, the chart, and the unifix cubes stayed on the science table for the entire unit on oviparous animals. In addition, the teacher brought in specimens of different-sized real eggs, and the children shaped Play-Doh eggs to correspond in size to the pictures in the book, from the tiny hummingbird egg to the huge ostrich egg (Raines & Canady, 1989).

Throughout the entire unit, the children manipulated the cubes to symbolize the quantity of egg-layers. The children looked at the pictures in the book from front to back, and, with each turn of the page, with each new animal, they placed a unifix cube on the table. At the end of the book, some of the children counted the cubes, while others simply made the one-to-one correspondence. Some counted the pictures, then counted the cubes to see if they got it right. Other children manipulated the objects, counted them, and wrote the numerals to represent them.

The teacher could have used cuisenaire rods for the graphic display, or could have strung a bead on a string for each animal mentioned, or could have stacked bristle blocks together; it really doesn't matter which manipulative is used, but it does matter that the teacher helped the children to symbolize their learning. The representation was a simple one-to-one correspondence, but five-year-olds need many of these types of experiences to help them begin to symbolize quantity. The science display is an excellent example of the teacher's use of real objects and abstract ones, or models. There were real eggs as well as semiabstract models such as Play-Doh eggs and pictures of animals, and the unifix cubes used to represent each animal constituted an abstract model. The printed words, the printed numerals, and the cubes were associated with each other, to help the children to build representations.

NUMBER CONCEPTS AND WRITING NUMERALS

Whole Language teachers think of numerals as language symbols and help their children associate the numerals and their corresponding number words with functional problems in the classroom environment and with activities associated with the themes or units of study. They also use them as manipulative representations. Whole Language kindergarten teachers expect children to grow in their use and understanding of numerals, as they grow in all other areas of symbolizing.

Children who are aware of numerals may incorporate them in their own printing at the writing center, without any association except that they have seen these graphic forms. Other children will write numerals first to tell how old they are. Most children will already know the number words and use them in their speaking vocabularies, before they use them correctly in their writing. All will invariably count by rote before they understand the concept of number.

Similarly, young children will write and talk about numbers and use numerals in their play activities. At times they will write numerals that indicate they understand number concepts, while on other occasions they appear to write the numerals simply to support their play. For example, while pretending to run a bakery, one child took her customer's order, wrote the numeral 5 on a small sheet of notepaper, and told her partner, "Quick, go get five cookies." Later, she wrote a string of fives on the same-sized paper and said, "She bought a million cookies."

When children's discussions contain number words during grouptime, during planned mathematics lessons in small groups, and during interactions with children during freeplay or center time, Whole Language kindergarten teachers call attention to the specificity and descriptiveness of language. Being specific and descriptive requires children to compare, classify, seriate, and describe. Descriptions of sets naturally moves to counting for comparison purposes.

Whole Language kindergarten teachers build concepts of number and use numerals and words in their presentations to the whole class and in interactions in small groups and with individuals. After children begin making one-to-one correspondence, teachers also provide many opportunties for children to count, read number words, and write numerals. The classroom must contain many practice materials for counting real objects and the symbols of those objects, such as mathematic manipulatives. There also must be opportunity for children to read the number words and associate the numerals, as well as to write the numerals on their own. However, even Whole Language teachers, who recognize the need for and value of practice, focus primarily on real problem solving. They use numerals in their own writing of group experience charts and in creating graphs associated with science themes, and they find many ways to make explicit their own use of numbers in the operation of the classroom.

SUMMARY

Whole Language kindergarten teachers keep small blocks in their classrooms because of their value for fine motor development, as well as for demonstration and manipulation to illustrate mathematical concepts. Direct instruction in prenumber and number activities does occur in the Whole Language kindergarten; however, it grows from meaningful problem solving which arises from everyday functions of the classroom, from materials and experiences that the children select for themselves, and from the interesting or captivating activities teachers design as a part of their units of study.

Whole Language teachers build connections among the underlying thinking processes of comparing, sequencing, and ordering, which children engage in naturally when they manipulate materials (Gibb & Castaneda, 1975). The teachers elicit specific and descriptive language from the children to express what their senses and perceptions tell them. Similarly, teachers find ways to extend the activities by posing interesting and challenging questions which by their very nature will include mathematical statements of the answers. Problem solving, however, is not relegated to the small-manipulatives and mathematics center, but is integrated across the curriculum. Many teachers are able to build connections between science activities and displays and the children's understanding and use of numbers.

Whole Language kindergarten teachers know young children need much practice with the language and symbols of mathematics, but this practice is never the focus of the mathematics curriculum. Practice in matching; in describing or naming; and in discriminating attributes, number words, and numerals is made possible through many manipulative and sensory materials, not isolated paper-and-pencil tasks. Teachers know that young children construct their own understanding of mathematical concepts and that the teacher's role is to provide the experiences and language that support and challenge the young thinker. Kindergartners will use the language and written symbols appropriately when they construct the underlying meaning for themselves in an environment that supports them as thinkers.

∗ 13 ∗

Parents and the
Whole Language Kindergarten

Kindergarten teachers have always felt a great sense of responsibility for communicating with the parents of their students. Every year, and particularly in years when the teacher plans to make significant changes in the curriculum, communication with parents on an individual and on a group basis is absolutely essential. Parents have a right to be informed about the curriculum, the social and emotional climate in the classroom, and the cognitive demands, as well as their individual child's growth in all areas of development. Parents have the right to know that their child is in a kindergarten with a teacher who is well informed, able to communicate about the curriculum, and willing to assume both the responsibilities and privileges of providing a learning environment that is developmentally appropriate for five-year-olds.

Whole Language kindergarten teachers are keenly aware of the importance of the home environment in young children's beginning reading and writing experiences. Many have acquired their knowledge of emergent literacy by studying the research conducted in home settings where youngsters have learned to read and write naturally (Taylor, 1983). However, as Lesley Morrow (1989) points out, the term *natural* when applied to readers and writers implies that the children accomplished literacy on their own, when in reality they were supported in their efforts by parents who communicated with them. They were also surrounded by literacy materials and lived in an emotional climate where they were free to risk making mistakes.

The basic principles of a Whole Language kindergarten come from these home studies and from descriptions of other environments rich in literacy materials (Holdaway, 1979). If teachers are to support children in their development as readers and writers, they must create a kindergarten environment with the same qualities found in the homes of "natural" readers and writers, the environment where children can communicate freely, where their questions will be answered, and where information will be provided in as meaningful a context as is possible. The children will be surrounded with interesting literacy materials, including books, magazines, pictures, and environmental print, as well as the tools and materials for writing. They will be encouraged to experiment and to take risks without an overcorrecting adult to criticize them. Instead they will be supported by an adult who recognizes that their emergence as readers and writers is a process similar to their development as speakers and listeners. Parents need to be aware that reading and writing emerge in natural stages, similar to the stages of speaking and listening, and that in a rich interactive environment children do learn to speak and listen. Likewise, in the rich literacy environment of the kindergarten, children will learn to read and write. In fact, as already stated, all five-year-olds have already begun the literacy process before they come to kindergarten. It is imperative that Whole Language teachers communicate the importance of the home environment to the children's continued success in school.

PARENTAL RIGHTS AND CONCERNS

The major concerns most parents have are whether or not their child will receive the personal attention he needs and whether he will be prepared for future success in school (Fields, 1988). The position papers from the NAEYC, ACEI, and IRA that form the basis for the recommendations for this book provide teachers with excellent descriptions of what constitutes quality programs. While copies of these documents certainly can be made available to parents, their understanding of what is "developmentally appropriate practice" can also be achieved by visiting good kindergarten classrooms.

Informing Parents About Developmentally Appropriate Practices

Some parents may not have attended kindergarten as children, and many who did attend were not in developmentally oriented classrooms. These parents' impressions of what constitutes a kindergarten program today may come from their initial contacts during the enrollment time in the spring or fall. If enrollment is held in the spring, teachers need to have each parent and child come to the classroom and stay at least through one grouptime and one freeplay or learning-center time. The teacher can ask the parent to write down any questions that may arise and arrange to have the aide take over the classroom for a few minutes at the end of the visit, to free the teacher to answer the parents' questions. The observations give the parents a chance to see how well five-year-olds—some of whom will be six years old by then—are progressing, and they can visualize their child making similar strides. A collection of newsletters to parents from the previous year should be made available, to help parents understand the goals and activities of a Whole Language kindergarten. The newsletters also help parents to understand what happens over the course of the year and establish the need for parental participation and set the tone of cooperation.

For parents who enroll their child in the fall, additional parent–teacher discussion and written information may be needed to help them understand the goals of a Whole Language kindergarten. At the large group meeting at the beginning of the year, parents from the previous years can be invited to share their children's success stories in the Whole Language program. These parents are always eager to share samples of their child's writing, their excitement about reading, and the changes that occurred over the course of the kindergarten year.

A parent information center can be created outside the classroom door, with a bulletin board, a display table, and a scrapbook of pictures from the previous year showing happy, enthusiastic learners using the centers in the classroom. Under the collection of pictures for each center, the teacher can write a few brief statements about the value of the materials and equipment in each area. Fall-orientation parents also need copies of the previous year's newsletters and any other brochures or handouts written specifically for parents.

KEEPING PARENTS INFORMED

An important element in the ongoing success of a Whole Language kindergarten is for teachers to insure that each parent is well informed at the beginning of the year and continues to be informed throughout the year. Although large-group presentations are needed for parents' meetings, teachers should plan regular meetings with parents on an individual basis. Regardless of how successful a Whole Language kindergarten program may be, teachers must always be aware that individual parents' primary concerns are with their own child's experience in that program. The Whole Language kindergarten program stresses the individuality of each child and allows each child to progress at her own rate. It is essential that all parents understand this characteristic of the program.

The parents' meetings should be conducted in the kindergarten classroom. Parents should be given a copy of the daily schedule and given a tour of the room. The teacher needs to explain the materials in each center, why they were selected, and how they fit into an integrated curriculum. Although the teaching of isolated reading and writing skills is not part of the Whole Language kindergarten program, parents are often skills oriented and need to know that skills will be learned. By examining the writing samples of previous years' students and the literacy materials in the classroom, they can gain a better understanding of the processes. Parents also need to know that, when they read to their children at home and when they encourage their children to experiment with writing, the children are learning "basic skills."

Parents need to know the kinds of materials their children will be bringing home. Teachers should explain the difference between the "worksheet" approach and what is meant by Whole Language. If necessary, teachers can show the parents a sample skills worksheet and then tell them how this skill will be learned in a Whole Language classroom. From the beginning of the year, parents need to be informed about how they can extend the experiences their child is having. A good place to begin is to talk with them about environmental print. They can help construct a bulletin board of environmental print that their kindergartners can already read. Parents can send in labels, cereal boxes, wrappers, and other environmental print that they notice their child reading. Many parents are unaware of the importance of environmental print in their child's early reading experiences.

After talking with the parents about the importance of reading to their children every day, teachers can lead the parents through a sample lesson of a shared reading experience with a big book or a predictable book. At subsequent parents' meetings, teachers can explain how young children's interests in books develop and how the books support the social studies and science themes that are the organizing units of the curriculum.

As their children become immersed in the language- and literacy-enriched kindergarten, many parents will begin to have questions about their children's writing. Whole Language kindergarten teachers often find it necessary not only to plan a large-group meeting on the topic of children's writing, where many examples of children's writing are discussed, but to summarize periodically the main points in a newsletter to parents.

The terms *Whole Language* and *emergent literacy* are new to many educators and certainly will be new to most parents. For the most part, parents are not aware of the extensive research data and professional literature that have led to the reshaping of kindergartens into Whole Language classrooms. Therefore, it is important that teachers continue to answer parents' questions and to plan for additional observations to keep parents informed of their children's successes.

ASSESSING PROGRESS IN THE WHOLE LANGUAGE KINDERGARTEN

Teachers who are planning to incorporate more of a Whole Language emphasis in their kindergartens will want to keep parents informed, not only of the goals of the program, but also of their own expectations and the children's progress. Parents need to realize that children come to school at different levels of literacy development and that an important objective of the Whole Language kindergarten program is to offer activities and instruction based on each child's needs. Parents who have provided a rich language environment for their child, where reading and writing have been given a high priority, need to recognize that their child has already been enrolling in a Whole Language program, even before coming to school. It is essential that parents understand that the Whole Language kindergarten is designed to help children from literacy-rich home environments to continue the development that has already begun, while providing less fortunate children with similarly rich experiences.

Parents have heard of the importance of reading to their children and will soon lose their apprehension concerning "basic-skills" learning when they witness the enthusiasm their children have for reading and writing. The children's progress is measured to a large degree by how well they understand the literacy process. Parents need to be made aware of how the observant teacher assesses literacy development, from their child's listening to "whole" stories being read; from the child's growing ability to write and to understand the process of becoming an author; and from the child's evolving sense of story, which includes story recall and comprehension through drama, puppetry, and other forms of story retellings. Many parents will need the teacher's guidance in making the transition from a skills orientation to a Whole Language attitude. Parents who insist on perfect word-by-word reading and correct spelling during their child's initial attempts to read and write need to be aware that they are working at cross-purposes with the Whole Language kindergarten teacher, who is stressing communication and comprehension, not perfect form.

SEARCHING FOR A MEANS OF COMMUNICATION

Many kindergarten teachers agree that a major problem in explaining the program, reporting children's progress, and enlisting the support of parents is that the parents of the children who are in the most need of help are the ones who do not come to group meetings and who fail to show up for conferences. Many efforts must be made to establish communication with these parents. Often the reason for the parents' lack of participation is not a lack of concern. It may be because they are working during the meeting times, or cannot afford a babysitter, or have unpleasant associations with school, or have such poor language skills that they feel they would not benefit from a meeting. Whatever the obstacle, teachers must continue to find ways to communicate with these parents, either through phone calls, another parent volunteer, or a home visit.

CONFERRING WITH PARENTS

In a Whole Language kindergarten, there are many ways to collect information about a child's progress, to be shared with parents. One of the most successful techniques kindergarten teachers use is to collect samples of a child's work, date the samples, and write anecdotal notes on the back. The resulting portfolio provides the teacher and the parents with a base for discussing the child's progress as an artist and as a writer. Observation notes of the child's listening behaviors and interest in books and stories, as well as notations on story retellings through drama, puppetry, and flannel board stories, can help parents realize that their child is comprehending well.

Although the portfolio provides important concrete and anecdotal examples of a child's literacy progress, the broad areas of a child's cognitive, language, socioemotional, and physical development also should be discussed. By explaining the child's activities throughout a typical day, each area of development can be discussed. The teacher can begin by mentioning the small motor activity the child chooses when entering the classroom, discuss how well the child participates during grouptime, mention the child's choices for free-play or learning-center activities, and continue with a description of the typical day. In addition, parents want to know about their child's friends and social interactions. While some parents may not think to ask about physical development, the teacher should also make observations about the child's fine and gross motor development. To help parents get some indication of the child's communication abilities, the teacher can discuss the child's listening and speaking. Notes on the child's interest in books, on writing samples, and on how well the child is able to represent what has been learned will help parents to see their child's progress in beginning symbolization and problem solving.

In a Whole Language kindergarten, teachers must continue to stress with parents that the progress their child is making should not be compared to the other children, because of the vast differences in children's abilities, home literacy, and preschool experiences. Unfortunately, many parents will insist on comparing their children with others in the classroom, but teachers should likewise insist on discouraging comparison and stressing the individual progress of each child. While many Whole Language kindergarten programs do not test children at all, if testing is required by the center or school district, parents should be informed of the test dates, what the test is designed to measure, and the strengths and weaknesses of the instrument.

If there is a serious problem or if a concern is brought up in the parents' meeting, rather than running overtime in a single conference, the teacher needs to plan a follow-up meeting and not keep other parents waiting. If needed, other resource people who have speical expertise can help answer the parents' questions, but it is most important that teachers not abdicate their responsibility for the child if another professional is brought in. Parents need reassurance that the entire team will work with them to solve problems collectively.

COMMUNICATING AS AN ONGOING PROCESS

Whole Language kindergarten teachers understand that children who live and learn in a rich language, literacy, and literature environment come to "own" the communication process. However, their ownership takes time and nurturing. Likewise, communication between the teacher and the parents is built over time. The enthusiasm, warmth, confidence, and caring that teachers express, which they communicate over the first few months, win the trust of parents. Trust is also established through the eyes of the child. When children come home happy and excited, showing their art and writing, taking an interest in books, counting, and discussing topics from science and social studies, as well as looking forward to the next day of playing with friends in the blocks and creative dramatics centers, then parents are reassured and impressed. When parents see their child learning, they may continue to have questions and concerns, but they will feel they have another partner in meeting their child's needs—the teacher.

SUMMARY

Parents have the need and the right to be made aware of the curriculum and the learning climate in their child's kindergarten. Teachers have the responsibility for establishing communication with the parents, from the time of the initial enrollment visit. While a fall enrollment period does not allow for visits to an operating classroom, as a spring enrollment does, there are numerous ways teachers can inform parents about their program. In addition to providing information through copies of old newsletters and a display of pictures and statements describing the program, teachers can conduct a well-planned parents' meeting at the beginning of the year. The schedule, room arrangement, and work that will be sent home can be discussed. The importance of an ongoing system of communication must be stressed with the parents, for the Whole Language kindergarten program to operate successfully.

Newsletters, additional parents' meetings, contacts with the home through telephone calls or home visits, and many opportunities to discuss the child's work are needed to win the parents' trust and confidence. Whole Language kindergarten teachers find ways to communicate with parents who are unable to attend school meetings.

When individual conferences are planned, it is imperative that the teacher discuss all areas of the child's development, keeping the focus on the child's strengths and reassuring the parent of the child's progress. Teachers speak in terms of the "whole child." They describe the child as a listener, speaker, and beginning reader and writer, and they also talk about the child as a thinker. They discuss the child's social and emotional development and fine and gross motor coordination. When problems do arise, teachers engage the parents' help, as well as that of other professionals. They continue to answer parents' questions and concerns cheerfully, realizing that real communication and trust are built over time. Whole Language kindergarten teachers share the responsibility and joy of being partners with the parents for the benefit of their kindergartners.

APPENDIXES

REFERENCES

CHILDREN'S BOOKS
AND RECORDINGS

INDEX

ABOUT THE AUTHORS

Excerpts from the NAEYC Position Paper: Developmentally Appropriate Practice in Programs for 4- and 5-Year Olds

The following are the NAEYC's integrated components of appropriate and inappropriate practice for four- and five-year-old children.

Component: Curriculum Goals

Appropriate practice: Experiences are provided that meet children's needs and stimulate learning in all developmental areas—physical, social, emotional, and intellectual.

Inappropriate practice: Experiences are narrowly focused on the child's intellectual development without recognition that all areas of a child's development are interrelated.

Appropriate practice: Each child is viewed as a unique person with an individual pattern and timing of growth and development. The curriculum and adults' interaction are responsive to individual differences in ability and interests. Different levels of ability, development, and learning styles are expected, accepted, and used to design appropriate activities.

Source: Bredekamp, S. (Ed.). (1987). *NAEYC position statement on developmentally appropriate practice in programs for 4- and 5-year-olds.* Washington, DC: National Association for the Education of Young Children. Copyright © National Association for the Education of Young Children. Reprinted by permission.

Inappropriate practice: Children are evaluated only against a predetermined measure, such as a standardized group norm or adult standard of behavior. All are expected to perform the same tasks and achieve the same narrowly defined, easily measured skills.

Appropriate practice: Interactions and activities are designed to develop children's self-esteem and positive feelings toward learning.

Inappropriate practice: Children's worth is measured by how well they conform to rigid expectations and perform on standardized tests.

Component: Teaching Strategies

Appropriate practice: Teachers prepare the environment for children to learn through active exploration and interaction with adults, other children, and materials.

Inappropriate practice: Teachers use highly structured teacher-directed lessons almost exclusively.

Appropriate practice: Children select many of their own activities from among a variety of learning areas the teacher prepares, including dramatic play, blocks, science, math, games and puzzles, books, recordings, art, and music.

Inappropriate practice: The teacher directs all the activity, deciding what children will do and when. The teacher does most of the activity for the children, such as cutting shapes, performing steps in an experiment.

Appropriate practice: Children are expected to be physically and mentally active. Children choose from among activities the teacher has set up or the children spontaneously initiate.

Inappropriate practice: Children are expected to sit down, watch, be quiet, and listen, or do paper-and-pencil tasks for inappropriately long periods of time. A major portion of time is spent passively sitting, listening, and waiting.

Appropriate practice: Children work individually or in small, informal groups most of the time.

Inappropriate practice: Large group, teacher-directed instruction is used most of the time.

Appropriate practice: Children are provided concrete learning activities with materials and people relevant to their own life experiences.

Inappropriate practice: Workbooks, ditto sheets, flashcards, and other similarly structured abstract materials dominate the curriculum.

Appropriate practice: Teachers move among groups and individuals to facilitate children's involvement with materials and activities by asking questions, offering suggestions, or adding more complex materials or ideas to a situation.

Inappropriate practice: Teachers dominate the environment by talking to the whole group most of the time and telling children what to do.

Appropriate practice: Teachers accept that there is often more than one right answer. Teachers recognize that children learn from self-directed problem solving and experimentation.

Inappropriate practice: Children are expected to respond correctly with one rigid answer. Rote memorization and drill are emphasized.

Component: Guidance of Socioemotional Development

Appropriate practice: Teachers facilitate the development of self-control in children by using positive guidance techniques such as modeling and encouraging expected behavior, redirecting children to a more acceptable activity, and setting clear limits. Teachers' expectations match and respect children's developing capabilities.

Inappropriate practice: Teachers spend a great deal of time enforcing rules, punishing unacceptable behavior, demeaning children who misbehave, making children sit and be quiet, or refereeing disagreements.

Appropriate practice: Children are provided many opportunities to develop social skills such as cooperating, helping, negotiating, and talking with the person involved to solve interpersonal problems.

Teachers facilitate the development of these positive social skills at all times.

Inappropriate practice: Children work individually at desks or tables most of the time or listen to teacher directions in the total group. Teachers intervene to resolve disputes or enforce classroom rules and schedule.

Component: Language Development and Literacy

Appropriate practice: Children are provided many opportunities to see how reading and writing are useful before they are instructed in letter names, sounds, and word identification. Basic skills develop when they are meaningful to children. An abundance of these types of activities is provided to develop language and literacy through meaningful experience: listening to and reading stories and poems; taking field trips; dictating stories; seeing classroom charts and other print in use; participating in dramatic play and other experiences requiring communication; talking informally with other children and adults; and experimenting with writing by drawing, copying, and inventing their own spelling.

Inappropriate practice: Reading and writing instruction stresses isolated skills development such as recognizing single letters, reciting the alphabet, singing the alphabet song, coloring within predefined lines, or being instructed in correct formation of letters on a printed line.

Component: Cognitive Development

Appropriate practice: Children develop understanding of concepts about themselves, others, and the world around them through observation, interacting with people and real objects, and seeking solutions to concrete problems. Learnings about math, science, social studies, health, and other content areas are all integrated through meaningful activities such as those when children build with blocks; measure sand, water, or ingredients for cooking; observe changes in the environment; work with wood and tools; sort objects for a purpose; explore animals, plants, water, wheels and gears; sign and listen to music from various cultures; and draw, paint, and work with clay. Routines are followed that help children keep themselves healthy and safe.

Inappropriate practice: Instruction stresses isolated skill development through memorization and rote, such as counting, circling an item on a worksheet, memorizing facts, watching demonstrations, drilling with flashcards, or looking at maps. Children's cognitive development is seen as fragmented in content areas such as math, science, or social studies, and times are set aside to concentrate on each area.

Component: Physical Development

Appropriate practice: Children have daily opportunities to use large muscles, including running, jumping, and balancing. Outdoor activity is planned daily so children can develop muscle skills, learn about outdoor environments, and express themselves freely and loudly.

Inappropriate practice: Opportunity for large muscle activity is limited. Outdoor time is limited because it is viewed as interfering with instructional time or, if provided, is viewed as recess (a way to get children to use up excess energy), rather than an integral part of children's learning environment.

Appropriate practice: Children have daily opportunities to develop small muscle skills through play activities such as pegboards, puzzles, painting, cutting, and other similar activities.

Inappropriate practice: Small motor activity is limited to writing with pencils, or coloring predrawn forms, or similar structured lessons.

Component: Aesthetic Development

Appropriate practice: Children have daily opportunities for aesthetic expression and appreciation through art and music. Children experiment and enjoy various forms of music. A variety of art media are available for creative expression, such as easel and finger painting and clay.

Inappropriate practice: Art and music are provided only when time permits. Art consists of coloring predrawn forms, copying an adult-made model of a product, or following other adult-prescribed directions.

Component: Motivation

Appropriate practice: Children's natural curiosity and desire to make sense of their world are used to motivate them to become involved in learning activities.

Inappropriate practice: Children are required to participate in all activities to obtain the teacher's approval, to obtain extrinsic rewards like stickers or privileges, or to avoid punishment.

Component: Parent–Teacher Relations

Appropriate practice: Teachers work in partnership with parents, communicating regularly to build mutual understanding and greater consistency for children.

Inappropriate practice: Teachers communicate with parents only about problems or conflicts. Parents view teachers as experts and feel isolated from their child's experiences.

Component: Assessment of Children

Appropriate practice: Decisions that have a major impact on children (such as enrollment, retention, assignment to remedial classes) are based primarily on information obtained from observations by teachers and parents, not on the basis of a single test score. Developmental assessments of children's progress and achievement are used to plan curriculum, identify children with special needs, communicate with parents, and evaluate the program's effectiveness.

Inappropriate practice: Psychometric tests are used as the sole criterion to prohibit entrance to the program or to recommend that children be retained or placed in remedial classrooms.

Component: Program Entry

Appropriate practice: In public schools, there is a place for every child of legal entry age, regardless of the developmental level of the child. No public school program should deny access to children on the basis of results of screening or other arbitrary determinations of the child's lack of readiness. The educational system adjusts to the developmental needs and levels of the children it serves; children are not expected to adapt to an inappropriate system.

Inappropriate practice: Eligible-age children are denied entry to kindergarten or retained in kindergarten because they are judged not ready on the basis of inappropriate and inflexible expectations.

Component: Teacher Qualifications

Appropriate practice: Teachers are qualified to work with 4- and 5-year-olds through college-level preparation in Early Childhood Education or Child Development and supervised experience with this age group.

Inappropriate practice: Teachers with no specialized training or supervised experience working with 4- and 5-year-olds are viewed as qualified because they are state certified, regardless of the level of certification.

Component: Staffing

Appropriate practice: The group size and ratio of teachers to children is limited to enable individualized and age-appropriate programming. Four- and 5-year-olds are in groups of no more than 20 children with 2 adults.

Inappropriate practice: Because older children can function reasonably well in large groups, it is assumed that group size and number of adults can be the same for 4- and 5-year-olds as for elementary grades.

Excerpts from the ACEI Position Paper: The Child-Centered Kindergarten

The ACEI Position

The Association for Childhood Education International (ACEI) recognizes the importance of kindergarten education and supports high quality kindergarten programs that provide developmentally appropriate experiences for children by:

- Providing for the education of the whole child including physical, social/emotional and intellectual development
- Organizing instruction around each child's developmental needs, interests and learning styles
- Emphasizing the processes of learning rather than focusing on finished products
- Recognizing that each child follows a unique pattern of development and that kindergarten children learn best through firsthand experiences with people and materials
- Affirming the importance of play to children's total development

These programs cannot survive in a climate requiring predetermined and universally applied objectives and routine use of standardized testing.

Source: Moyer, J., Egertson, H., & Isenberg, J. (1987). The child-centered kindergarten. *Childhood Education, 63*(4), 235–242. Reprinted by permission from the Association for Childhood Education International, ACEI.

Program Implementation

An effective, developmentally appropriate kindergarten program (both curriculum and learning environment):

- Recognizes and accepts individual differences in children's growth patterns and rates by setting realistic curriculum goals that are appropriate to their development.
- Educates the whole child—with attention to physical, social/ emotional and intellectual developmental needs and interests.
- Responds to needs of children as developing, thinking individuals by focusing on the processes of learning rather than disparate skills, content and products.
- Provides multiple opportunities for learning with concrete, manipulative materials that 1) are relevant to children's experiential background and 2) keep them actively engaged in learning and discovering through use of all the senses, leading to more input upon which thought is constructed.
- Provides a variety of activities and materials by incorporating 1) learning activities that encourage active participation through "hands-on" activity, communication and dialogue; 2) large blocks of time to pursue interests; 3) time to ask questions and receive answers that develop concepts and ideas for use at varying levels of difficulty and complexity; and 4) time to reflect upon and abstract information when encountering different viewpoints from peers.
- Views play as fundamental to children's learning, growth and development, enabling them to develop and clarify concepts, roles and ideas by testing and evaluating them through use of open-ended materials and role-enactment. Play further enables children to develop fine and gross motor skills, to learn to share with others, to see others' points of view and to be in control of their thoughts and feelings.
- Provides opportunities for the use of multicultural and nonsexist experiences, materials and equipment that enhance children's acceptance of self and others and enable them to accept differences and similarities among people, including those handicapped in some way.
- Embraces the teaching of all content areas, presented as integrated experiences that develop and extend concepts, strengthen skills and provide a solid foundation for learning in language, literacy, math, science, health, art and music.

- Allows children to make choices and decisions within the limits of the materials provided, resulting in increased independence, attention, joy in learning and feelings of success necessary for growth and development.

Appropriate Physical Environment

The following environmental principles address spatial organization, use of materials and adults in the kindergarten:

- Rooms should be arranged to accommodate individual, small group and large group activities.
- Interest areas should be clearly defined; differ in size, shape and location; and attend to traffic patterns while permitting continuity of activity and reducing distractibility. All spaces should be clearly visible to the teacher.
- Rooms should be arranged to facilitate the activity and movements of children at work by attending to available paths for their use and minimizing the amount of interference they receive.
- Learning materials should be arranged and displayed so that they are inviting to children and suggest multiple possibilities for use by being clearly visible and also accessible, enabling children to return and replace materials as easily as they can get them. Clear, well-organized materials facilitate children's ability to use them and explore with them.
- Materials should be changed and combined to increase levels of complexity, thus helping children become more self-directed and increasing their level of involvement.
- Children perceive space they can see, reach and touch. Teachers can support, stimulate and maintain children's involvement in learning by providing a variety of raw materials for exploration, tools for manipulation, containers for storage and display, adequate work spaces, inviting displays at eye level and appropriate sources of information within children's reach.

Teachers for Kindergartens

ACEI advocates developmentally appropriate kindergartens staffed with early childhood teachers who:

- Are knowledgeable in child development, committed to children and able to plan a curriculum that will promote the full development of each child—enabling them to have a profound influence on children's lives.

- Listen thoughtfully to children, extend children's language about ideas and feelings, ask questions that encourage insights and highlight contradictions, and promote and value creative, divergent responses of all children.
- Regularly assess children's interests, needs and skill levels—enabling them to plan continuous, flexible and realistic activities for each child.
- Design learning environments that provide for successful daily experiences by matching activities to each child's developmental level and using positive interactions, encouragement and praise for children's efforts.
- Promote a positive self-image by helping children be successful in a variety of activities and experiences and providing techniques to help children establish their own limits. How children feel about themselves affects what they do, say and think.
- Utilize a variety of instructional approaches including individual, small group, large group, role-enactment activities and activity centers—all suited to kindergarten children's wide range of ability, interests and needs.
- Provide varied experiences about which kindergarten children can communicate by: 1) encouraging them to use their own experiences as a basis for developing language activities through individual and small group interactions with peers and adults; 2) arranging for periodic change of materials, equipment and activities in the environment; and 3) providing experiences for children to use their senses as they interact with people and materials.

Such teachers provide effective interaction with children, as well as encouragement, support and guidance.

Conclusion

ACEI advocates child-centered kindergarten programs that encourage active experiential learning, are developmentally appropriate, increase independence and promote joy in learning—staffed by teachers who are professionally prepared to work with young children.

The IRA Position Paper:
Literacy Development and Prefirst Grade

A Joint Statement of Concerns about Present Practices in Prefirst Grade Reading Instruction and Recommendations for Improvement
    Association for Childhood Education International
    Association for Supervision and Curriculum Development
    International Reading Association
    National Association for the Education of Young Children
    National Association of Elementary School Principals
    National Council of Teachers of English
Prepared by the Early Childhood and Literacy Development Committee of the International Reading Association.

Literacy learning begins in infancy. Children have many experiences with oral and written language before they come to school.

- Children have had many experiences from which they can build ideas about the functions and uses of oral and written language.
- Children have a command of language and of processes for learning and using language.
- Many children can differentiate between drawing and writing.
- Many children are reading environmental print, such as road signs, grocery labels, and fast food signs.
- Many children associate books with reading.
- Children's knowledge about language and communication is influenced by their social and cultural backgrounds.

Source: Early Childhood and Literacy Development Committee. (1988). *Literacy development and prefirst grade.* Newark, DE: International Reading Association. Reprinted by permission of the International Reading Association.

- Many children expect that reading and writing will be sense-making activities.

Basic premises of a sound prefirst grade reading program:

- Reading and writing at school should permit children to build upon their already existing knowledge of oral and written language.
- Learning should take place in a supportive environment where children can build a positive attitude toward themselves and toward language and literacy.
- For optimal learning, teachers should involve children actively in many thoughtful, functional language experiences, including speaking, listening, writing and reading.
- Teachers of young children should be prepared in ways that acknowledge differences in language and cultural backgrounds, and should emphasize reading as an integral part of the language arts as well as of the total curriculum.

Concerns:

- Many prefirst grade children are subjected to rigid, formal prereading programs with inappropriate expectations and experiences for their levels of development.
- Little attention is given to individual development of individual learning styles.
- The pressures of accelerated programs do not allow children to be risk takers as they experiment with written language.
- Too much attention is focused upon isolated skill development and abstract parts of the reading process, rather than on the integration of talking, writing and listening with reading.
- Too little attention is placed on reading for pleasure; therefore, children do not associate reading with enjoyment.
- Decisions related to reading programs are often based on political and economic considerations rather than on knowledge of how young children learn.
- The pressure to achieve high scores on tests inappropriate for the kindergarten child has led to undesirable changes in the content of the programs.
- Activities that deny curiosity, critical thinking and creative expression are all too frequent, and can foster negative attitudes toward language communication.
- As a result of declining enrollment and reduction in staff, individ-

uals with little or no knowledge of early childhood education are sometimes assigned to teach young children. Such teachers often select inappropriate methods.

- Teachers who are conducting prefirst grade programs without depending on commercial readers and workbooks sometimes fail to articulate for parents and other members of the public what they are doing and why.

Recommendations:

1. Build instruction on what the child already knows about oral language, reading and writing. Focus on meaningful experiences and meaningful language rather than on isolated skill development.
2. Respect the language the child brings to school, and use it as a base for language and literacy activities.
3. Ensure feelings of success for all children, helping them to see themselves as people who enjoy exploring both oral and written language.
4. Provide reading experiences as an integrated part of the communication process, which includes speaking, listening and writing, as well as art, math and music.
5. Encourage children's first attempts at writing, without concern for the proper formation of letters or correct conventional spelling.
6. Encourage risk taking in first attempts at reading and writing, and accept what appear to be errors as part of the children's natural growth and development.
7. Use reading materials that are familiar or predictable, such as well known stories, as they provide children with a sense of control and confidence in their ability to learn.
8. Present a model for children to emulate. In the classroom, teachers should use language appropriately, listen and respond to children's talk, and engage in their own reading and writing.
9. Take time regularly to read to children from a wide variety of poetry, fiction and nonfiction.
10. Provide time regularly for children's independent reading and writing.
11. Foster children's affective and cognitive development by providing them with opportunities to communicate what they know, think and feel.
12. Use developmentally and culturally appropriate procedures for

evaluation, ones that are based on the objectives of the program and that consider each child's total development.

13. Make parents aware of the reasons for a broader language program at school and provide them with ideas for activities to carry out at home.

14. Alert parents to the limitations of formal assessments and standardized tests of prefirst graders' reading and writing skills.

15. Encourage children to be active participants in the learning process rather than passive recipients, by using activities that allow for experimentation with talking, listening, writing and reading.

Steps in Binding a Book

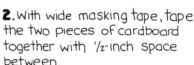

1. Cut two pieces of heavy cardboard slightly larger than the pages of the book.

2. With wide masking tape, tape the two pieces of cardboard together with ½-inch space between.

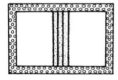

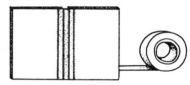

3. Cut outside cover 1½ inches larger than the cardboard and stick to cardboard (use thinned white glue if cover material is not self-adhesive.)

4. Fold corners over first, then the sides.

5. Measure and cut inside cover material and apply as shown.

6. Place stapled pages of the book in the center of the cover. Secure with two strips of inside cover material, one at the front of the book and the other at the back.

Source: S. C. Raines and R. J. Canady, *Story s-t-r-e-t-c-h-e-r-s: Activities to expand children's favorite books*, p. 240. Mt. Rainier, MD: Gryphon House, 1989. Used with permission of the publisher.

References

Allen, R. V. (1974). *Language experiences in reading. Teacher's resource guide, level 1.* Chicago: Encyclopedia Britannica Educational Corporation.

Allen, R. V. (1986). Hitching posts for literacy learning in the computer age. In M. R. Sampson (Ed.), *The pursuit of literacy: Early reading and writing* (pp. 145–149). Dubuque, IA: Kendall/Hunt.

Allen, R. V., & Canady, R. J. (1979). *Reading: A language experience approach* (Film). Birmingham, AL: Promethean Films South.

Altwerger, B., Edelsky, C., & Flores, B. M. (1987). Whole Language: What's new? *The Reading Teacher, 41*(2), 145–154.

Anderson, R. C., Hiebert, E. H., Scott, J. A., & Wilkinson, I. A. G. (1984). *Becoming a nation of readers.* Washington, DC: U.S. Department of Education, National Institute of Education.

Arnaud, S. (1971). Introduction: Polish for play's tarnished reputation. In S. Arnaud (Ed.), *Play: The child strives toward self realization* (pp. 5–12). Washington, DC: National Association for the Education of Young Children.

Ashton-Warner, S. (1963). *Teacher.* New York: Bantam.

Atkins, C. (1984). Writing: Doing something constructive. *Young Children, 40*(1), 3–7.

Auckerman, R. C. (1984). *Approaches to beginning reading.* New York: John Wiley.

Baghban, M. J. M. (1984). *Our daughter learns to read and write: A case study from birth to three.* Newark, DE: International Reading Association.

Bayless, K. M., & Ramsey, M. E. (1978). *Music: A way of life for the young child.* St. Louis: C. V. Mosby.

Bettelheim, B., & Zelan, K. (1981). *On learning to read: The child's fascination with meaning.* New York: Vintage Press.

Bissex, G. L. (1980). *Gyns at wrk: A child learns to write and read.* Cambridge, MA: Harvard University Press.

Bredekamp, S. (Ed.), (1987). *NAEYC position statement on developmentally appropriate practice in programs for 4- and 5-year-olds.* Washington, DC: National Association for the Education of Young Children.

Brittain, W. L. (1979). *Creativity, art, and the young child.* New York: Macmillan.

Bromley, K. D. (1988). *Language arts: Exploring connections.* Boston: Allyn & Bacon.

Bruner, J. (1976). *Play: Its role in development and evolution.* New York: Basic Books.

Calkins, L. M. (1986). *The art of teaching writing.* Portsmouth, NH: Heinemann.

Cambourne, B. (1988). *The whole story: Natural learning and the acquisition of literacy in the classroom.* Auckland, New Zealand: Ashton Scholastic.

Canady, R. J. (1982a, August). *I am reading now: A study of environmental print in a book structure.* Paper presented at Catskills Reading Conference, Oneonta, NY.

Canady, R. J. (1982b, August). *Young children's use of environmental print to construct meaning.* Paper presented at Catskills Reading Conference, Oneonta, NY.

Canady, R. J. (1983). Beginning reading programs: How can we begin what has already begun? In S. Raines (Ed.), *The Wesleyan papers: Keeping the child in childhood* (pp. 19–28). Rocky Mount, NC: North Carolina Wesleyan College Press.

Chall, J. S. (1967). *Learning to read: The great debate.* New York: McGraw-Hill.

Chapman, L. H. (1978). *Approaches to art in education.* New York: Harcourt Brace Jovanovich.

Chomsky, C. (1972). Stages in language development and reading exposure. *Harvard Educational Review, 42*(1), 1–33.

Clark, M. (1976). *Young fluent readers: What can they teach us.* London: Heinemann.

Clay, M. M. (1972). *Reading: The patterning of complex behavior.* London: Heinemann.

Clay, M. M. (1975). *What did I write?* Auckland, New Zealand: Heinemann.

Cohen, D. H. (1968). The effect of literature on vocabulary and reading achievement. *Elementary English, 45*(2), 209–213, 217.

Copple, C., Sigel, I. E., & Saunders, R. (1979). *Educating the young thinker: Classroom strategies for cognitive growth.* New York: Van Nostrand.

Cullinan, B. E. (1987). Inviting readers to literature. In B. E. Cullinan (Ed.), *Children's literature in the reading program* (pp. 2–14). Newark, DE: International Reading Association.

D'Amboise, J. (1989, August 4). I show a child what is possible. *Parade magazine*, pp. 4–6.

Delacato, C. H. (1959). *The treatment and prevention of reading problems.* Springfield, IL: Charles C. Thomas.

Dewey, J. (1900). *School and society.* Chicago: University of Chicago Press.

Dewey, J. (1902). *The child and the curriculum.* Chicago: University of Chicago Press.

Dewey, J. (1916). *Democracy and education.* New York: Free Press.

Dodge, M. K., & Frost, J. L. (1986). Children's dramatic play: Influence of thematic and nonthematic settings. *Childhood Education, 62*(3), 166–170.

Dorman, P. (1989, April). *Learning from the inside out.* Presentation at the annual study conference of the Association for Childhood Education International, Indianapolis, IN.

Dorman, P., & Alvarez, B. J. (1989). In S. Hoffman & L. L. Lamme (Eds.), *Learning from the inside out: The expressive arts* (pp. 52–61). Wheaton, MD: Association for Childhood Education International.

Durkin, D. (1966). *Children who read early.* New York: Teachers College Press.

Durkin, D. (1970). What does research say about the time to begin reading instruction? *Journal of Educational Research, 64*(1), 52–56.

Dyson, A. H. (1985). Individual differences in emerging writing. In M. Farr (Ed.), *Advances in writing research: Vol. I. Children's early writing development* (pp. 59–125). Norwood, NJ: Ablex.

Early Childhood and Literacy Development Committee. (1988). *Literacy development and prefirst grade.* Newark, DE: International Reading Association.

Elkind, D. (1987). *Miseducation: Preschoolers at risk.* New York: Alfred A. Knopf.

Feldman, C. (1980). Two functions of language. In M. Wolf, M. K. McQuillan, & E. Radwin (Eds.), *Thought & language/language and reading* (pp. 72–85). Cambridge, MA: Harvard Educational Review, Reprint Series No. 14.

Ferreiro, E. (1986). The interplay between information and assimilation in beginning literacy. In W. H. Teale & E. Sulzby (Eds.), *Emergent literacy: Writing and reading* (pp. 15–49). Norwood, NJ: Ablex.

Ferreiro, E., & Teberosky, A. (1982). *Literacy before schooling.* Exeter: Heinemann.

Fields, M. V. (1988). Talking and writing: Explaining the whole language approach to parents. *The reading teacher, 41*(9), 898–903.

Flesch, R. (1955). *Why Johnny can't read.* New York: Harper.

Fromberg, D. (1988). *The full-day kindergarten.* New York: Teachers College Press.

Garvey, C. (1977). *Play.* Cambridge, MA: Harvard University Press.

Genishi, C. (1985). Talking to learn: The child takes charge of literacy. *Dimensions, 13*(3), 9–11.

Gentry, J. C., & Henderson, E. H. (1978). Three steps to teaching beginning readers to spell. *The Reading Teacher, 31*(6), 632–637.

Gibb, G., & Castaneda, A. M. (1975). Experiences for young children. In J. N. Payne (Ed.), *Mathematics learning in early childhood* (pp. 95–120). Reston, VA: National Council of Teachers of Mathematics.

Gibson, L. (1989). *Literacy learning in the early years: Through children's eyes.* New York: Teachers College Press.

Goodman, K. S. (1968). The psycholinguistic nature of the reading process. In K. S. Goodman (Ed.), *The psycholinguistic nature of the reading process* (pp. 13–26). Detroit: Wayne State University.

Goodman, K. S. (1969). Analysis of oral reading miscues: Applied psycholinguistics. *Reading Research Quarterly, 5*(1), 9–30.

Goodman, K. S. (1982). What is universal about the reading process? In F. V. Gollasch (Ed.), *Language and literacy: The selected writings of Kenneth S. Goodman* (Vol. 1, pp. 71–75). Boston: Routledge & Kegan Paul.

Goodman, K. S. (1986). *What's whole in whole language?* Portsmouth, NH: Heinemann.

Goodman, Y. M. (1978). Kidwatching: An alternative to testing. *National Elementary School Principal, 57*(4), 41–45.

Goodman, Y. M. (1983). Beginning reading development: Strategies and principles. In R. P. Parker & F. A. Davis (Eds.), *Developing literacy: Young children's use of language* (pp. 68–83). Newark, DE: International Reading Association.

Goodman, Y. M. (1986). Children coming to know literacy. In W. H. Teale & E. Sulzby (Eds.), *Emergent literacy: Writing and reading* (pp. 1–14). Norwood, NJ: Ablex.

Goodman, Y. M., & Watson, D. (1977). A reading program to live with: Focus on comprehension. *Language arts, 54*(8), 868–879.

Graves, D. H. (1983). *Writing: Teachers & children at work.* Exeter, NH: Heinemann.

Griffing, P. (1983). Encouraging dramatic play in early childhood. *Young Children, 38*(1), 13–22.

Hall, M. (1981). *Teaching reading as a language experience.* Columbus: Charles E. Merrill.

Halliday, M. A. K. (1973). *Explorations in the functions of language.* London: Arnold.

Hansen, J. (1987). *When writers read.* Portsmouth, NH: Heinemann.

Harste, J. C., Short, K., & Burke, C. (1988). *Creating classrooms for authors: The reading-writing connection.* Portsmouth, NH: Heinemann.

Harste, J., Woodward, V., & Burke, C. (1984). *Language stories and literacy lessons.* Portsmouth, NH: Heinemann.

Henderson, E. H. (1980). Developmental concepts of word. In E. H. Henderson & J. W. Beers (Eds.), *Developmental and cognitive aspects of learning to spell: A reflection of word knowledge* (pp. 1–14). Newark, DE: International Reading Association.

Henke, L. (1988). Beyond basal reading: A district's commitment to change. *The New Advocate, 1*(1), 42–51.

Hildreth, G. (1936). Developmental sequences in name writing. *Child Development, 7,* 291–303.

Hill, P. S. (Ed.) (1923). *A conduct curriculum for the kindergarten for the first grade.* New York: Charles Scribner's Sons.

Hirsch, E. S. (1974). *The block book.* Washington, DC: National Association for the Education of Young Children.

Hittleman, D. R. (1988). *Developmental reading, K–8: Teaching from a whole language perspective.* Columbus, OH: Merrill.

Hoffman, S. (1987). The language of teaching: Responses to children's developing literacy. *Childhood Education, 63*(5), 356–361.

Hoffman, S., & Knipping, N. (1988). Spelling revisited: The child's way. *Childhood Education, 64*(5), 284–287.

Holdaway, D. (1979). *The foundations of literacy.* Sydney: Ashton Scholastic.

Holdaway, D. (1986). The structure of natural learning as a basis for literacy instruction. In M. R. Sampson (Ed.), *The pursuit of literacy: Early reading and writing* (pp. 56–72). Dubuque, IA: Kendall/Hunt.

Hornsby, D., Sukarna, D., & Parry, J. (1986). *Read on: A conference approach to reading.* Portsmouth, NH: Heinemann.

Hudson, B., Speight, B., & Salisbury, G. (1988, November). *Props for enriching children's play themes.* Paper presented at the annual conference of the American Association for the Child's Right to Play, Washington, DC.

Isaacs, S. (1948). *The social development of young children.* London: Routledge.

Isaacs, S. (1972). *Intellectual growth in young children.* New York: Schocken Books.

Isbell, R., Floyd, S., Peters, V., & Raines, S. C. (1988, November). *Ideas to stimulate sociodramatic play.* Paper presented at the annual conference of the American Association for the Child's Right to Play, Washington, DC.

Isbell, R., & Raines, S. C. (1989, April). *Helping young children develop language during center time.* Paper presented at the annual conference of the Southern Association on Children Under Six, Richmond, VA.

Isenberg, J., & Jacob, E. (1983, June). *Playful literacy activities and learning: Preliminary observations.* Paper presented at the International Conference on Play and Play Environments, Austin, TX.

Isenberg, J., & Quisenberry, N. L. (1988). Play: A necessity for all children. *Childhood Education, 64*(3), 138–145.

Jalongo, M. R., & Zeigler, S. (1987). Writing in kindergarten and first grade. *Childhood Education, 64*(2), 97–104.

Jarolimek, J., & Foster, C. D. (1989). *Teaching and learning in the elementary school.* New York: Macmillan.

Jensen, M. A. (1985). Story awareness: A critical skill for early reading. *Young Children, 41*(1), 20–24.

Jewell, M. G., & Zintz, M. (1986). *Learning to read naturally.* Dubuque, IA: Kendall/Hunt.

Kamii, C. (1982). *Number in preschool and kindergarten: Educational implications of Piaget's theory.* Washington, DC: National Association for the Education of Young Children.

Lamme, L. L. (1984). *Growing up writing.* Honesdale, PA: Highlights for Children.

Leeb-Lundberg, K. (1974). The block building mathematician. In E. S. Hirsch (Ed.), *The block book.* Washington, DC: National Association for the Education of Young Children.

Long, R., Manning, M., Manning, G., Martin, K., Williams, C., & Wolfson, B. (1982). *Indices of literacy in preschool children.* Unpublished research report, University of Alabama, Birmingham.

Loughlin, C. E., & Martin, M. D. (1987). *Supporting literacy: Developing effective learning environments.* New York: Teachers College Press.

Lowenfeld, V. (1957). *Creative and mental growth.* New York: Macmillan.

Lowenfeld, V., & Brittain, W. L. (1982). *Creative and mental growth.* New York: Macmillan.

Lynch, P. (1986). *Using big books and predictable books.* New York: Scholastic.

Mandler, J. M., & Johnson, N. S. (1977). Remembrance of things past: Story structure and recall. *Cognitive Psychology, 9*(1), 111–151.

Martin, B. (1988, April). *Language, literature, and reading.* Keynote address at the Children's Literature Conference, George Mason University, Fairfax, VA.

Martinez, M., & Roser, N. (1985). Read it again: The value of repeated readings during storytime. *The Reading Teacher, 38*(8), 782–786.

Martinez, M., & Teale, W. H. (1987). The ins and outs of a kindergarten writing program. *The Reading Teacher, 40*(4), 444–451.

Martinez, M., & Teale, W. H. (1988). Reading in a kindergarten classroom library. *The Reading Teacher, 41*(6), 568–572.

McLuhan, M., & Fiore, Q. (1967). *The medium is the message: An inventory of effects.* New York: Bantam.

Moffitt, M. W. (1974). Children learn about science through block building. In E. S. Hirsch (Ed.), *The block book* (pp. 25–32). Washington, DC: National Association for the Education of Young Children.

Montebello, M. (1988, September). *The story lamp is on.* Workshop in Children's Literature, George Mason University, Fairfax, VA.

Montessori, M. (1964). *Spontaneous activity in education.* Cambridge, MA: Robert Bentley.

Moomaw, S. (1984). *Discovering music in early childhood.* Boston: Allyn & Bacon.

Morrow, L. M. (1985). Retelling stories: A strategy for improving young children's comprehension, concept of story structure, and oral language complexity. *The Elementary School Journal, 85*(5), 647–656.

Morrow, L. M. (1989). Designing the classroom to promote literacy development. In D. S. Strickland & L. M. Morrow (Eds.), *Emerging literacy: Young children learn to read and write* (pp. 121–134). Newark, DE: International Reading Association.

Morrow, L., & Weinstein, C. (1982). Increasing children's use of literature through program and physical design changes. *Elementary School Journal, 83*(2), 131–137.

Moyer, J., Egertson, H., & Isenberg, J. (1987). The child-centered kindergarten. *Childhood Education, 63*(4), 235–242.

Nurss, J. R., & Hough, R. A. (1986). Reading aloud in early childhood classrooms. *Dimensions, 14*(2), 7–9.

Olszewski, P., & Fuson, K. (1982). Verbally expressed fantasy play. *Developmental Psychology, 13*(1), 57–61.

Ornstein, A. C., & Hunkins, F. P. (1988). *Curriculum: Foundations, principles, and issues.* Englewood Cliffs, NJ: Prentice-Hall.

Osborn, J. D., & Osborn, D. K. (1983). *Cognition in early childhood.* Athens, GA: Education Associates.

Parker, F. W. (1894). *Talks on pedagogics.* New York: Kellogg.

Parry, J., & Hornsby, D. (1985). *Write on: A conference approach to writing.* Portsmouth, NH: Heinemann.

Parten, M. B. (1932). Social participation among preschool children. *Journal of Abnormal and Social Psychology, 27*(3), 243–269.

Pellegrini, A., & Galda, L. (1985). Social dramatic play and literacy. *Dimensions, 13*(3), 12–14.

Piaget, J. (1926). *The language and thought of the child.* London: Routledge & Kegan Paul.

Piaget, J. (1965). *The child's conception of the world.* Totowa, NJ: Littlefield.

Piaget, J. (1974). *The language and thought of the child,* M. Gabain, Trans. New York: New American Library.

Piaget, J. (1977). *The development of thought: Equilibration of cognitive structures.* New York: Viking.

Piaget, J., Inhelder, B., & Szeminska, A. (1964). *The child's conception of geometry.* New York: Harper & Row.

Quay, L. C., Weaver, J. H., & Neel, J. J. (1986). The effects of play materials on positive and negative social behaviors in preschool boys and girls. *Child Study Journal, 16*(1), 67–75.

Raines, S. C. (1982). *A guide to early learning.* Palo Alto, CA: R. & E. Research Associates.

Raines, S. C. (1983, April). *Children learn to write: A cross-cultural field study of nineteen young writers.* Paper presented at the annual study conference of the Association for Childhood Education International, Cleveland.

Raines, S. C. (1986). Teacher educator learns from first and second grade readers and writers. *Childhood Education, 62*(4), 260–264.

Raines, S. C. (1990a). Representational competence: (Re)presenting experiences through words, action, and images. *Childhood Education, 66*(3), 139–144.

Raines, S. C. (1990b, April). *Study of the effects of literacy materials in play centers.* Paper presented at Literacy Forum sponsored by Center for Applied Research and Development, George Mason University, Fairfax, VA.

Raines, S. C., & Canady, R. J. (1982, July). *An analysis of young children's beginning writing.* Paper presented at the Catskills Reading Conference, Oneonta, NY.

Raines, S. C., & Canady, R. J. (1989). *Story s-t-r-e-t-c-h-e-r-s: Activities to expand children's favorite books.* Mt. Rainier, MD: Gryphon House.

Raines, S. C., & Isbell, R. (1988, April). *The wordless picture book: A valued but neglected resource.* Paper presented at the annual study conference of the Association for Childhood Education International, Salt Lake City.

Raines, S. C., & Isbell, R. (1988). Tuck talking about wordless picture books into your classroom. *Young Children, 43*(6), 24–25.

Raines, S. C., & Isbell, R. (1989, April). *A descriptive study of the book interest behaviors of young children.* Paper presented at the annual study conference of the Association for Childhood Education International, Indianapolis.

Read, C. (1975). *Children's categorization of speech sounds in English.* Urbana, IL: National Council of Teachers of English.

Rhodes, L. K. (1981). I can read! Predictable books as resources for reading and writing instruction. *The Reading Teacher, 34*(5), 511–518.

Robinson, D., Mahaffey, M., & Nelson, D. (1975). Measurement. In J. D. Payne (Ed.), *Mathematics learning in early childhood* (pp. 227–250). Reston, VA: National Council of Teachers of Mathematics.

Robison, H. F. (1971). The decline of play in urban kindergartens. *Young Children, 26*(6), 333–341.

Roskos, K. (1988). Literacy at work in play. *The Reading Teacher, 41*(6), 562–566.

Routman, R. (1988). *Transitions: From literature to literacy.* Portsmouth, NH: Heinemann.

Rudolph, M., & Cohen, D. H. (1984). *Kindergarten and early schooling.* Englewood Cliffs, NJ: Prentice-Hall.

Schickedanz, J. A. (1978). Please read that story again: Exploring relationships between story reading and learning to read. *Young Children, 33*(5), 48–55.

Seefeldt, C., & Barbour, N. (1986). *Early childhood education: An introduction.* Columbus, OH: Charles E. Merrill.

Sinatra, R. (1986). *Visual literacy connections to thinking, reading, and writing.* Springfield, IL: Charles C. Thomas.

Smilansky, S. (1968). *The effects of sociodramatic play on disadvantaged preschool children.* New York: John Wiley.

Smith, B. O., Stanley, W. O., & Shores, J. H. (1957). *Fundamentals of curriculum development.* New York: Harcourt Brace Jovanovich.

Smith, F. (1976). Learning to read by reading. *Language Arts, 53*(3), 297–299, 322.

Smith, F. (1982). *Understanding reading.* New York: Holt Rinehart & Winston.

Smith, F. (1983). *Essays into literacy.* Exeter, NH: Heinemann.

Smith, F. (1985). *Reading without nonsense.* New York: Teachers College Press.

Snyder, A. (1972). Patty Smith Hill (1868–1946): Dynamic leadership in new directions. In M. Rasmussen (Ed.), *Dauntless women in childhood education, 1856–1931* (pp. 233–270). Washington, DC: Association for Childhood Education International.

Spodek, B., Saracho, O., & Davis, M. D. (1987). *Foundations of early childhood education: Teaching three-, four-, and five-year-old children.* Englewood Cliffs, NJ: Prentice-Hall.

Stanton, J., Weisberg, A., & Faculty of Bank Street School for Children. (1974). Suggested equipment for block building. In E. S. Hirsch (Ed.), *The block book* (pp. 105–108). Washington, DC: National Association for the Education of Young Children.

Stauffer, R. G. (1980). *The language experience approach to the teaching of reading.* New York: Harper & Row.

Sulzby, E. (1986). Writing and reading: Signs of oral and written organization in the young child. In W. H. Teale & E. Sulzby (Eds.), *Emergent literacy: Writing and reading* (pp. 50–89). Norwood, NJ: Ablex.

Taba, H. (1962). *Curriculum development: Theory into practice.* New York: Harcourt Brace Jovanovich.

Taylor, D. (1983). *Family literacy: Young children learn to read and write.* Exeter, NH: Heinemann.

Teale, W. H. (1985). The beginnings of literacy. *Dimensions, 13*(3), 5–8.

Teale, W. H., Hiebert, E. H., & Chittenden, E. A. (1987). Assessing young children's literacy development. *The Reading Teacher, 40*(8), 772–777.

Teale, W. H., & Sulzby, E. (Eds.). (1986). Introduction: Emergent literacy as a perspective for examining how young children become writers and readers. In W. H. Teale & E. Sulzby (Eds.), *Emergent literacy: Writing and reading* (pp. vii–xxv). Norwood, NJ: Ablex Publishing.

Temple, C., Nathan, R., Burris, N., & Temple, F. (1988). *The beginnings of writing.* Boston: Allyn & Bacon.

Torrey, J. W. (1969). Learning to read without a teacher. *Elementary English, 46*(5), 550–556, 658.

Trelease, J. (1989). *The read-aloud handbook.* New York: Penguin Books.

Veatch, J., Sawicki, F., Elliott, G., Barnette, E., & Blakey, J. (1973). *Key words to reading: The language experience approach begins.* New York: Harper & Row.

Vukelich, C., & Golden, J. (1984). Early writing development and teaching strategies. *Young Children, 39*(2), 3–8.

Vygotsky, L. S. (1962). *Thought and language.* Cambridge, MA: MIT Press.

Wachowiak, F. (1985). *Emphasis art.* New York: Thomas Y. Crowell.

Watson, D. J. (Ed.), (1987). *Ideas and insights: Language arts in the elementary school.* Urbana, IL: National Council of Teachers of English.

Willert, M. K., & Kamii, C. (1985). Reading in kindergarten: Direct vs. indirect teaching. *Young Children, 40*(4), 3–9.

Winsor, C. B. (1974). Blocks as a material for learning through play—The contribution of Caroline Pratt. In E. S. Hirsch (Ed.), *The block book* (pp. 1–8). Washington, DC: National Association for the Education of Young Children.

Yaden, D. (1988). Understanding stories through repeated read-alouds: How many does it take? *The Reading Teacher, 41*(6), 556–560.

Yawkey, T. D. (1983). Pretend play and language growth in young children (Report No. PSO13774). University Park, PA: College of Education, Division of Curriculum and Instruction. (ERIC Document Reproduction Service No. ED 231 552).

Ylisto, I. P. (1967). *An empirical investigation of early reading responses of young children.* Unpublished doctoral dissertation, University of Michigan, Ann Arbor.

Children's Books and Recordings

Allen, R. V. (1985). *I love ladybugs.* Allen, TX: DLM Teaching Resources.

Anno, M. (1975). *Anno's counting book.* New York: Thomas Y. Crowell Company.

Arnold, T. (1987). *No jumping on the bed!* New York: Dial.

Asbjørnsen, P. C., & Moe, J. E. (1981). *The three billy goats gruff.* New York: Clarion.

Balian, L. (1986). *Amelia's nine lives.* Nashville, TN: Abingdon Press.

Bennett, J. (1986). *Teeny tiny.* New York: Putnam.

Carle, E. (1981). *The very hungry caterpillar.* New York: Philomel Books.

Carlstrom, N. W. (1986). *Jesse bear, what will you wear?* New York: Macmillan.

Cauley, L. B. (1981). *Goldilocks and the three bears.* New York: Putnam.

Crews, D. (1980). *Truck.* New York: Greenwillow Books.

Crews, D. (1986). *Flying.* New York: Greenwillow Books.

Degen, B. (1983). *Jamberry.* New York: Harper & Row, Publishers.

Ehlert, L. (1987). *Growing vegetable soup.* San Diego: Harcourt Brace Jovanovich.

Freeman, D. (1964). *Dandelion.* New York: Viking Press.

Freeman, D. (1968). *Corduroy.* New York: Viking Press.

Gag, W. (1923). *Millions of cats.* New York: Coward, McCann, Putnam Publishing Group.

Galdone, P. (1961). *The house that Jack built.* New York: McGraw-Hill.

Galdone, P. (1973). *The little red hen.* Boston: Houghton Mifflin Company.

Galdone, P. (1975). *The gingerbread boy.* New York: Seabury.

Galdone, P. (1984). *The three little pigs.* New York: Clarion.

Galdone, P. (1986). *The three little kittens.* New York: Clarion.

Gibbons, G. (1984). *The seasons of Arnold's apple tree.* San Diego: Harcourt Brace Jovanovich.

Hayes, S. (1986). *This is the bear.* New York: J. P. Lippincott.

Heller, R. (1981). *Chickens aren't the only ones.* New York: Grosset & Dunlap.

Hoban, R. (1964). *A baby sister for Frances.* New York: Harper & Row.

Hoban, T. (1978). *Is it red? Is it yellow? Is it blue?* New York: Greenwillow Books.

Hoffman, H. (1968). *The green grass grows all around.* New York: Macmillan.

Howard, E. F. (1988). *The train to Lulu's.* New York: Bradbury Press.

Hutchins, P. (1986). *The doorbell rang.* New York: Greenwillow Books.

Jacobs, J. (1983). *Jack and the beanstalk*. New York: Clarion.

Keats, E. J. (1970). *Hi, cat*. New York: Macmillan Publishing.

Kennedy, J. (1983). *The teddy bears' picnic*. San Diego: Green Tiger Press.

Krauss, R. (1945). *The carrot seed*. New York: Harper & Row Publishers.

Martin, B. (1983). *Brown bear, brown bear, what do you see?* New York: Holt, Rinehart & Winston.

Mayer, M. (1974). *Frog goes to dinner*. New York: Dial.

Mayer, M. (1983). *Me too!* New York: Golden Books.

McCully, E. (1984). *Picnic*. New York: Harper and Row.

Murphy, J. (1986). *Five minutes' peace*. New York: G. P. Putnam's.

Ormerod, J. (1982). *Moonlight*. New York: Lothrop.

Peek, M. (1981). *Roll over! A counting book*. New York: Clarion Books.

Peek, M. (1985). *Mary wore her red dress, and Henry wore his green sneakers*. New York: Clarion Books.

Palmer, H. (1969). Colors. (Recording). *Learning basic skills through music* (Vol. 1). Freeport, NY: Educational Activities.

Rey, H. A. (1941). *Curious George*. Boston: Houghton Mifflin.

Ryder, J. (1987). *Chipmunk song*. New York: Lodestar Books, E. P. Dutton.

Siebert, D. (1984). *Truck song*. New York: Harper & Row.

Simon, N. (1982). *Where does my cat sleep?* Niles, IL: Albert Whitman.

Simon, N. (1986). *Cats do, dogs don't*. Niles, IL: Albert Whitman.

Testa, F. (1980). (Naomi Lewis, Trans.) *Leaves*. New York: Peter Bedrick Books.

Wadsworth, O. A. (1986). *Over in the meadow: A counting rhyme*. New York: Penguin.

Wildsmith, B. (1970). *Brian Wildsmith's circus*. New York: Oxford University Press.

Index

About the Authors

Shirley C. Raines is Professor of Education at the University of South Florida in Tampa where she also chairs the departments of Childhood Education, Language Arts, and Reading. She is the executive board member of the Association for Childhood Education International. Her research focuses on young children's acquisition of written language and their interest in books. She completed her Ed.D. at the University of Tennessee, where she specialized in early childhood education. Before becoming a teacher educator, she was a classroom teacher, and she has directed a child care center as well as a Head Start program.

Robert J. Canady is Professor of Education at Marymount University in Arlington, Virginia, where he teaches graduate students in language arts and reading and researches young children's literacy development. He consults with school districts on language-based reading programs. Bob received his Ed.D. from the University of Arizona. He has both taught in and directed preschool programs.

Drs. Raines and Canady are a husband-and-wife writing team. In addition to this book, they have written *Story S-t-r-e-t-c-h-e-r-s: Activities to Expand Children's Favorite Books* (1989). Bob spends his spare time restoring antique cars and flying his own airplane. Shirley does photography and watercolor painting. They have four children, Brian, Lynnette, Scott, and Lark, and three grandchildren, Michelle, Damien, and Tina.